David K. Carson, PhD
Kent W. Becker, EdD

Creativity in Psychotherapy
Reaching New Heights with Individuals, Couples, and Families

Pre-publication
REVIEWS,
COMMENTARIES,
EVALUATIONS . . .

"*Creativity in Psychotherapy* is an outstanding new addition to the therapy literature. Long overlooked or trivialized by professionals in many disciplines, creativity may well be our best hope for a healthy and rewarding future. Carson and Becker have produced a very readable, yet thoroughly researched and well-organized text that is based on sound professional concepts. It ties together the long-debated beliefs concerning the art versus the science of psychotherapy. What a creative idea to survey counseling professionals about their own creative processes.

The beginning section of the text orients the reader to the creative process, which the authors identify as dynamic, interactive, innovative, and systemic. In the several intervention chapters, there is a good review of prominent techniques in major models of family therapy, and a long list of ideas (garnered from the authors' survey) to create your own activities and interventions. The chapter on creativity in supervision also emphasizes the reader's personal creative process, and gives unusual depth and breadth to a book about learning and practicing therapy. The supervision process is conceptualized as being positive, developmental, and solution-focused.

This is a unique book for teachers, students, supervisors, and clinicians. If you are one of these, reading this book, or even parts of it, will cause you to reflect on your own life and your professional practice, and you will come away stimulated and enriched. It will refresh your mind and energize your work. What more can you ask?"

William M. Walsh, PhD
Professor of Counseling Psychology,
Director of Marriage and Family Therapy,
University of Northern Colorado

More pre-publication
REVIEWS, COMMENTARIES, EVALUATIONS . . .

"**N**o two clients or life situations are the same. Therapists need to use improvisation and creativity to be effective. Creativity is also needed to develop different problem formulations and solutions. This important variable has not received enough attention in the professional psychotherapy literature until this gem of a book. The authors have thoroughly researched the role of creativity in counseling and provide practical suggestions as to how to increase your divergent thinking ability. A book well worth reading."

Jon Carlson, PsyD, EdD, ABPP
Distinguished Professor,
Governors State University

"**E**xciting, inviting, intriguing, informative, and innovative are just a few of the words that describe the content of *Creativity in Psychotherapy*. Carson and Becker have explored a vital, but often ignored, concept in therapeutically working with individuals, couples, and families—creativity. In the process, they

have offered new insight on the subject and how it contributes to health and healing. This book is based on classic research in the field as well as that generated by the authors in a national survey.

Within these pages are ideas that will spark ideas. The authors orient readers at the beginning of each chapter with a 'creative incubation' exercise. They also help readers become more creative in breaking out of their set ways of seeing and being in the world by offering them opportunities for further growth at the end of every chapter. Thus, this work, unlike other books on the subject, simultaneously operates on cognitive, affective, and behavioral levels and presents its material to readers through interactive means. So read this text with an expectation and a realization that in your journey through these pages you will emerge not just more informed, but different, and most likely better, than when you first began."

Samuel T. Gladding, PhD
Professor and Chair,
Department of Counseling,
Wake Forest University

The Haworth Clinical Practice Press
An Imprint of The Haworth Press, Inc.
New York • London • Oxford

Creativity in Psychotherapy
Reaching New Heights
with Individuals, Couples,
and Families

HAWORTH Marriage and the Family
Terry S. Trepper, PhD
Executive Editor

Creativity in Psychotherapy
Reaching New Heights with Individuals, Couples, and Families

David K. Carson, PhD
Kent W. Becker, EdD

The Haworth Clinical Practice Press
An Imprint of The Haworth Press, Inc.
New York • London • Oxford

Published by

The Haworth Clinical Practice Press, an imprint of The Haworth Press, Inc., 10 Alice Street, Binghamton, NY 13904-1580.

PUBLISHER'S NOTE
Identities and circumstances of individuals discussed in this book have been invented or changed to protect confidentiality. Any resemblance to actual persons, living or dead, is entirely coincidental.

Cover design by Brooke R. Stiles.

Library of Congress Cataloging-in-Publication Data

Carson, David K.
    Creativity in psychotherapy : reaching new heights with individuals, couples, and families / David K. Carson, Kent W. Becker.
      p. ; cm.
Includes bibliographical references and index.
    ISBN 0-7890-1578-1 (hardcover : alk. paper)—ISBN 0-7890-1579-X (softcover : alk. paper)
    1. Psychotherapy. 2. Family psychotherapy. 3. Creative thinking. [DNLM: 1. Creativeness. 2. Psychotherapy—methods. WM 420 C321c 2003] I. Becker, Kent W. II. Title.
    RC480.5 .C364 2003
    616.89'14—dc21
                                                 2002015322

To my wife, Cecyle: my passion and wonder,
my children, Seth and Sanya: pearls of great price who fill my soul,
and my stepchildren, Farah, Brock, and Shena:
shining stars who brighten our lives
D. K. C.

To my wife, Carol, and daughter, Katie,
for all their patience and love, and the creativity
they have brought to our family
K. W. B.

The more I take risks with my own creativity, the more I learn about myself as well as others, and the more I build associative connections within myself to be used as both verbal and enacted metaphor. I then begin to find ways of bridging to generic situations with people, creating a storehouse of metaphoric processes that later someone else labels as "technique." Yet, for the therapist-creator, tapping one's own resources in this fashion keeps oneself and therapy and training alive, interesting, fresh, and even fun at times. And, it invites clients and trainees to tap their own creativity, which is after all, the highest function of a human mind. It is also the goal in therapy for people to "do something different" than what holds them prisoner to their habitual behaviors, thought patterns, and feelings.

Bunny Duhl
in D. J. Weiner's *Beyond Talk Therapy*,
1999, pp. 95-96

CONTENTS

ABOUT THE AUTHORS

David K. Carson, PhD, is Professor of Child and Family Studies in the Department of Family and Consumer Sciences at the University of Wyoming, where he also co-coordinates the Interdisciplinary Graduate Specialization in Marriage and Family Therapy. He is a licensed marriage and family therapist, a clinical member of the American Association for Marriage and Family Therapy, an AAMFT-approved supervisor, and a certified diplomate in psychotherapy with the American Psychotherapy Association. Dr. Carson has authored or co-authored more than 70 publications and has served on the editorial board of the *Journal of Counseling and Development* and other counseling-related journals.

Kent W. Becker, EdD, is Assistant Professor of Counselor Education and Supervision at the University of Wyoming. In addition to co-coordinating the Interdisciplinary Graduate Specialization in Marriage and Therapy with Dr. Carson, he serves as the doctoral program coordinator for Counselor Education and Supervision. Dr. Becker is a licensed marriage and family therapist and a licensed professional counselor.

Preface

In the new millennium, as Dacey and Lennon (1998) have argued, the most valued ability in much of the world will not be intelligence (the capacity to learn and to use existing knowledge), but creativity (the ability to produce new ideas and knowledge). Such an assertion may be especially true in the helping professions, including individual, couple/marital, and family therapy. In this book, therapists' characteristics and techniques that might be labeled as creative or associated with the notion of creativity are carefully examined. Special areas of coverage include

- the concept of creativity in some prominent theories of counseling and family therapy;
- the relation of divergent thinking (central to the notion of creativity) to healthy human development and functioning and its role in the practice of therapy;
- the dynamic, interactive nature of creativity in therapy;
- the circumstances in which increased creative abilities in clients is or should be a goal in therapy;
- some threats or blocks to the development and expression of creativity in therapists and their clients;
- the role of creativity in psychotherapy and family therapy training; and
- the degree to which creativity in therapy is linked to the counseling office.

The importance a therapist places on creativity is no doubt based to a large degree on his or her theoretical persuasions, style of relating, and approaches to helping. On the other hand, although not all experienced clinicians are necessarily creative, it is our view that creativity in all types of counseling tends to correlate positively with the therapist's training, areas of expertise, and experiences in working with individuals and families.

We believe this book fills a crucial gap in both the creativity and psychotherapy literature. It is needed because there has been no inclusive examination to date of creativity in the treatment of individual, couple, and family difficulties. A unique feature of the book is its solid basis in established theoretical principles and empirical research, coupled with its readability and practical utility. It is our contention that the book will be intellectually stimulating and personally enlightening to academicians, practitioners, and therapists-in-training. It is both narrow (specific creative processes and interventions, including, for example, the role of humor and intuition) and broad (creativity related to diversity issues; institutional barriers to creative innovations) in scope. The book also includes a solid integration of both the popular and research-based knowledge on the interface between creativity, resiliency, and pathology—little of which can be found in the literature. Another unique feature of the book is the summary of findings from a large survey of therapists around the United States (conducted by the authors) that highlights various ways in which they view the importance and role of creativity in their work, as well as creative interventions they have found useful. These chapters are extremely important in that they provide viewpoints and information extending far beyond the authors' limited notions and perspectives on creativity. Finally, we believe a chapter on creative supervision will help provide some important closure to the book and address a crucial gap in the literature. It is our hope that through reading this book clinicians will be encouraged to further contemplate the role of creativity, both theoretically and pragmatically, in their approach to working with individuals, couples, and families.

For Whom Is This Book Appropriate?

This book should be considered as the main text in an advanced psychotherapy or marriage and family therapy course that focuses on techniques/applications more than theory, as a supplemental text in an introductory graduate-level (master's or doctoral) marriage and family counseling or therapy course, or as the sole text in a graduate seminar that examines the specific role of creativity in therapy. The book could also be adopted as one of the readings in a graduate-level social work, counselor education, human development and family studies, or counseling or clinical psychology class. Indeed, creativity is a hot topic these days, and interest is growing rapidly among students and professors in the helping and human services professions.

Although we believe that the book will be a popular text in graduate-level counseling courses, it may find an even stronger audience among practicing family therapists, counselors, psychotherapists, social workers, psychologists, and other human service professionals. This is because of its emphasis on application, as well as the fact that it is replete with examples and illustrations of creative intervention techniques.

There are not many books like this one. We can think of only a few—all of which are distantly related to ours. First, a number of books on the market deal with the creative arts in counseling and other experiential techniques. For example, Sam Gladding's (1998) book, *Counseling As an Art: The Creative Arts in Counseling,* is an excellent compilation. Rosemary Thompson's (1996) *Counseling Techniques* and Ed Jacobs's (1992) *Creative Counseling Techniques: An Illustrated Guide,* are packed with a variety of interventions (and creative ideas for props and other materials), some of which are tailored for working with couples and families. Daniel Wiener's (1999) edited book, *Beyond Talk Therapy: Using Movement and Expressive Techniques in Clinical Practice,* is another superb resource for the general practitioner and includes chapters dealing with drama therapy interventions, expressive art therapies (including music and dance/ movement therapy), and body psychotherapies such as yoga.

One excellent book that does provide some examination of the role of creativity in family therapy is Robert Taibbi's (1996) *Doing Family Therapy: Craft and Creativity in Clinical Practice.* This book has a number of strengths (such as readability, inclusion of pertinent illustrations and case study material, survival tips, and lessons of therapy for therapists). However, our book includes a thorough discussion of several additional dimensions to creativity in individual and family work. These include

- the role of creative and divergent thinking in therapy;
- creativity within the broader contexts of therapy (including organizational and institutional, insurance/third-party payment related, dealing with sensitive ethical issues in therapy, etc.);
- personal, social, cultural, and institutional barriers to creativity in therapy;

- the role of creativity in individual and family dysfunction and resiliency;
- applications of creative concepts and interventions gleaned from contemporary schools of therapy;
- how other therapists view creativity in their work; and
- the role of creativity in the supervision of therapists-in-training.

Taibbi also has little to say about the connection between creativity and humor, creativity and intuition, and other close correlates of creativity in family work. This book includes an engaging discussion of each of these areas and much more.

Other edited books that include creative approaches to family therapy have been edited by Thorana S. Nelson and Terry S. Trepper, including *101 Interventions in Family Therapy* (1993) and *101 More Interventions in Family Therapy* (1998). Both books are published by The Haworth Press, Inc. These edited books are an excellent collection of interventions into a variety of marital and family problems— many of which appear to be innovative, thought provoking, and useful to practicing family therapists. Most chapters are two to five pages in length and include a brief introduction and/or conceptual framework for the intervention, a short description of the intervention itself, a highlighted case study, and, in some chapters, mention of the limitations of the intervention. The strength of these books is their extensiveness of coverage, including the variety of interventions presented and relevance of marital and family difficulties discussed. We sincerely compliment these authors on their work. However, our goal was to write with a guiding theme and purpose in mind (i.e., creativity), blending diverse components of a complex picture into hopefully a meaningful whole. This included an exploration of the cognitive aspects of creative thinking and its importance and role in therapy and client change.

Another book, edited by Lorna Hecker and Sharon Deacon, *The Therapist's Notebook* (1998), is an extensive collection (over 400 pages) of homework, handouts, and activities for use in psychotherapy. This book includes numerous illustrations of practical interventions for use with couples, families, and children ranging from play therapy techniques to imagery to nonverbal/movement exercises. It is a veritable storehouse of information for creative interventions with children, adults, couples, and families.

Jackie Gerstein's (1999) *Sticking Together: Experiential Activities for Family Counseling* not only lays a solid foundation for experiential family therapy but also instructs therapists as to how to set up an experiential program or protocol with couples and families who have children in differing age groups. Most of the experiential games, activities, and techniques involve a fairly high level of physical movement, contact, cooperation, and teamwork among family members in which learning and growing happens as much by seeing and doing as talking with one another.

Two recent books by Angela Hobday and Kate Ollier contain a wealth of creative and experiential interventions. These include *Creative Therapy with Children and Adolescents* (1999) and *Creative Therapy 2: Working with Parents* (Ollier and Hobday, 2001). These books provide therapists with a variety of ideas for helping clients get in touch with and express their feelings, enhance self-esteem and motivation to change, reduce stress, improve coping and problem-solving skills, come to terms with loss, and find creative ways of enjoying one another as family members. However, these resources are generally geared toward working individually with children and adults rather than conjointly in the context of couple and family therapy.

Finally, two recent books by Bill O'Hanlon and associates (one in particular) probably approximate most closely what we have tried to accomplish in this book. *Invitation to Possibility Land* (Bertolino and O'Hanlon, 1999) is a quasi-verbatim account of an intensive weeklong training seminar held in Portland, Maine, in 1996. This book introduces readers to possibility thinking and solutioning, especially as conducted in a pedagogical and experiential format. However, O'Hanlon's other book, *A Guide to Possibility Land: Fifty-One Methods for Doing Brief, Respectful Therapy* (O'Hanlon and Beadle, 1997), captures the essence of possibility techniques. Although we have found both of these books remarkably interesting and useful both in our teaching and clinical practice, they are different from our book in several notable ways. These include: (a) our linkage to the constructs of creativity and creative thinking; (b) our groundedness in a number of theoretical perspectives; (c) our emphasis on creativity as a process of self-discovery; and (d) our strict adherence to a discussion of tools and techniques used in individual, couple, and family therapy.

In sum, our book is different from others in that it addresses the processes of creativity within the broad practice of psychotherapy, as well as couple and family therapy. Its emphasis is on the centrality of creativity to the field of therapy and the dynamic role of creativity in individual and family health/illness and couple relationships.

Premise of the Book

The premise of this book is that creativity in therapy primarily involves a mind-set, a way of thinking about oneself in relation to the individual, couple, or family. This mind-set includes unique ways of conceptualizing presenting difficulties, as well as working cooperatively with clients in discovering and formulating creative solutions, and not simply a grab bag of techniques. However, we also believe that therapy is as much an experience as it is a dialogue. In this regard, techniques and interventions are definitely important components of the therapist's repertoire of skills. The creative therapist continually thinks and acts in fresh ways in response to the constant ebbs and flows of client dynamics and interactions, and employs creative techniques and interventions when they are timely and appropriate. Creative interventions become part of the therapy at that moment and have ripple effects throughout the remaining course of therapy. However, their effectiveness is lessened or lost when clinicians use them in a scattered manner that does not fit into the whole of the therapy process with clients (i.e., as a compartmentalized segment of the session). In sum, more than anything this book illustrates a philosophy of working with individuals, couples, and families. The creative interventions described are but illustrations of our overarching approach to working with those whom we serve.

Surveying the Terrain of Creative Interventions As a Centerpiece of the Book

Part of this book (Chapters 4 through 7) includes responses from therapists across the United States (thirty-six total states to be exact) to a questionnaire that was designed to capture their perceptions of creativity in their work with clients. Using an online methodology we surveyed 142 marriage and family therapists (MFTs). All of these clinicians identified themselves as having a specialized interest and training in couple and family therapy. However, like many therapists, participants in our study reported that they spent a considerable amount of time (more than 60 percent) conducting therapy with individuals, including children and adults. Hence, although the focus of the study was on their work with couples and families, it is our conviction that responses of these participants can be generalized to psychotherapy practice with individuals. This assertion is based partly on our belief that all therapy is systemic in nature and is not dependent on the number of people in the room.

We constructed an instrument in which both quantitative and qualitative questions were asked (see Chapter 4). The research was based in part on our conviction that approaches to therapy that are more creative/experiential allow couples and families to communicate their thoughts and feelings freely and in a less threatening way. This process often facilitates deeper awareness of relational conflicts and difficulties, empathic understanding, and emotional healing. These interventions can also assist in uncovering unconscious material, including motivations, projective identifications, intrapsychic conflicts and defenses, and anxieties resulting from past experiences. Further, creative experiencing can enhance the ability of clients to think more divergently, as well as brainstorm potential solutions to real problems. Although the best interventions tend to arise out of the therapist's own creativity in the moment more than in any preconstructed interventions (Whitaker and Keith, 1981), it is our view that spontaneity and careful planning of creative interventions can go hand in hand.

Along with tapping respondents about what creativity meant to them in the context of couple and family therapy, what they thought were the most important qualities or characteristics of a creative family therapist, and blocks, barriers, or inhibitors that kept them from being as creative as they would like to be, we asked them to list three of their most creative interventions in working with couples and families. The participants provided some unique and unconventional responses to this question, in addition to listing a number of techniques and interventions that have frequently appeared in the family therapy and psychotherapy literature. A thorough presentation of quantitative findings from this study is reported elsewhere (Carson et al., 2003).

Outline of the Book

This book is divided into three sections. The Introduction and first three chapters lay the foundation for the book. In Chapter 1 we explore the meaning, role, and various dimensions of creativity in individual, couple, and family therapy. In Chapters 2 and 3 we provide an overview of the relationship between creativity and both healthy and pathological individual functioning, as well as family resiliency and dysfunction. Section II deals with the therapists' perceptions of creativity in their work (obtained in our empirical study) and applications to working more creatively with couples and families gleaned from the information provided by our 142 study participants. In Section III, Chapters 8 and 9 include an in-depth discussion, accompanied by examples, of creative interventions derived from ten popular therapy approaches or schools of thought. Chapter 10 examines the role of creativity in supervision. Here we discuss some creative principles and methods of supervising trainees that we have found exciting and effective over our years of doing clinical supervision.

Each chapter of the book begins with a Creative Incubation exercise intended to help prepare the reader for the material in that chapter, thus increasing the likelihood that some creative experiencing will occur as the information is ingested. We then conclude each chapter with one or more suggestions for how readers might begin Breaking Out of the Box and unleashing their creativity as therapists. Our hope is that this book will provide a variety of topographic maps and supplies for therapists and clients as they climb and conquer new peaks together.

Acknowledgments

The danger in writing acknowledgments is that authors will forget to pay tribute to individuals who have played a pivotal role in the book's inception, development, or completion. Ideas are inspired by many people, from former professors and supervisors to colleagues, clients, family members, and friends. However, our short list must include the following. For all those who are not acknowledged here, we trust you will know who you are.

We wish to thank the 142 therapists across the United States who were willing to serve as participants in our study. It is their creativity that makes up a portion of this book. Without their time, effort, and incredible insights, this book would have never come to fruition. We also want to thank the American Association for Marriage and Family Therapy (AAMFT) for allowing us to tap some of its members for participation in the study.

It is our pleasure to acknowledge the many creative students we have had the honor of teaching, training, and supervising over the years. Our sincere appreciation is also extended to the individuals, couples, and families who, as clients, have entrusted us with their struggles, hopes, and dreams.

Thanks also to two special friends and colleagues who offered their assistance and many insightful ideas in the writing of two chapters of the book, Heidi Bellis (Chapter 3) and Dr. Penny Dahlen (Chapter 10).

We are grateful to Mona Gupton for her help with the initial production of the manuscript. Her technical assistance has been second to none. Also, to my (DKC) department chair and good friend, Dr. Bernita Quoss, for her personal encouragement and profound sense of duty, professionalism, and character that have influenced me for a good portion of my academic career.

The first author would also like to acknowledge Dr. Mark Runco at California State University, Fullerton, for his unique contributions to the study of creativity in children, adults, and families. Years ago, without knowing, he inspired me to take the plunge into this fascinating sphere, and for that I will always be grateful.

We want as well to offer our sincere thanks to Dr. Lorna Hecker at Purdue University Calumet for encouraging us to pursue this project. Her ideas, particularly in the early phases of this undertaking, were most helpful. We are also grateful to Peg Marr for her suggestions and assistance throughout the later stages of the editing process.

Finally, we want to thank The Haworth Press, Inc., for taking a chance on us from the very beginning. It is our sincere hope that this book will be of great benefit to many. Our special thanks goes to Dr. Terry S. Trepper, editor in chief of The Haworth Clinical Practice Press. His extensive clinical experience, broad-based understanding of the family therapy field, encouragement, and keen editorial skills have been invaluable throughout the publication process.

Introduction:
Psychotherapy with Individuals, Couples, and Families As a Creative Enterprise

OLD WINE IN NEW WINESKINS:
WHAT IS CREATIVITY IN THE CONTEXT OF THERAPY?

The history of the psychotherapy field, and family therapy in particular, reads like an exciting novel, with creative twists and turns at practically every juncture. Creative ideas abound in the now numerous theories and models of therapy, and an abundance of new interventions have been proposed. The creative wizardry of pioneers such as Minuchin, Ackerman, Whitaker, Haley, and Satir (among many others) is ever apparent and reminds us that clinicians need a rich foundation of theory and technique from which to conduct their work. Taibbi (1996, p. 3) asserts that family therapy in particular "requires a flexibility, a creativity, an ability to fly by the seat of your pants that exponentially increases with the number of people in the room and their level of distress and conflict." Since change in close relationships is typically a slow and painful process, creative thinking and maneuvering are often necessary to break therapeutic impasses, help clients resolve conflicts, and empower individuals and families toward positive growth. Yet the role of various dimensions of creativity, including creative or divergent thinking, has received limited attention in the psychotherapy literature. Personality traits of highly creative therapists also need to be further explored. In addition, therapists can benefit greatly from a careful and thorough analysis of the creative processes in therapy.

Creativity has been defined by Barron as

> essentially the ability to bring something new into existence purposefully, though the process may have unconscious, or subliminally conscious, as well as fully conscious components.

1

Novel adaptation is seen to be in the service of increased flexibility and increased power to grow and/or to survive. (1988, p. 80)

Creativity involves both the processes and products of an individual in a complex interpersonal and sociocultural context that includes reciprocal interactions of people, cultural domains, and social institutions. It generally refers to activities or products that are truly original and break new ground. Dowd (1989) indicated that creative endeavors generally result in "strikingly new formulations that are not derived from what preceded them and in that sense represent a discontinuity" (p. 233). Creativity involves the production of something and is not just pure mental activity; hence, it is difficult to measure creativity in advance of an actual creative product.

Counseling in its broadest sense is a process that involves the use of psychological methods in giving professional guidance and assistance to individuals, couples, families, or groups. It is a speciality in which the therapist helps others alleviate their distress, resolve their crises, increase their ability to solve problems and make decisions, and improve their well-being. Systems-based therapy broadly encompasses therapeutic interventions conducted with some or all immediate family members conjointly, couples, and children within the context of parent education and counseling.

Providing a meaningful discussion of the relationship between creativity and therapy is an onerous task, given the abstract nature and seemingly countless definitions of creativity and schools of therapy that have appeared in both the classical and contemporary literature. To complicate the matter, notions of creativity as a construct are absent in most psychotherapy theories. Although a host of modern counseling interventions have been touted as creative, our personal belief is that many contemporary techniques are not all that helpful to individuals, couples, and families in the short or long run. Indeed, change is a slow and often painful process, especially for adult clients, and quick fixes, results, or products are probably rare in both creative and psychotherapeutic endeavors.

It is not our intention to discuss which approaches we think are less creative or noncreative but rather to elaborate on creative elements in a variety of therapeutic approaches. Such an assessment might be presumptuous, since creativity, like beauty, probably is largely in the eye of the beholder. On the other hand, we are convinced that certain components of and parameters surrounding the construct of creativity can be useful to therapists in determining which approaches include creative modes of thinking and skill when working with children, adults, couples, and families. Although one could argue that all counseling is creative to some extent, there is little doubt that some therapists operate at a much higher level of creativity with their clients, as well as engage their clients in creative thought and action more frequently and purposefully (both during and beyond the context of therapy) than other therapists. This book explores some of the reasons why this is so. Hence, our approach is integrative and systemic.

In our view, therapeutic approaches that promote mental health often parallel methods which enhance creativity, with similar desired outcomes or products. Humanistic writers such as Maslow (1968, 1971), May (1975), and Rogers (1961) have suggested that therapeutic approaches that promote good mental health often parallel activities or behaviors which typify highly creative individuals. Common characteristics of creative people include autonomy; acceptance of self, others, and nature; a democratic character structure; confidence; intrinsic motivation; a wide range of interests; and tolerance for ambiguity (see also Runco and Bahleda, 1986). Aspects or manifestations of positive mental health include (a) increased personal growth, awareness, and self-confidence; (b) improved problem-solving abilities (such as through the generation of multiple ways to look at a phenomenon or approach a situation); (c) enhanced human relationships; (d) a strong but balanced internal locus of control and responsibility; and (e) giving up traditional patterns of living and acquisition of new perceptions and roles.

Traditionally, counseling has been less often defined as a process of creation than of helping, education, personal development, and repair. However, Frey notes that (1975), "in the broadest sense, counseling is actually a creative enterprise within which client and counselor combine their resources to generate a new plan, develop a different outlook, formulate alternative behaviors, begin a new life" (p. 23). According to Frey, many times in counseling the therapist cannot rely on technical skill alone (or the latest gimmicks) but has to turn to inventiveness and creativity. Moreover, clients are not just consumers of services but are coproducers of both the processes and the products of counseling. Hence, counseling may be viewed as a creative interaction. Heppner, Fitzgerald, and Jones (1989) discussed the two major areas of counseling in which creativity occurs. These include understanding a client's problem and facilitating client change. These investigators suggested that, since counseling has been said to involve both scientific and artistic elements, "creativity within counseling can be the link between the predictable and the mysterious in human interaction, the known and the unknown" (p. 272). Lewis (1983) goes so far as to say that, in one way or another, every school of psychotherapy acknowledges the centrality of creativity in the therapeutic process. These sentiments have been echoed by those in the field of family therapy. For instance, Deacon and Thomas (2000) assert that family therapy is an art, a creative process that, "when broken down, is essentially the growth and development of creativity in clients and therapists" (p. 4).

STRENGTHS AND LIMITATIONS OF CREATIVITY IN THE THERAPEUTIC PROCESS

In case the reader assumes that we are elevating creativity to the level of the divine or positing that creativity is *the* primary component of therapy, we want to make it clear at the outset that this is not the case. It is our view that creativity on the part of the therapist (and of clients) is but one of several key factors in working successfully with couples, family units, and individuals. However, we feel equally strong that creativity is a crucially missing piece in many psychotherapeutic endeavors, especially in couple and family therapy, and that both novice and veteran therapists often overlook or underestimate the unique and important role that creativity plays in the process of working with clients. More than ever in today's world of unprecedented instability and uncertainty in the lives of children and adults, therapy requires inventiveness and strategic effort and skill. However, clinicians should not necessarily use techniques just because they are new, intriguing, or popular. Moreover, creative thinking entails sound judgment as much as the ability to break conventional boundaries. Creativity in therapy is also important because of the ever-increasing pressure to employ brief, short-term, solution-focused therapies due in part to restrictions posed by managed care. Clients too seem to expect more from therapy than ever before (and rightly so), even in the early stages. Thus, therapists generally no longer have the luxury of taking their time or being too cautious or non-innovative. Simply put, they need to be able to more fervently and effectively facilitate creative thought and action in their clients, using themselves and their skills as creative agents of change.

GETTING THE MOST FROM THE INCUBATION AND BREAKING OUT OF THE BOX EXERCISES

At the beginning of each chapter we have designed a brief Creative Incubation Exercise. The first exercise sets the stage for reading the book, and the remaining activities were created to assist the reader in switching gears and preparing to welcome the next chapter in a manner that is purposeful and personal. We believe (from our own journeys and teaching) that by giving oneself permission to slow down and undertake each exercise, readers will benefit by preparing their hearts and minds to be open, flexible, and ready for change (incubation). These are the same conditions therapists seek to create with their clients.

At the end of each chapter we invite readers to begin "Breaking Out of the Box" and join us for a variety of activities designed to further unleash their own personal creativity. As therapists become more adept at breaking out of their own self-constructed boxes, they are more likely to model and facilitate creative problem solving in session. The idea is to have fun with these activities. Readers should not take themselves too seriously. If what we ask feels strange and awkward—GREAT! This may be just what is needed.

SECTION I:
THE IMPORTANCE OF CREATIVITY
IN INDIVIDUAL, COUPLE,
AND FAMILY THERAPY:
HEALTH, DYSFUNCTION,
AND RESILIENCY

Chapter 1

Essential Components of Creativity in Individual, Couple, and Family Treatment

CREATIVE INCUBATION EXERCISE #1: SETTING THE TONE

We invite you to embrace this book in a manner that may be a bit different for some of you. This book is about you, your creative self, and energizing (or reenergizing) the potential within. As helpers we spend endless time (and energy) creating safe and therapeutic environments for others. We are thoughtful about how we arrange our office, greet our clients, pace the session, and put our ideas into actions. Now it is your time. It is time for you to be just as thoughtful about your own time and space. You deserve it!

We offer the following ideas to set the stage as you continue your reading:

- Accept that you are a creative individual. If you have ever been told otherwise, make a conscious decision now to say, "I am creative. Watch out world!" Life and society can dump a lot of barriers in our path. It is time to start your backhoe and push that debris aside. You are in the driver's seat and you make the rules.
- Read this book in places of personal energy. Honor your creativity by spending time reading in areas that nurture your soul. Be thoughtful about the where as well as the what. You may find yourself at your favorite coffee shop, next to a babbling brook, or on the sunny side of your favorite hill or peak. If you read indoors one week, venture out the next week. If you read in a place of solitude one week, read amid a group of young children playing the next week. Mix it up.

- Be kind to yourself and your personal life. Although getting professionally reenergized is exciting, it will never replace the power that creativity can infuse in our personal and spiritual journeys. Periodically ask yourself if your creative juices are flowing at home as well as at work. Share your creative energies with those you love and yourself first.
- Finally, have fun with your journey. Remember that creativity and experience go hand in hand. This book is intentionally a blend of words and actions. Absorb both, and as Dave often says, "Let the big dog eat!"

CREATIVITY AS AN ECOLOGICAL, CONTEXTUAL, AND SYSTEMIC CONCEPT

Creativity is contextual, systemic, and interactive in nature. It is not simply a feature of a person but rather a phenomenon resulting from the interactions of people with their physical environment, social institutions, and cultural domains in space and time (Mellou, 1995). Creativity can be viewed as a product of reciprocal influences of the person and the sociocultural context. Indeed, newer models of creativity have tended to reflect this ecological/systemic orientation. For example, Harrington's (1990) ecosystem model involves a complex interaction between an individual's personal resources (both as objectively and subjectively perceived) and the relevancy and use of other resources in the person's ecosystem, including functional relationships among creatively active persons. Barron's (1995) systems/ecological perspective on creativity focuses on the interplay of the individual's conscious and unconscious with certain societal factors such as spirituality/religiosity and gender stereotyping. Gruber (1988, 1995) also discusses the numerous influences on creativity (historical, societal, institutional), as well as how creators in various fields and endeavors both influence and are influenced by one another. Arieti (1976) indicates that some cultures value and are much more facilitative of creativity in children and adults than are other cultures and are, hence, more "creativogenic."

One of the most thorough analyses of how the social context influences the development and expression of creativity in children and adults has come from Teresa Amabile, especially with regard to intrinsic and extrinsic motivation. In her earlier work, Amabile (1983,

1987) placed much greater emphasis on intrinsic motivation in creative endeavor. According to Amabile, both creativity and intrinsic motivation can be discouraged or eliminated when there is an overabundance of extrinsic motivation (pay, praise, or promotion at work, home, or school). However, in her later writings, Amabile (1996, 1997) stresses the importance of a particular kind of extrinsic motivation in the genesis and manifestation of creativity. These "synergistic extrinsic motivators," in combination with intrinsic motivation, can enhance creativity, including socioenvironmental factors supporting an individual's autonomy, competence, or task involvement (e.g., additional materials or equipment to further one's creative endeavors), modeling from creative significant others, certain nonthreatening types of competition, and validation from others concerning the novelty or originality of the task or product.

In Dacey and Lennon's (1998) model, the sources of creativity include not only biological (e.g., genetic, hormonal, hemispheric dominance and intercoordination), cognitive (e.g., intelligence, remote associations, lateral thinking), and personality (e.g., tolerance of ambiguity, risk taking) characteristics, but also microsocietal (family relationships, home environment) and macrosocietal (work, economic, neighborhood/community, educational, ethnic, religious, political) features. These factors operate in a complex, interactive/multiplicative manner and in a temporal/historical context. Hence, notions of eminent and everyday creativity change throughout time and vary across cultures and social environments. Earlier, Dacey (1989a,b) postulated that during certain critical periods throughout the life span, creative ability can be cultivated most effectively. According to Dacey, creativity is most likely to develop during periods of crisis and change, such as early or late adolescence, or perhaps during the early to mid-forties. This notion has a direct implication for counseling and family therapy, in that couples and families often go for professional help during periods of crisis and change in the family life cycle.

According to Dacey and Lennon (1998), nothing is necessarily fixed about our perceptions or evaluations of what is creative, including what happens in the counseling milieu. Socioeconomic status, coupled with resources in the physical and social environment, the political climate, and the quality and availability of education, provide both affordances (opportunities) and restrictions in terms of the development and expression of individual creativity. It can easily be argued, for example, that restraints on creativity are much greater in resource-limited families living in more disadvantaged communities. Such is the plight of millions of ethnic minority families in the United States. Poverty, prejudice, and discrimination are generally not favorable to the development and expression of creativity in children or adults, even though exceptions to this rule have always been evident in our society. Creativity can (and has been known to) flourish in less than optimal societal environments, albeit often not without great obstacles and challenges.

One of the most powerful macrosocietal influences on the development of creativity in children and adolescents is the educational system. The same might be said for students in college and graduate or professional school. Although schools no doubt have the capacity to facilitate creativity in students (and sometimes do), the literature on creativity and schooling generally paints a negative picture. Elementary and secondary schools in the United States and other Western nations are viewed as institutions that tend to suppress creativity from the early grades onward (Csikszentmihalyi, 1996; Sternberg and Lubart, 1995; Torrance, 1995). This occurs for many reasons, including

- the strong emphasis on content learning, a competency-based curriculum, and convergent thinking;
- the failure of teachers and administrators to recognize and encourage creativity in their students;
- teachers' fears that when students are allowed or challenged to be creative the instructors will lose control of their classroom, fueled by an emphasis on dominance, subordination, and student conformity;
- a failure on the part of school personnel to understand and appreciate the value of creativity with regard to both individual and cooperative learning, as well as self-management, coping, and life skills;
- teachers already feeling pulled in too many directions ("You want us to facilitate creative thinking and expression also?!"); and
- rigid rules of school districts and punitive actions sometimes taken against innovative teachers.

However, research has demonstrated that teachers can be taught how to cultivate children's creativity in the context of their assigned responsibilities (Torrance, 1975, 1982).

These influences of the educational system on the lack of creativity development in students has some interesting implications for individual and family therapy. First, since everyday creativity is generally not nurtured, much less valued, in most schools, children grow up deficient in creative thoughts and skills. This may have important ramifications to problem solving and other areas of personal adjustment and relationships. Second, therapists are just as unlikely to have had enriching creative experiences at school or in the home. Hence, they may underestimate or not recognize the importance of creative thinking and behavior to client health or psychopathology, or to their work as clinicians. Third, therapists may have difficulty discerning the differences in their clients' thinking, behavior, or personality between the highly gifted or creative person and those with particular disorders or presenting with certain symptoms, for example, the highly creative person who is incorrectly diagnosed with cyclothymia.

EMINENT AND EVERYDAY CREATIVITY

Creativity theorists and researchers generally distinguish between two major types of creativity: eminent and everyday. Eminent (extraordinary) creativity entails individual accomplishments that have received some form of special recognition or notoriety from society at large or from a major professional group (e.g., arts, sciences, political leadership). Included in this category would be those possessing creative genius, although many eminent creators would not necessarily be labeled as geniuses. A list of eminent personality theorists/clinicians would no doubt include individuals such as Sigmund Freud, Carl Jung, Abraham Maslow, Carl Rogers, Fritz Perls, Harry Stack Sullivan, Henry Murray, and Rollo May, to name a few. The field of family therapy, too, has had its share of creative gurus (to be elaborated on later). However, although the practice of psychotherapy (including couples and family work) sometimes entails expressions of extraordinary creativity by both eminent therapists and those without widespread recognition, our emphasis here is on the development and use of everyday creativity in the therapeutic setting by "ordinary" individuals, those who make up the vast majority of professionals involved in counseling and family therapy.

In a general sense everyday creativity involves the full range of original outcomes derived from one's day-to-day activities, including those at work and play. This type of creativity carries with it no requirement for social recognition but is identified solely in terms of the widely accepted criteria of originality and meaningfulness to self and/or others (including hobbies or special talents). As will be illustrated, this kind of creativity in therapy occurs in bursts of creative breakthrough as well as through slow, methodical creative actions on the part of both therapist and clients. And, as Dacey and Lennon (1998) have observed, thinking and producing creatively do not always involve a major restructuring of acquired knowledge or the creation of something entirely new, but often simply the reproductive application of past methods in useful ways.

CREATIVITY IN SOME PROMINENT THEORIES
OF COUNSELING

Gladding (1995a) describes how some prominent and enduring counseling theories have acknowledged the importance of creativity, especially with regard to the counseling process and the nature of change. For instance, according to Freud (1940) creativity is central to the generally positive defense mechanism of sublimation. From Adler's (1968) perspective, the counselor encourages innovative responses from clients, with creative expression being one indicator of growth. In accordance with humanistic and existential theories (e.g., Fromm, May, Maslow, Allport), the readjustment of personality tensions has been equated with creativity, in that the process of change involves both risks and creative acts (Bugental and Sterling, 1995; Corey, 1991). Gestalt theorists view creativity (e.g., trying out new behaviors that may seem strange or unconventional) as a means toward integration and change (Yontef, 1995). From some cognitive psychology perspectives, enhancement of divergent thinking and/or new visual images is often a prerequisite to behavioral change and emotional relief (Corey, 1991; Freeman and Reinecke, 1995). Finally, according to some linguistic and communications adherents (e.g., Fisch, Weakland, and Segal, 1982; Haley, 1987), the "language of change" essential to psychotherapy may involve the creative use of metaphors, stories, parables, fairy tales, and other methods that, according to Gladding, "can open up a whole new world to clients and offer them choices and ways of looking at the world that they would not otherwise discover" (1995a, p. 4). Gladding discusses a number of "specific creative exercises in counseling" embraced within the domains of music, visual arts, and writing. These include such creative techniques as guided imagery, idea journals, one-minute free writes, genograms, early recollections, collage and other art mediums, analysis of heroes and heroines, timeline analyses, and life mapping (see also Heppner et al., 1994).

Some Conceptual Commonalities Between Creativity and Family Therapy

Gladding and Henderson (2000) examined areas of overlap between Eberle's (1971) SCAMPER (substitute, combine, adapt or alter, modify or magnify, put to other uses, eliminate [or minimize], and reverse or rearrange) model of creativity and the practice of family therapy. Although creativity is a cornerstone of family counseling, Gladding and Henderson assert that many therapists do not have the time or natural inclination to consistently use methods that are original and creative while at the same time clinically sound. However, the SCAMPER model can be a convenient and effective way of promoting change in families.

Substitution is a principle similar to reframing and relabeling in family therapy. Here, negative or destructive words and images can be substituted with positive and empowering ones. Combining has to do with helping family members join and work together with a certain focus as a single unit rather than against one another. Adapting and altering homeostatic ways of thinking and behaving is often how families make positive changes, such as when unrealistic expectations of children or adolescents are replaced by realistic expectations. Further, couples and family members can learn how to modify or magnify their comments toward one another, including tipping the scales in favor of positive interchanges even if they continue to argue on a regular basis. Family members can also enhance their relationships by rechanneling personal characteristics or putting them to other uses, such as when parents help a shy child continue developing his or her nonverbal communication and keen observational skills. Negative family scripts or histories can also be eliminated, minimized, or rewritten in an effort to create a new family paradigm or dominant story. Finally, families can be helped to reverse or rearrange destructive patterns of interacting by changing routines and rituals, or sometimes doing the opposite of what they have been doing. Although the SCAMPER model should never be adopted as a stand-alone approach to working more creatively with families, it provides an eclectic and atheoretical road map that can be extremely useful to practitioners.

Deacon and Thomas (2000) have recently examined the construct commonalities between creativity theories and systems-oriented approaches to family therapy. According to these authors, positive change is always at the center of therapy and any creative endeavor, including problem solving and resolution (therapy) and problem finding and invention (creativity). In particular, first-order change in family therapy is to convergent thinking in creativity theories (resolution within the rules of the problem) as second-order change is to divergent thinking (resolution that works outside the rules of the problem or changes the problem definition itself). Although such components of divergent thinking as originality, flexibility, and elaboration are central to creativity, family therapy often involves related cognitive processes (e.g., examining family members' expectations, assumptions, stories, rules, and meanings within the family and reframing perspectives). Other parallel processes include affect as a catalyst to change in family therapy and the role that affect plays in creativity (e.g., emotional flexibility and intrinsic motivation). Moreover, the general steps involved in therapy (e.g., assess, define, intervene, evaluate) are similar to those highlighted in many theories of creativity (e.g., preparation, definition, incubation, illumination, and verification). What creativity and family therapy ultimately have in common, however, is that for change to occur there must be safety, optimal support and challenge, and a "flow" experience. Flow in a creativity sense has to do with being completely enveloped with an activity in the moment that is both goal directed and enjoyable (Csikszentmihalyi, 1996, 1997). Here, action and awareness are merged, and challenge and skill are balanced. In a process in which time is forgotten, self-consciousness is transcended, and there is little worry over failure, the activity becomes an end in itself. In transforming episodes of family therapy, the flow between therapist and clients is highly similar (Deacon and Thomas, 2000; Piercy and Nelson, 1999).

Papp (1984) discussed the connection between artistic creativity and clinical creativity. According to her, an artist survives neither by means of inspiration nor favorable circumstance but by persistence. Hence, a large part of creativity is habit—the habit of doing something difficult. Both artists and clinicians have as their goal the breaking of frames and wanting people to see things differently. Moreover, as with artistic inspiration, creativity in clinical work sometimes, perhaps often, involves breakthroughs. Indeed, "in the family therapy literature, many examples of breakthroughs are celebrated" (Openlander, 1991, p. 69). According to Openlander, this is often the result of the creative efforts of therapist and clients. However, the main difference between artists and therapists is that artists explore human experience, not needing to answer questions about life's dilemmas and ambiguities but only to raise them. Therapists are called upon to help put back together what life experiences have broken. In this context, they ask questions with the intent that they will, along with their clients, find solutions to problems or ways to make the intolerant more tolerable and hopefully meaningful. Although artists observe and record inevitabilities, therapists attempt to influence them. Clinical creativity, particularly in couples and family work, also differs from artistic creativity in that it frequently involves an attempt at second-order change. However, like art, in creative family therapy truth is pursued in a circuitous manner. This often occurs through tasks, rituals, metaphors, and stories that serve as devices that keep clients from being blind to the truth. What must be remembered is that change is as much a function of clients' creativity as it is that of the therapist. As Papp (1984, p. 24) notes, "A therapist's creativity is systemic and cannot be separated from the creativity of the client or family. A brilliant intervention only becomes brilliant through the brilliant use made of it by other people."

In sum, creativity is an essential part of marriage and family work. Without novel experiences, clients are likely to continue approaching their life issues from the same perspectives. If the therapist's goal is to identify patterns that are not working and assist clients in replacing these ineffective patterns with more efficacious ones, and if one assumes that new experiences are necessary for change to occur, then it can safely be concluded that creativity is an essential part of the therapeutic process.

The Notion of Creativity in Some Approaches to Individual and Family Therapy

Although most theories of family therapy have not directly stressed the importance of creativity, we would argue that creative ideas and interventions are inherent to all major family therapy schools of thought. These include such diverse approaches as narrative therapy (White, 1995; White and Epston, 1990; Zimmerman and Dickerson, 1996), internal family systems therapy (Schwartz, 1995), solution-focused therapy (de Shazer, 1985, 1988), and strategic family play therapy (Ariel, 1992), to name a few. For example, the idea of concentrating on what *is* working in the family and identifying exceptions to the time the problem exists (de Shazer, 1985, 1988, 1991, 1994), allowing problems to talk (Zimmerman and Dickerson, 1996), identifying subpersonalities or "parts" of the self that inhibit individual growth and family functioning (Schwartz, 1995), and providing opportunities for family members to construct things together and freely interact in fun and exciting ways (Ariel, 1992) are creative frameworks from which to conduct therapy.

Experiential approaches to therapy, perhaps more than any other type of approach, employ techniques and interventions that are intended to facilitate creative experiencing. Indeed, spontaneous and creative experiencing is an important goal of experiential family therapy (Piercy et al., 1996), so much so that Whitaker and Keith (1981) suggest that nonrational, right-brain experiencing is an indicator of health in both therapist and clients. Moreover, problems are often created and maintained, at least in part, because clients' creative problem-solving abilities are nonexistent or have ceased to function. As Piercy and colleagues have indicated, techniques such as sculpturing, art therapy, puppetry, drawings, psychodramatic techniques, and certain Gestalt interventions are all applied in order to free clients to experience significant others and life more creatively and personally. Other techniques include journaling and other forms of writing, music, play therapy and therapeutic games, guided imagery, genograms, early recollections, analysis of heroes and heroines, and life mapping (Heppner et al., 1994). Creative approaches to therapy allow clients to communicate their thoughts and feelings spontaneously in a caring and nonthreatening environment. The use of techniques that allow people to create and express themselves in nonverbal ways are often less threatening and can facilitate an understanding of their strengths as well as their weaknesses and conflicts. These techniques can also help clients become aware of and express feelings and unconscious material (e.g., due to traumatic experiences) in ways that allow them time before taking ownership of these thoughts and feelings (Gladding, 1998; Whitaker and Keith, 1981). Further, creative products, such as an increased ability to brainstorm potential solutions to a problem, can provide a permanent, tangible record of progress throughout the course of therapy (Gardner and Moran, 1997; Taibbi, 1996).

As important as creative techniques can be, Piercy and colleagues (1996) have correctly observed that techniques are not the essence of effective therapy because the best interventions (especially in the later sessions) tend to arise out of the therapist's own creativity in the moment and not in any preplanned interventions (see also Neill and Kniskern, 1982). Hence, the "objective of all techniques is to eliminate techniques" (Whitaker and Keith, 1981, p. 218). What then are the components of creativity in the context and process of therapy? Creativity is often a core feature of the assessment and engagement, middle, and termination phases of therapy (Taibbi, 1996; Worden, 1994). One of the most significant ways creativity is manifested in all counseling endeavors, including family therapy, is through divergent thinking in therapist and clients (Flach, 1990; Taibbi, 1996). This type of thinking is multifaceted and involves both problem-solving and problem-finding abilities.

CREATIVE PROBLEM FINDING
AND PROBLEM SOLVING

Central to the construct of creativity are the notions of creative problem finding/generation (the ability to generate whole new problems to solve or issues to explore) and creative problem solving (the ability to entertain a wide range of possible options or solutions and then select the *best* action or response) (Brown, 1989; Isaksen, Dorval, and Treffinger, 1994; Runco, 1994b; Wolin and Wolin, 1993). Creative problem finding (CPF) and creative problem solving (CPS) are in one sense two sides of the same coin. CPF involves sensing gaps and missing elements, identifying discrepancies and apparent contradictions, and entertaining new hypotheses about old problems/issues or generating entirely novel questions or problems to be solved (Runco, 1994b). CPS, on the other hand, entails the use of original or unconventional means of resolving personal dilemmas or reaching tentative conclusions about intellectual questions, issues, or challenges. CPS is central to the creative process and often involves such mental operations as preparation, concentration, incubation, ideation, illumination, and verification/production (Noller, 1979; Witmer, 1985).

The association between CPF and CPS and counseling or family therapy seems obvious. It could easily be argued that individuals and families sometimes (perhaps often) present for therapy because of a lack of personal creative problem-solving abilities, the incapacity to employ these abilities in a way that is effective or helpful, or limitations of others with whom they are interacting which make it difficult or impossible for everyone to experience a positive outcome. However, in many cases CPF precedes CPS, in that individuals and families often have to first identify and clarify their problems or issues, or explore the underlying patterns, behaviors, or emotions that may be the source of pain or difficulties, before they can engage in a creative way of dealing with them. In addition, as will be elaborated on later, creative problem solving is believed to be essential to the resolution of tension or disequilibrium (Runco, 1994b) and for successful adaptation (Cohen, 1989; Flach, 1990). Hence, problem-finding and problem-solving abilities can be linked to positive mental health, provided they are operating on approximately the same level of efficiency. Some empirical evidence, for example, suggests that individuals who are high in problem-finding but low in problem-solving capacities are more likely to report greater personal difficulties (Cropley, 1990; Mraz and Runco, 1994; Richards, 1990).

A number of models of creativity have been based upon problem-solving abilities that include, for example, an interaction of prior knowledge, search strategies, personal values, and affect (Voss and Means, 1989). Treffinger, Isaksen, and Dorval's (1994) creative learning model entails basic thinking tools that can be acquired and practiced by people of all ages in order to solve real-world problems. Others (e.g., Edwards and Sproul, 1984) have viewed creative thinking and problem solving as parallel if not identical processes, since both result in useful solutions to either old or new problems. Smith and Van der Meer (1990) referred to creativity as a high-level coping strategy, since creativity is the only behavior that contributes to successful adaptation while at the same time leading directly to original results. However, this does not imply that creativity is exclusively an adaptive function or coping strategy, but simply that in some cases it might be (Runco, 1994a). Nevertheless, although creative problem-solving abilities do not automatically lead to effective coping, in many human situations they appear to be a necessary condition for adaptive behavior.

THE IMPORTANCE OF DIVERGENT THINKING IN THERAPY

Divergent thinking (DT) (a term that is sometimes mistakenly used interchangeably with creative thinking) is a central component of creativity. Tests of DT are often commonly used measures of creative potential (Baer, 1993; Runco, 1991). DT is characterized by thought processes that radiate outward and explore new ideas that are generated from the original notion. It often entails achievement of conclusions open to individual interpretation through the synthesizing or integration of pieces of information initially thought to be unrelated or even antithetical. In contrast, convergent thinking (CT) is characterized by reasoning that brings together relevant information and arrives at a firm conclusion based on this information—often through the recognition and expression of preestablished or externally dictated criteria. It tends to be analytical and focuses on reaching a correct solution to a problem or issue. Although creativity is often associated with divergent thinking processes, convergent thinking is not necessarily detrimental to creative production or the creative process. Sometimes convergent thinking is an important aspect of creative problem solving. However, often in therapy clients become too focused on the problem or their own failed attempts to resolve difficulties. Thus, although their convergent-thinking skills may be operating on an extremely high level, their divergent-thinking abilities are nonfunctional or dysfunctional.

There are several key components of divergent thinking according to Torrance (1974, 1988)—all of which can be assessed in individuals through both verbal and figural methods. These include fluency (the ability to produce a large number of ideas), flexibility (the ability to produce a large variety of ideas), originality (the ability to produce ideas that are novel, unusual, unconventional, or not obvious; believed to be the centerpiece of creativity), elaboration (the ability to develop, embellish, or complete an idea or concept), and resistance to premature closure (resistance to leap to conclusions prematurely without considering the available information). In resisting premature closure the creative person is able to stay open and delay closure long enough to make the mental ascent that makes original ideas possible. Since these modes of thinking often appear to precede or accompany corresponding modes of behavior, it is not surprising that DT is generally associated with coping abilities (Carson and Runco, 1999) and good mental health (Cropley, 1990; Richards, 1990). Moreover, divergent feeling (DF) is often a product or concomitant of divergent thinking. DF has to do with the ability and presumed freedom one has (including inside the marriage and family unit) to express the full range of human emotions in ways that are not damaging to self or others. Feelings that accompany, or are a part of, risk taking, curiosity, and imagination are also manifestations of DF.

Divergent thinking, then, tends to be tentative and exploratory. It is oriented to the development of possibilities rather than data, to speculation rather than conclusions. Other characteristics of DT include a tolerance for ambiguity and inconsistency, the ability to hold contradictory ideas simultaneously in one's mind, resistance to premature closure in one's thinking and judgments, intuitive thought, and the capacity to incorporate and modify new ideas (Baer, 1993; Runco, 1991). Dowd (1989) describes DT as the ability to maintain flexible constructs and avoid a premature "hardening of the categories" or "immaculate perception." Thus, DT can be thought of as more intuitive and less data based (or data bound) than convergent thinking. These characteristics appear to be associated with the client's ability to master his or her environment *and* the therapist's skill at his or her craft.

Frey (1975) suggests that therapeutic innovators are consistently able to focus on the interplay of convergent and divergent thinking, alternately "busting out" by combining what was before not combinable and then carefully evaluating these combinations for the best ideas and approaches with their clients. Moreover, personal or relational difficulties of clients often seem to be augmented by an imbalance in convergent and divergent thinking (e.g., a deficiency in DT and overuse of CT). Thus, some clients and families become paralyzed in their own paradigms (Reiss, 1981). Rather than being able to imagine alternatives or try out new behaviors or methods of problem solving, they may become too locked in on the problem(s), blame someone for making others miserable, or obsess over their own repeated failed attempts to resolve the difficulties or to feel better. After a while the attempted solutions themselves may become part of the symptom picture. In many therapy situations an increase in divergent thinking seems to be essential in breaking unhealthy patterns of perceiving, behaving, and contemplating options, alternatives, and possible solutions. In other situations, however, difficulties might be augmented by a deficiency in CT and an overuse of DT, such as in some high-energy chaotic families. Hence, change in individuals, as well as family systems, may require shifts or increases in both convergent and divergent thinking. It is possible that the divergent thinking component is often overlooked (or sometimes underemphasized) by both therapists and clients.

THE CREATIVE PROCESS IN THERAPY

The creative process in therapy involves the act of creating, often in several stages or phases. This process is dynamic and interactional. Included are various dimensions of creative thinking and emotional expression or involvement (Baer, 1993; Witmer, 1985):

1. *Preparation*—acquiring skills and background information; resources; sensing and defining a problem
2. *Concentration*—focusing intensely on the problem to the exclusion of other demands; a trial and error phase that includes false starts and frustration
3. *Incubation*—withdrawing from the problem; sorting, integrating, clarifying at an unconscious level; relaxation and solitude
4. *Ideation*—generation of ideas that are not judged or evaluated
5. *Illumination*—an "Aha!" stage; often sudden, involving the emergence of an image, idea, or perspective that suggests a solution or direction for further work
6. *Verification*, *Elaboration*, and *Production*—testing out the new idea; evaluating, developing, implementing, and convincing others of the worth of the idea

These stages may parallel the general process of therapy. For example, preparation entails the building of a safe and secure therapeutic environment (analogous to the establishment of the creative environment discussed earlier). Concentration and incubation become key components of the assessment and problem exploration phase, whether one is focusing on understanding the developmental history of problems and/or the homeostatic maintenance of problems in the present. Gradually, then, old ideas or behaviors are often reframed so that clients can develop new ways of looking at things, seeing alternatives, and feeling more empowered to make changes in their lives (ideation and illumination). Reframing thus involves a combination or transformation of information, often in unique or novel ways, that is used to elucidate or resolve a client's problem by extending the client's experiential world in some manner. New ideas and behaviors are then practiced or tested out in real-life situations (evaluation). Finally, verification/production can be seen in increased problem-solving abilities, open and healthy expression of emotions, closer and more meaningful relationships, and the promotion of individual competence and self-esteem within the family over time (the creative product).

It is important to note that these stages of the creative process in therapy are not necessarily linear but may operate in a cybernetic fashion. Further, what often appears as resistance in therapy may actually be a failure on the part of therapist and clients to find a creative solution to the impasses that are common in many helping situations. There are also both content and process variables affecting the clinician's creative thinking and actions. According to Heppner, Fitzgerald, and Jones (1989), process variables include the therapist's knowledge bases, self-efficacy, mental and emotional well-being, ability to remain open to new information, receptiveness to one's own experiences in therapy (e.g., dealing with countertransference issues), and effort and involvement. Sometimes therapists try too hard, become overinvolved with clients, get too concerned about their own performance, or miss important information because of narrowly focused attention. However, Heppner, Fitzgerald, and Jones (1989) suggest that creative insight is most likely to occur during periods of relaxed tension when solutions are not forced. From this perspective, therapy in general, and family therapy in particular, becomes one of the most productive settings to study creativity within the context of interpersonal relationships. Moreover, Cole and Sarnoff (1980) indicate that "the modeling of creativity by the counselor may well have transfer effects beyond those consciously perceived by the client" (p. 144).

Lest we overemphasize the importance of the cognitive and behavioral aspects of creativity in family therapy, it is crucial to remember that change on the emotional level in clients is equally important. In fact, it is often through corrective emotional experiences in therapy that individuals, couples, and families are able to move forward. Getting in touch with one's own feelings and seeing the full impact of one's behavior on the feelings of others are often paramount to empathic understanding. Further, breaking free of power imbalances and emotional controls or manipulation in intimate relationships (including the family) and learning how (or allowing oneself and others) to express the full range of human emotions in constructive ways and in an environment that is safe and reinforcing are all essential ingredients of creative therapy. These are aspects of what might be called divergent feeling. Indeed, emotional experiences and releases are often keys to change in relationships and family systems. Emotional creativity, or the affectional release of creative energy, has the potential to help individuals and close relationships heal. This is because positive emotional experiences often lead to enhanced efforts in problem solving, imagination, flexibility, and playfulness in family systems (Deacon and Thomas, 2000). Reciprocally, when these behaviors are augmented, emotional security and positive emotional expressions tend to increase. Hence, the emotional engagement of the therapist with clients, coupled with opportunities to experience and express emotions toward one another in therapy, may be important first steps in developing new patterns of relating in people's everyday lives.

The creative process in therapy may include other cognitive operations associated with divergent thinking. Present in many effective approaches to counseling is the facilitation of deferred judgment in the face of strong feelings and perceptions on the part of the client and the initiation of processes that lead to divergent thoughts and emotions. As Cole and Sarnoff (1980) have indicated, "Divergent production and deferred judgment are means to insure large numbers of diverse responses increasing the likelihood of finding a problem's 'good solution'" (p. 145). For example, therapists who have a capacity to intuit and state hunches, recognize connections and patterns in family systems, integrate and synthesize information, use metaphorical logic and communication, and engage in frequent checking and hypothesizing with clients (e.g., "It seems to me that . . ." or "I wonder if . . .") often seem to facilitate the process of discovery and change, regardless of whether their stated hunches are accurate.

As mentioned earlier, the role of creativity in therapy has less to do with techniques per se than with dynamic process. Creativity in counseling involves a complex interaction of counselor training and qualities, client personalities and presenting problems, structural and systemic considerations, the understanding and healthy expression of human emotions, and the circumstances under which counseling is taking place. For instance, a highly creative and well-trained therapist whose personality combines well with that of a particular teenager and her parents may still be met with a great deal of resistance from parents who find it difficult to remove their child from the role of identified patient and face the reality of serious difficulties in their marriage. Persistent marital patterns, together with parent denial, may make it difficult for the therapist to assist the struggling adolescent and help the family gradually transform itself. One could argue that creative solutions to problems are more likely to occur under more ideal conditions (e.g., therapist and clients like each other, clients are bright, problems do not seem insurmountable). If, for example, parents and teenager are able and willing to engage in creative thinking and experience, change may be more probable even if they are somewhat resistant to change. In other cases, creativity might best be expressed and enhanced in families where conditions are far from optimal and problems are numerous. There is little doubt that the outcomes depend on a multitude of factors unique to each family and situation and are often not easy (or always necessary) for the therapist to predict or control.

In terms of the counselor and creativity, creative interventions require that counselors devote time and energy to being flexible, spontaneous, and sometimes provocative. One such creative intervention is enactment. Gladding (1995a) notes that enactment "is a creative procedure for making the covert overt and informing clients of possibilities they either failed to recognize or were afraid to try previously" (p. 8). The circumstances, however, have to be right for a given intervention to be successful. According to Gladding,

> One way of setting up circumstances so therapeutic creativity is possible is to make therapeutic sessions more similar to play than to work. By doing so, clients are attracted to participating in activities the counselor may suggest because therapeutic directives are seen as non-threatening and even fun. (1995a, p. 9)

This is not to diminish clients' pain or the struggle required in most cases for change but to simply suggest that successful therapy may involve a combination of play and hard work, and that creativity at some level may be a requirement for successful intervention. Therapists who work regularly with children and/or families may find this especially true. It is also to suggest that it is easy for clients and sometimes therapists to become more problem oriented than solution oriented and to focus on clients' limitations rather than areas of resiliency, in other words, to concentrate more on resolving clients' difficulties than building on strengths, opportunities, and possibilities. Being able to see beyond the problems and utilize existing strengths requires that clients think divergently.

Finally, it is our contention that the creative process in therapy extends beyond the one-hour session (Frey, 1975; Gladding, 1995a; Taibbi, 1996). Creative therapists tend to engage clients in activities outside the office (e.g., homework assignments which can be interesting and insightful, family fun nights, marital dates) that allow them to practice and extend what they are gaining in therapy. These activities may sometimes elicit the participation of others in the life of the client or family (e.g., peer helpers, extended family members, coupled friends). However, it is important to emphasize that increased creativity in clients or use of creative insight or techniques in therapy do not automatically result in therapeutic change. The volitional/motivational aspects of counseling remain perhaps the most perplexing with regard to modifications or transformations in family systems. However, it is in this domain that creativity can play a unique and strategic role. Although couple and family therapy in particular presents some of the greatest challenges in the mental health field, it also provides a fruitful forum for the nurturing and expression of creativity in family members and the therapists who are dedicated to helping them.

In summary, despite the importance of creativity in family therapy and individual counseling, Gladding (1995a) suggests that the most vital role of creativity in people helping might be that it instills hope within clients that their lives can be better. As Frey aptly concludes:

The redefinition of counseling as an exercise in creativity allows us to draw on more resources in our struggle to help our clients, including such resources as intuition and our own ingenuity. We can be more sure of ourselves and our ability to provide help because we can more fully enter the relationship. (1975, p. 27)

However, therapists and clients must be aware of the many threats or blocks to creativity before the creative process can flow freely and creative solutions can be found.

The Creative Environment and Therapy

The creative therapeutic environment is one that encourages spontaneity and free expression (verbal, behavioral, emotional) of clients and therapist, often through intense, invigorating stimulation and interaction. Part of the creative environment entails the therapist's unconditional acceptance of and regard for clients as unique individuals (Rogers, 1961, 1986). The creative environment may also include a comfortable and aesthetically pleasing physical setting in which to work. Clients, too, are partially responsible for establishing a creative environment through their willingness to self-transpose, learn, and grow. Sometimes changing the environment, either in the context of therapy or in clients' living, employment, or educational situations, may free up creative energy. For example, working with children and adolescents in milieus other than one's office (e.g., the park or basketball court), or with families in groups, may not only help therapist and clients build a greater rapport, but also release creative potential. Freeing creative energy in children and adults may also involve making some basic but often overlooked changes in clients' eating, sleeping, leisure, and exercise patterns.

According to Deacon and Thomas (2000), the creative therapeutic environment includes several characteristics of the flow process. That is, the creative environment is safe, invites challenges and risk taking, is emotionally intense, involves being and doing, and allows the therapeutic process to be an experience in itself. The creative environment also utilizes clients' gifts and talents, invites divergent thinking and problem solving, and involves systemic interaction. In short, the creative environment is one that encourages a freedom and diversity of thinking, action, and emotional expression in a private and secure place. One goal is that as clients learn how to create and participate in this type of environment in therapy, they will eventually be able to replicate it at home.

The Importance of Intuition in Therapy

Intuition is the ability to attain direct knowledge or insight without evident rational thought and inference. Experienced therapists seem to rely heavily on their intuition when seeking to understand problematic relationships and facilitate change in individuals, couples, and family systems. Sometimes they seek to elicit or enhance the intuitive abilities of clients. Intuition has been described by Hans Selye (1988) as a major component of the creative process (a "gift of the creative process," p. 253). Selye suggests that intuition is the unconscious intelligence that leads to knowledge without reasoning or inference. Thus, intuition is closely linked to creative thinking—the "flash needed to connect conscious thought with imagination" (1988, p. 253)—which is, in turn, a key component of immediacy. However, according to Selye, although intuition may seem to appear suddenly and without provocation, it is actually the result of careful preparation. In scientific inquiry this is commonly supported by intensive study, keen observation, and a fruitful memory. Such is also likely the case in therapy. Indeed, just as chance favors the prepared mind, advantage and good fortune, in all probability, favor the prepared therapist. Although it is impossible to verify, teach, or regulate unconscious intuitive logic, intuitive thinking "must be carefully checked and its error repaired above the surface of consciousness" (Selye, 1988, p. 253).

In many counseling situations, intuition appears to be denied full expression or is simply underdeveloped in therapists and in our clients. This can limit the effectiveness of our interventions. There are several possible reasons that intuition gets blocked or fails to be useful. First, intuition is obscure and nonverbal. It is an understanding that may develop through "feelings, moods, dreams, fantasies, reveries, and in personal images and symbols" (Fisher, 1981, p. 21). For example, when we have a feeling with no apparent cause, it may be a clue for us to be aware of oncoming intuition since emotions, moods, and body feelings are often the basic minimal cues to intuition. Intuition also expresses itself in allegories, metaphors, puns, and other forms of humor. Second, because we usually do not expect intuition,

we are not ready for it when it comes. Third, this process is compli-
cated by the fact that the intuitive thought or feeling is often faint
and/or ephemeral, and unless a thought or feeling is strong, we tend
to ignore or fail to recognize it. Finally, because intuition may be dis-
turbing and unwelcome to the conscious mind, it may be squelched
by the defenses (e.g., denial, suppression, rationalization). Hence, we
frequently tend to dismiss intuitive knowledge as "trivial, frivolous,
or inconsequential" (Fisher, 1981, p. 23).

Throughout the counseling process, it is imperative that therapists
differentiate intuition from (1) wishful thinking, (2) impulsiveness,
(3) image making (the need to appear to others as strong, decisive,
confident, self-assured, etc.), (4) rebelliousness (the need to be unorthodox), (5) intellectual laziness, (6) fear of uncertainty (adopting a
solution solely because it provides relief from indecision or ambiguity), and (7) simply an emotion that carries one away (e.g., being angry at someone and "intuiting" that the person is doing something
evil). How, then, are we to validate intuition?

Just as self-deception is a notorious deterrent to intuition, so it follows that "self-awareness would be a prime asset. Understanding
your strengths, weaknesses, tendencies, habits, vulnerabilities, and
minor neuroses is the best way to keep psychological nuisances from
contaminating intuition" (Goldberg, 1983, p. 210). Careful observation of self, keeping a journal, and eliciting regular feedback from
trusted friends and colleagues can help us understand the mental and
physical correlates of our good intuitions, as well as the difference
between intuitions and needs, desires, fears, expectations, and other
aspects of selective perception and perceptual defense. Helpful checks
and balances can also include standing aside and asking ourselves
how we would feel if the intuitive thought or feeling belonged to
someone else and had nothing to do with us. In addition, forcing ourselves to defend an intuitive idea logically, as though we were the
only member of a jury, can serve as a safeguard against incorrect assumptions and interpretations.

The functions of intuition in therapy are multifaceted. Intuition is
important in clarifying problems, stating hunches (hypothesis formu-
lation and testing), helping clients identify feelings, reading subtle,
nonverbal behaviors, and picking up on what is not being communicated by clients (Carson, 1999c). For instance, systemic therapists
(Boscolo et al., 1987; Selvini Palazzoli et al., 1989) employ various

kinds of circular questions that involve introducing hypotheses ("If you get angry to protect yourself, does your family interpret that as you being hostile?") and hypothetical future queries ("If you were to leave him, what would he do?") (Lawson and Prevatt, 1999). Circular questioning often occurs spontaneously during the course of therapy. Hence, clinicians must often use their intuitive knowledge in conjunction with conscious, rational, and carefully planned inquiries because of the subtleties of feelings and nonverbal behaviors expressed by family members and the speed and complexity of interactions in family therapy.

Intuition also plays a key role in creative problem solving. Clients often become more problem focused than solution oriented, and the attempted solutions themselves can easily become part of the symptom picture (de Shazer, 1985, 1988). Indeed, intuition can be the spark for all forms of originality, inventiveness, and ingenuity. It can often be triggered during the counseling process. For example, when clients say they have little or no understanding of the problem, the therapist can suggest, "Pretend you knew what that was about. What would you say about it?" Or, with an individual having difficulty labeling or expressing a particular emotion, "If you were to give your anger/shame/worry a voice, what would it say right now?" Giving problems a voice or allowing them to talk is a central feature of narrative family therapy (Zimmerman and Dickerson, 1996). Since the intuitive system often expresses itself in allegories, stories, and metaphors, narrative approaches can provide avenues for intuitive expression, thus allowing intuitive knowledge to become conscious and useful to clients. For example, in working with a family that runs its own business, the family might be encouraged to brainstorm the kinds of activities it typically does to ensure the greatest output of goods/services and provide routine preventive maintenance in the business (e.g., in advertising, marketing, or servicing equipment). Families may then be able to make useful connections. Procedures such as family drawings, guided imagery exercises (e.g., "the hidden advisor"), reading and writing poetry, and dream interpretation can also facilitate a connection between clients' intuitive voices and their current realities.

In sum, intuition is an important part of creative problem solving, with creativity and intuition often being inextricably intertwined. Fisher (1981) notes that "creative people seem to have an innate and apparently untutored ability to put aside their judgmental or self-critical faculty when their intuition bombards them with ideas" (p. 73). Incubation (a pause in the process of problem solving when conscious thinking about the problem is dormant and the intuitive voice has a chance to break through) is often what enables us to make connections between present knowledge and stored unconscious information (i.e., intuitive knowledge), thus reaching a creative solution to both scientific and real-life problems. Access to intuitive knowledge can be gained with practice and experience. Once we as therapists are aware of the sensation or experience of intuition, we can build on it and learn to trust it with greater confidence, such as a sixth sense. As we develop greater and faster input from our intuition, it is possible that we can help clients reach creative solutions more quickly and with more precision and success.

THE CREATIVE USE OF PLAY
AND HUMOR IN THERAPY

The importance of play and humor to good mental health, and to working therapeutically with children, adolescents, and adults, has been a consistent theme in the medical and psychotherapy literature for several decades. Creativity researchers have also written extensively about the unique relationship between play, humor, and creativity. Play and humor are essential components of the creative process in individual psychotherapy as well as couples and family therapy. Play and humor have long been recognized as significant to individual health and functioning. Humor has been shown to play a powerful role in enhancing the immune system in fighting physical illnesses (Black, 1984; Cousins, 1979; Siegel, 1986), reducing stress (Ditlow, 1993; Dugan, 1989), and promoting positive mental health (Galloway and Cropley, 1999; Haig, 1988; Nilsen, 1991). Play and humor are also central to healthy couple (Christensen and Jacobson, 2000; McBrien, 1993) and family (Beavers and Hampson, 1990; Walsh, 1998; Wuerffel, DeFrain, and Stinnett, 1990) relationships. For example, humor has been shown to reduce tension in marriages and family relationships, enhance communication, help people express feelings of warmth and caring, augment positive parenting practices, facilitate enjoyment of one another, and reduce quarreling and conflict (Bleedorn, 1982; Kane, Suls, and Tedeschi, 1977; LaGaipa, 1977; Winick, 1976; Wuerffel, DeFrain, and Stinnett, 1990).

A strong relationship also exists between creativity and humor (Amabile, 1987; Nilsen, 1991). Humor involves open, alert, relaxed, and playful modes of thinking where boundaries are offset, conventional rules are suspended, and one's imagination is allowed to run wild (Ditlow, 1993). In any educational experience, humor can serve as a conduit between teaching and learning by connecting feeling states with cognitive strategies and memory processes. Moreover, flashes of insight or heightened awareness are sometimes triggered or accompanied by something that people find funny or amusing—something that tickles or penetrates their viscera as much as stimulates their neurons. The connection between humor and creativity has been demonstrated empirically in studies of both children and adults (Cornelius and Casler, 1991; Humke and Schaefer, 1996; McGhee and Goldstein, 1983). For example, both humor and creative thinking often involve the recognition of cognitive or conceptual *incongruities,* and the *integration* of pieces of a larger puzzle into a more holistic framework (Murdock and Ganim, 1993). Murdock and Ganim's overview of the research on humor and creativity reveals a number of similarities with regard to the processes involved. These include such elements as spontaneity, play, bisociation, recognition of incongruities (both intellectual and emotional), appreciation of appropriate absurdity, and unexpected discovery of relationships among both natural and human phenomena. Further, this review of research indicated several common *personal characteristics* involved in humor and creative thinking and endeavors. These included imagination, curiosity, surprise (i.e., the ability to be surprised and allow oneself to be surprised), intuition, reason, inspiration, positive emotions (e.g., hope, faith, love), an open and playful attitude toward life (and an appropriate comic perspective), intellectual flexibility, an ability to recognize and appreciate irony and paradox, good mental health and the ability to handle high levels of stress, the ability to see oneself in a detached and distant way, and the capacity to laugh at oneself. Finally, *environmental factors* contributing to the expression of humor and creativity included a more open and tension-free atmosphere in which laughter, playfulness, and experimentation/exploratory behavior were not simply permitted but encouraged. As will be seen, all of these ingredients are, in one way or another, integral to creative therapy with individuals, couples, and families. First, however, we shall briefly discuss the role and importance of humor in the broader domains of counseling and psychotherapy.

Humor in Individual Counseling and Psychotherapy

There is a vast body of literature on the subject of humor in counseling and psychotherapy. One might say that humor has unlimited creative uses in therapy and is often a key component of *immediacy*. One of our favorite books is Harold Mosak's (1987) *Ha Ha and Aha: The Role of Humor in Psychotherapy*. Mosak discusses the role of humor in establishing a therapeutic relationship with clients; in diagnosis, interpretation, and "turning clients around"; as a criterion for termination; and as an important component of the therapist's repertoire of skills. He also shares from his arsenal of jokes used in psychotherapy. Another excellent resource is Fry and Salameh's (1987) *Handbook of Humor and Psychotherapy*. Some other useful discussions on this topic are provided by Dimmer, Carroll, and Wyatt (1990), Richman (1996a,b), and Rutherford (1994). As with all effective psychotherapy, the use of humor by the therapist requires sensitivity (e.g., to client's age, gender, ethnic/cultural background, unique personalities and presenting problems, etc.), appropriateness, timing, skill, caring, and empathy (Corey, 1991).

Gladding (1995b, 1998) highlights the potential power of using humor in counseling, as well as some of the problems. One premise, set forth by Albert Ellis (1977), is that a fair portion of emotional disturbance in clients (as well as therapists) consists of taking life too seriously. This corresponds with Corey's (1991) notion that therapy need not always be serious; in fact, when it is, progress can be slowed or blocked. Gladding discusses a number of advantages to using humor in counseling. Humor can reduce tension (in or between clients, as well as between therapist and clients), promote insight and teamwork, foster creativity (e.g., as when moments of levity stimulate problem-solving skills), facilitate calculated risks that need to be taken by clients and/or therapist, help therapists reduce or overcome client resistance, assist clients in being able to talk about taboo subjects (e.g., sexual difficulties), help clients realize more fully that a situation may be serious but not hopeless, and, finally, help the therapist maintain balance and good mental health in dealing with people's pain and conflicts. Gladding's notions fit well with Rutherford's (1994) assertion that humor often provides a temporary lift of clients' depressed mood or alleviation of anxiety. In counseling, more objective appraisals of one's difficulties, divergent thinking, and renewed efforts at creative problem solving cannot occur until clients experience some momentary shifts in their emotional states. Humor can also be used to help clients understand and appreciate symbolic, metaphorical, and multiple meanings, and may even serve as a means of unconscious communication, acceptance, and understanding between therapist and clients (Richman, 1996b).

Humor and Play in Couples and Family Therapy

Humor

As McBrien (1993) notes, humor is central to strengthening the cooperative efforts of couples in therapy. The same could be said for working with families. Humor is a natural social lubricant in working with children and adolescents, in or out of the context of family therapy. Humor has an almost mystical way of helping couples and family members see one another or their problem(s) differently and encouraging them to begin again or try new things.

Based on the work of Fry and Salameh (1987) and Mosek (1987), McBrien summarizes the positive uses of humor with couples (all of which, in our opinion, apply to families as well). These include establishing rapport, maintaining focus on the couple (i.e., perceived by clients that the therapist is 100 percent with them), unblocking creativity (i.e., by freeing cognitive and emotional energy), releasing tension (which helps clients detach from the emotions associated with the events or difficulties and experience renewed hope), and avoiding burnout in both therapist and clients. Moreover, the therapist can use jokes, cartoons, and anecdotes to augment corrective feedback from clients. Some additional benefits for clients can include the therapist's role modeling of humor, which can be powerful in the eyes of clients, and the assignment of humor-oriented homework for couples (e.g., watching comedies or reading a joke book together). A first cousin of humor, play, is equally important and useful in working with couples and families.

Play

Play is an essential aspect of normal childhood development and contains healing power for both children and adults (Ackerman, 1999; Elkind, 1988; Terr, 1999). Botkin (2000) has recently observed that "playfulness in children has been found to be a stable personality trait that is related to creativity, imaginativeness, positive affect, emotional expressiveness, and physical activity . . . all of which are resources for creative solutions to problems" (p. 32). She reminds us that play in adults reduces stress, stimulates fantasy and releases the imagination, lowers the defenses, promotes group cohesion, allows for experimentation with and exchange of roles, and provides an avenue for the expression of metaphorical and symbolic thinking and interaction. All of these benefits of play can and often do play out during the process of family therapy. Hence, it is no accident that in recent years practitioners have discovered the many uses of play in assessing (Sweeney and Rocha, 2000) and working with families (Ariel, 1992; Gil, 1994; Schaefer and Carey, 1994; VanFleet, 1994).

Play serves many purposes in family therapy. First, it provides a forum for the active inclusion of even young (preschool-aged) children in the therapy process (Schaefer, 1993). As Gerstein (1999, p. 7) notes, "Serious discussion and methodical problem solving impose on children's communication, shutting out their voices, and inhibiting their special abilities, knowledge, and creative resources." Play and other experiential activities provide opportunities for children to express themselves in ways that reflect their view of the world and through behaviors that are more natural to them. Moreover, play is often less threatening than verbal discourse, not only to children but to adults. Second, as Botkin (2000) notes, family dynamics are often mirrored through children's play in the context of family therapy, as well as the family playing together. Third, play encourages the free expression of emotions among family members and facilitates emotional closeness, open communication, and improved interactions (Gil, 1994; Schaefer, 1993). Fourth, play allows the family members, to a large extent, to direct the course of their own therapy, thus empowering them to have confidence in their ability to learn new ways of solving problems and managing their lives (Ariel, 1992; Gil, 1994). Finally, play helps families feel a new sense of hope and optimism through helping them focus more on areas of existing strength and potential solutions than on problems. Hence, it activates the family's innate creativity (Schaefer and Carey, 1994).

Botkin (2000) indicates that family play therapy can be both directive and nondirective. In nondirective therapy, the therapist simply supplies a variety of play objects and expressive materials and asks the family to choose what they would like to use and in what manner of play they would like to engage. Observing what families decide to do, their process of decision making, and how they interact provides insight into a variety of family patterns, dynamics, and roles. This form of play is not only cathartic to family members but is an exceedingly useful part of the assessment process to the therapist. In family play therapy that is more directive, the therapist chooses the materials and activity for the family (e.g., "I want you to plan a fun family vacation together by drawing it on the canvas board"; "I am going to create part of a story with this puppet family, and then I would like you all to continue the story with your puppets"). Directive family play therapy allows the therapist to participate with the family or remain separate and simply observe and comment.

The most important prerequisite to effective play therapy with families, of course, is that the therapist feels comfortable with and enjoys playing with children and adults (Botkin, 2000). The therapist must know when and how to let out the child within while at the same time managing or staying on top of the therapeutic process, in other words, balancing this area of connectedness with the family with one's professional role as the therapist. Hence, characteristics such as creativity, flexibility, curiosity, imagination, sensitivity, open-mindedness, and a sense of humor are central to the family play therapist's personal repertoire.

The successful family play therapist must also know how to overcome the family's resistance to play. Botkin (2000) suggests ways in which this can be done. These include, for example, having the adults revisit pleasant aspects of their own childhood (i.e., favorite places, playmates, or toys) and ask them what experiences they enjoyed most, how they liked to pretend, and so forth. The therapist can then connect the past with the present by asking them how play is a part of their life now and what beliefs keep them from being able to play openly and freely with their child(ren). The therapist can also model various ways of playing in session. Of course, having adequate space as well as a variety of play objects and materials (e.g., drawing and coloring materials, sand tray with miniatures, puppets and dolls, a variety of children's toys and books, building blocks and other construction items, modeling clay, etc.) is useful if not essential to being able to engage in the full array of play therapy modalities discussed by Botkin and the other authors cited previously.

In sum, many are the seeds of creativity planted through the free expression of play and humor in close relationships, and therapy can be a forum for doing so. Indeed, the lack of creative problem solving in individuals and families often lies in the clients' focus on the ultra-serious and their inability to renew or cultivate that which they once found, or could discover, as playful and fun.

BREAKING OUT OF THE BOX: CREATING MY BOX

The box is one of the most common visual images referred to when discussing creativity. We all have a box that has been created and restructured over time. For some of us our box is constructed of childhood messages (can't, shouldn't, don't) or previous constraining professional experiences. This activity is designed to assist you in taking a clear and concentrated look at your box. You will revisit your box in Chapter 7 with an invitation to consciously decide what you want to do with your box. The following steps are provided as a guide only. As new or better ideas come to you, seize them and incorporate them. This is your box.

Step 1: Find or construct a box of any shape or size. Spend the time to come up with a box that represents you, your potential, and the messages or realities that provide obstacles to your creativity.

Step 2: Draw or paste images, words, or pictures that bring your box to life. You may want the inside of the box to symbolize your untapped creative potential while the outside represents both your current creative endeavors as well as your personal or professional barriers. Feel free to use any objects or materials that seem right for you.

Step 3: Put your box in the middle of the room and slowly walk around it to view your box from as many perspectives as possible. What do you notice from each angle? What do you experience as you look inside your box? Now pick up your box. What does it feel like? What does the size, weight, and texture communicate to you? What are you learning about your box, yourself, and your potential?

Step 4: Share this experience with a friend or colleague (or in your journal).

Step 5: As you proceed through your readings, feel free to add or modify your box. And remember—we will revisit your box in Chapter 7, so keep it in a safe place.

Chapter 2

An Overview of the Role of Creativity in Individual Mental Health, Psychopathology, and Family Dysfunction

CREATIVE INCUBATION EXERCISE #2: CHANGING LENSES

Wyoming is truly an amazing place. We are blessed to live in a gorgeous area. With several major mountain ranges and the beauty of the plains, the views are endless. As novice photographers who frequent the high slopes year-round, we are also constantly taking mental photographs of our clients. We find ourselves often switching between our therapist and photographer hats. At times we opt to view our couples and families through a wide-angle lens allowing us to capture the big picture of their lives, relationships, community, and culture. At other times we find ourselves changing to a macro (or close-up) lens. As if looking at the petals of a small flower, this lens allows us to better understand individuals in more depth, including their thoughts, emotions, personal history, and hopes. We are also aware that from time to time a filter is added to our lens. Although at times this filter may assist us in better seeing our clients by filtering out distractions, at other times the filter may contort our view to show only the negatives or problems of our clients. We call this a "pathological filter." It greatly limits our perception and must be replaced by a filter that allows for both strengths (solutions) and problems (challenges). So as we sit with our couples and families, we find ourselves "zooming" in and out several times throughout the course of each session. As we become aware of our own personal biases, we seek to find a filter that invites a more complete picture of our clients.

It is now time for you to become a photographer in session as you respond to the following questions:

1. Describe the benefits and limitations of viewing your clients through a wide-angle lens.
2. Describe the benefits and limitations of viewing your clients through a macro (or close-up) lens.
3. How will you decide when to change lenses in session?
4. What are your filters (biases) that may limit your view?

THE IMPORTANCE OF CREATIVITY
TO MENTAL HEALTH

One definition of mental health is the ability to love, work, and play. Creativity is central to all of these endeavors. This chapter provides a bird's-eye view of the theoretical, clinical, and empirical literature examining the relevance of creativity to individual mental health and to couple and family relationships. Specifically, we discuss how and why ordinary (or everyday) creativity, as distinguished from eminent (or genius-type) creativity, is believed to be a central component of resiliency and good mental health in children and adults, as well as marital and family relationships. There is ample evidence that everyday creativity plays a unique role in our ability to cope with stress, learn, develop, and connect with others. Conversely, deficits in everyday creativity may be associated with decreased resiliency and less satisfying couple and family relationships. Potential benefits of facilitating creativity with regard to both personal mental health and relationship enhancement, primarily within the context of the family, will be discussed. Practical suggestions for enhancing everyday creativity in the lives of children, adults, couples, and families are made, including ways of augmenting creative thinking.

Creativity is a relatively new concept in the field of mental health research and practice, particularly as it relates to stress, coping, resiliency, and psychopathology in children and adults. What, for example, is the connection between creativity and mental illness or creativity and high-level functioning? In the creativity literature, it is eminent rather than everyday (or ordinary) creativity that has been commonly linked to mental illness. Eminent creativity is that of genius, or exceptional creation, as seen in famous artists, musicians, writers, or scientists, both today and throughout history. However, there are many misconceptions about the role that eminent creativity plays in individual health and illness, and there is a range of opinions in the empirical and clinical literature. Everyday creativity, which refers to unconventional but highly adaptive coping of people in everyday life, has not commonly been associated with poor mental health or psychopathology. Instead, this type of creativity may serve as a protective factor in individuals at any point in the life cycle.

Creative Thinking, Stress, Coping, and Mental Health in Children

The extent to which children cope effectively with daily hassles and stressful life events is directly associated with their experience of developmental delays or emotional and behavioral disturbances. Daily hassles and major life stressors have been linked to problems in children's academic performances and cognitive development (e.g., difficulties with concentration or memory, learning disabilities), socioemotional development (e.g., lower social competence, emotional disturbances, mood swings, immaturity), and a variety of behavior problems and manifestations of psychopathology (e.g., conduct disorders, anxiety disorders, childhood depression, psychosomatic symptoms) (Anthony, 1987; Carson et al., 1992; Dickey and Henderson, 1989; Rutter, 1983, 1987; Sears and Milburn, 1990). However, the empirical study of children's stress and coping is still relatively very new, and little is known about the personality factors that may influence whether children are able to successfully adapt to both major and minor stressors they encounter (Carson and Skarpness, 1988; Cohler, 1987; Werner, 1990).

It would seem that creative thinking should be directly associated with various areas of child development and behavior, including how children adapt to their everyday world. Theoretically, children who are able to think more creatively should cope more effectively with major stressful life events and daily hassles. For instance, if a child can think more fluently, flexibly, and with a high degree of originality, then that child should exhibit more effective coping skills in different social milieus. Furthermore, various aspects of creative thinking may be related to intellectual problem-solving capabilities. Hence, one might expect that more creative-minded children would not only cope better with stress on a daily basis but also adapt more effectively to major life events.

The current literature has focused on the unique ways in which children respond to stressful events and daily hassles, how stress can influence children in negative ways, and various predictors of resiliency (protective factors) and vulnerability (vulnerability factors) in children (Garmezy, 1985; Garmezy and Masten, 1990; Kimchi and Schaffner, 1990; Sears and Milburn, 1990). Creative thinking may be associated with children's coping in terms of their ability to think more divergently about both minor and major life events. Divergent thinking may in turn be related to higher-level problem-solving skills with regard to everyday life situations and people (Hennessey and Amabile, 1988). There may also be a connection between children's creative thinking and self-esteem (Jaquish and Ripple, 1980), which might also be associated with their coping abilities. Although intellectual problem-solving capacities do not in themselves translate into more successful coping, they may be a necessary (although insufficient) condition for successful coping.

Some empirical evidence supports these assertions. Studies have established a connection between children's creativity and interpersonal problem solving (Miller, Serifica, and Clark, 1989; Shondrick et al., 1992), as well as creativity, stress, and coping abilities (Carson et al., 1994). For example, Carson and colleagues (1994) administered the verbal and figural portions of the Torrance Tests of Creative Thinking (Form A) and the Stress Impact Scale (SIS) to sixty nine- to twelve-year-old children. An observational rating scale of coping behavior, the Coping Inventory (CI), was also completed on each child in the school setting by trained observers, and the Stress Response Scale (SRS) was completed by mothers. Age and several Torrance figural indicators of creative thinking, including fluency, originality, elaboration, and resistance to premature closure as measured on the figural portion of the Torrance test were most predictive of coping abilities and less overall problematic responses to stress as reported by mothers. The investigators drew several tentative conclusions. First, the expectation that creative thinking would be associated with better coping in the school milieu, as well as fewer problematic responses to stress and behavioral difficulties, was generally supported. Hence, any effort on the part of parents, teachers, or other professionals to encourage and provide opportunities for the enhancement of children's creative-thinking skills may have secondary payoffs with regard to their coping abilities. In this regard, children may respond much more readily to creative-thinking opportunities than to stress management or social skills training workshops or classes. Second, the data showed that although verbal indicators of creative thinking were largely unrelated to children's coping and stress responses, several figural indicators (including fluency, originality, elaboration, and resistance to premature closure) were strongly associated with their coping abilities. Further, the regression analyses indicated that, of the various dimensions of creative thinking, resistance to premature closure was the most powerful predictor of coping behavior. This aspect of creative thinking needs to be further explored. Data from the Carson and colleagues (1994) study also suggest that verbal approaches to assessing creative thinking may be less reliable than figural approaches or that, because they are perhaps confounded with language development and proficiency, they are a poorer indicator of creative thought and hence less predictive of adaptive behavior. Finally, the findings suggest that although age may not be a major factor in the manifestation of problem behaviors (SRS) or perception of stressful life events (SIS) at this period of childhood, the developmental progression from third to sixth grade seems to entail an increase in coping abilities (CI)—at least as exhibited in the school environment.

Children today find themselves in school systems that emphasize convergent thinking and conventional production of ideas much more than the development of creative-thinking skills. This approach to education can lead to a compartmentalization of some intellectual abilities and restriction of others (e.g., divergent thinking). Moreover, even in many American homes the importance of creative and divergent thinking may not be recognized or valued by parents, nor opportunities for creative expression abundant. Our high-tech society deemphasizes the importance of creative thinking by elevating the value and necessity of fact learning and concrete thinking as steps toward academic success, job obtainment, and materialistic security. It may be that the ability to think and live creatively is a much-needed skill in today's world—not only in coping effectively in social, academic, and vocational arenas but also in combating the mundaneness and hassles of everyday life. The provision of environments (particularly family and school) in which children's creative-thinking skills are encouraged may be a crucial step toward enhancing their resiliency.

Creative Thinking, Stress, Coping, and Mental Health in Adults

An abundance of research has supported the notion that it is not objective stressful events per se which influence one's mental and emotional health, relational functioning, and physical well-being but how individuals perceive, subjectively experience, and successfully cope with the stress in their lives (Lazarus and Folkman, 1984). In recent years stress and coping research has focused on the mechanisms that facilitate or impede the development of psychological resiliency in both children and adults (Aldwin, 1994; Rutter, 1987). A central component of resiliency is how people cope with major life stressors and crises, as well as the accumulation of daily hassles or strains. Coping is an action-oriented process that includes, but is not limited to, intellectual problem-solving abilities and internal regulation of thoughts, emotions, and defenses. More vulnerable persons have been described as having ineffective coping skills or a limited repertoire of coping abilities. Deficiencies in coping can contribute to an array of relationship problems, family conflicts, and psychological disturbances (Cowan, Cowan, and Schulz, 1996).

Contrary to the idea that creativity is strongly associated with emotional instability and personal dysfunction, there is some empirical evidence that, although some eminently creative individuals have been shown to exhibit mild mood disorders (Richards, 1990), as a general rule highly creative men and women tend to have well-integrated personalities (Martindale, 1989; Mellou, 1995; Simonton, 1988). Everyday creativity may be particularly associated with one's ability to cope with stress (Flach, 1990; Richards, 1990; Runco and Richards, 1998; Smith and Van der Meer, 1990; Woodman and Schoenfeldt, 1990). Crucial links in the chain of successful coping and adaptation include creative problem finding/generation and problem solving (Brown, 1989; Isaksen, Dorval, and Treffinger, 1994; Runco, 1994b; Wolin and Wolin, 1993). During the course of any heightened creative process an individual may experience depression, anxiety, or feelings of inadequacy (Flach, 1988; Stein, 1988). However, creativity is a mechanism that, over the course of time, might buffer or compensate for at least some of the potential negative influences of life stressors and traumatic experiences on both children and adults (Carson and Runco, 1999; Carson et al., 1994; Cohen, 1989; Wolin and Wolin, 1993).

Investigations into the relationship between creativity and coping have been scarce. Earlier studies are limited because researchers did not employ direct measures of coping ability but instead used measures of psychological maladjustment as dependent variables and indicators of coping. For example, Schubert (1988) found that college students with high creativity scores (as measured by Guilford's creativity scales) had significantly lower scores on the Minnesota Multiphasic Personality Inventory (MMPI) scales of hysteria, paranoia, psychasthenia, schizophrenia, social introversion, anxiety, and repression. Creativity scores were inversely related to scores on the responsibility scale, which suggested that the more creative students may have been somewhat more resistant to social pressure and conformity. Further, the more creative students were less likely to withdraw from college or fail academically. A study of architects by MacKinnon (1965), again using the MMPI and peer nomination for the assessment of creativity, yielded similar findings, as have other studies using either the MMPI or the Rorschach as measures of adjustment/coping (e.g., Barron, 1963; Cashdan and Welsh, 1966; Kubie, 1961; Pine and Holt, 1960; Wild, 1965). One problem with these studies is that the mere absence of symptoms or psychopathology did not mean that the more creative individuals were necessarily better at coping than were their less creative counterparts.

More recent investigations of adults have also tended to focus on indicators of mental and emotional health in relation to creativity or divergent-thinking capacities, rather than examining coping strategies, processes, or abilities per se (Richards, 1990, 1996; Runco and Richards, 1998). Blissett and McGrath (1996) found a strong association between creativity and interpersonal problem-solving skills in an adult sample. However, this was a program evaluation study in which undergraduate students received training in both creative thinking and interpersonal problem solving. The results suggested that creativity and problem solving represented complementary skills, and that increases in one domain appeared to have spillover effects into the other. According to Blissett and McGrath, although conceptually different, creativity and interpersonal problem solving are similar in that they often involve the production of novel outcomes.

A recent study of college undergraduates by Carson and Runco (1999) examined the relationship among creative problem-solving (PS) and problem-generation (PG) abilities, stress and daily hassles, and coping skills. Hierarchical regression analyses indicated that separate sets of both PS and PG task scores were predictive of scores on certain coping scales even after the variance accounted for by indices of stress and hassles was removed. Specifically, PG and PS abilities were negatively related to such coping processes as confrontation, distancing, escape/avoidance tendencies, and excessive acceptance of responsibility, and positively associated with more general adaptive qualities. The findings suggest that PS and PG abilities are important components of an individual's overall capacity to cope with both major and minor stresses of life. Further, as expected, both generic and student-related stressful life events, as well as daily hassles, were strongly predictive of less adaptive coping behaviors, with events rated by students and those pertaining to college life being the most common predictors. The results suggest that although problem-solving and problem-generation abilities are both important to an individual's overall ability to cope with hassles and stress, these abilities appear to operate in a relatively independent manner.

Everyday creativity has been shown to be advantageous to those adults with a personal or family history of bipolar disorders (Richards, 1999). According to Richards, everyday creativity may help individuals with familial or personal predispositions to mood disorders, such as depression or bipolar disorder, overcome or buffer the effects of these disorders. Another potential mental health benefit associated with creativity is self-actualization. Individuals who are more self-actualized also tend to be more creative (Runco, 1999). Thus, creativity and self-actualization are mutually reinforcing in both children and adults. Highly creative people are more likely to explore, question, and confidently process their environment. However, Wink (1999) postulates that creativity is not so much a path toward self-actualization as a by-product of it. Since self-actualized individuals are, by definition, generally mentally healthy and more altruistically oriented, Wink's theory indirectly supports the notion that there is a connection between sufficient everyday creativity and good mental health.

CREATIVITY, MENTAL HEALTH, AND PSYCHOPATHOLOGY IN ADULTS: AN OVERVIEW

Historically in the literature, eminent creativity has been consistently linked with notions of psychopathology in adults. Since this type of creativity by definition refers to exceptional thinking and/or products that lie at the outer spheres of conventional norms or expectations, it is a small leap to believe that many, if not most, eminent creators are bizarre, if not pathological. However, a careful review of the literature reveals that although there are some connections between eminent creativity and some manifestations of psychopathology (e.g., mood and anxiety disorders) in some adults, this association may not be normative. Moreover, evidence suggests that high levels of creative thinking are predictive of both coping and good mental health in children and adults.

Runco (1990) postulates that there are two overlapping possibilities when looking at the relationship between creativity and mental health: (a) creativity derives from aspects of health or (b) creativity leads to health. According to Richards (1990, p. 320), "Either type of relationship can occur directly or through the mediation of a third factor (which itself can be multivariate and complex)." Richards suggests that motivation is one factor that independently enhances both health and creativity, and thus is an important link between them. An extensive analysis of the literature by Cropley (1990) indicates a generally positive association between high levels of everyday creativity and good mental health. For example, "creativity is connected with personal qualities such as flexibility, openness, autonomy, humor, playfulness, willingness to try things, elaborations of ideas, realistic self-assessment, and similar characteristics" (p. 240). Cropley notes that these traits are typically seen as some of the core elements of a healthy personality. MacKinnon (1978) lists several factors that describe the mental health of the creative person, including significantly above-average intelligence; alertness and adaptability; absence of repression and suppression; and a tendency toward introversion, along with the downside of a theme of remembered unhappiness in childhood and a considerable amount of psychic turbulence at various points in one's life. Other reviewers, including Rhodes (1990), view creative expression as a force for mental health and positive growth (particularly as individuals move from "deficiency creativity" to "being creativity"), and there is some empirical evidence of a strong positive association between creativity and self-actualization in adults (Runco, Ebersole, and Mraz, 1991). However, as will become evident later, the relationship between creativity and mental health may be different in eminently creative individuals.

Researchers such as Richards (1990, 1997) have identified five different ways of looking at the relationship between creativity and health, particularly with regard to everyday creativity and healthy functioning. These are summarized and briefly commented on as follows.

Healthy functioning directly enhances creativity. Aspects of healthy functioning may include physical health, acute perceptual and cognitive abilities, and emotional expressiveness/appropriate affect. However, although this may be true in some cases, the world seems filled with high-functioning children and adults who are not overly creative. Hence, healthy functioning may not necessarily lead to creativity.

Healthy functioning indirectly enhances creativity. These factors may include early developmental advantages and success, and societal opportunities and stability. Conversely, as we have demonstrated earlier, high levels of stress can lower overall coping and subsequent creativity. The problem with this possibility is that the childhood backgrounds of creative geniuses were often troubled and traumatic, as were the physical resources available.

Creativity directly enhances healthy functioning. These factors might include increased everyday creativity that can directly improve mental health and more flexible and less negative and defensive attitudes toward aging. Yet some highly creative individuals are not terribly healthy psychologically or emotionally.

Creativity indirectly enhances healthy functioning. Creative activities and responses can decrease intrapersonal or interpersonal conflict or morbidity, thus increasing resilience and, subsequently, health. Moreover, creative mental imagery and meditation can have an impact on immune function and, hence, health and survival. In contrast, psychological inflexibility and distress can contribute to several forms of physical illness. This possibility seems a bit more plausible, in that there are not as many problems with exceptions as were noted in the first three.

A third factor independently affects creativity and health. These factors can include positive subclinical traits such as confidence, sociability, and energy. Further, ease of thinking may enhance overall social and occupational adjustment, which may in turn influence or raise creative potential. This too seems plausible, although exceedingly difficult to substantiate.

The relationship between creativity and mental health is systemic and multifaceted. In adults, everyday creativity appears to be much more closely related to positive mental health than does eminent creativity. Increasing an individual's everyday creative thinking and behavior has interesting implications for the treatment and prevention of mental illness, as well as marital and family conflicts. Eminent creators, on the other hand, often face greater difficulties with social acceptance and labeling and perhaps are more mentally unstable, sensitive, and emotionally labile. In addition, a decrease in or lack of creativity can be viewed as a common precursor to psychological or relationship difficulties, just as emotional or psychological disturbance can disrupt creative thinking, process, and production.

According to Andreasen (1987) and Richards (1990), findings from various studies support the assertion that there is some relationship between eminent creativity and psychopathology, especially mood disorders such as depression and bipolar disorders, certain anxiety disorders, and possibly schizotypal and hypomanic conditions. Although criticized by a number of investigators, some theorists such as Eysenck (1982, 1993, 1995) assert that psychoticism (not psychosis, but a dispositional trait underlying susceptibility to the development of psychotic symptoms) underscores the creative personality. Whether these influences are genetic/predispositional, neurological, or environmental (e.g., social stigmatism due to a severe departure from "normalcy") is a matter of debate (Hoppe and Kyle, 1997; Richards, 1997). However, Richards (1990) indicates that eminently creative people who are mentally or emotionally ill, or socially maladjusted, are probably the exceptions, rather than the rule. Highly creative individuals are not usually in the clinical range of these disorders, and when they are, they are generally less disturbed than their less creative counterparts (Richards, 1990, 1997).

The association between eminent creativity and psychopathology has also been discussed in several different ways (Richards, 1990, 1997). These are summarized as follows.

Features of pathology directly enhance creativity. For example, symptoms and symptom complexes such as hypomanic or soft bipolar traits may affect the creative process, including intense inner and outer experiences that provide material for creative expression. Periods of heightened anxiety may also trigger neurons in complex ways that contribute to creative thinking and products.

Features of pathology indirectly enhance creativity. These features may include conflict-based motivation to create, the effects of particular levels of stress or anxiety, the obsessive work-oriented nature associated with bipolar disorders, and extreme risk-taking behaviors sometimes associated with already being different or standing apart.

Creativity leads directly to pathology. This process may entail anxiety or possible decomposition (e.g., use of alcohol to contain the anxiety) when creative efforts elicit painful material. Also, experiential sources of illness associated with lowered resiliency may include the inability to experience creative disruption, a maladaptive experience of disruption, and the ultimate inability to reintegrate.

Creativity leads indirectly to pathology. Involved here may be expectations, affectation, or exaggeration of one's own deviancy based on popular stereotypes of the eminent creator that is followed by possible exacerbation or triggering of latent problems. This process may also include the stigma of being different or socially deviant, or the actual disapproval or ostracism sometimes encountered by highly creative people.

A third factor independently affects creativity and psychopathology. These factors include stressors such as personal loss, physical disability, or economic deprivation that may sometimes motivate creative expression but may also independently lead to physical or psychological decompensation. In addition, a genetic predisposition for bipolar mood disorders may produce symptoms such as rapid thinking, impulsivity, and restlessness that can contribute to creative accomplishment while at the same time promoting a degree of psychological distress.

It is evident that the relationship between creativity, health, and mental illness is extremely complex and that investigators sometimes differ considerably in their views. Rothenberg (1990), for example, indicates that high-level functions of creative thinking such as homospatial and janusian processes (see Chapter 4) tend to be healthy and adaptive. This suggests that mental illness does not generally facili-, tate creativity but interferes with it. Thus, according to Rothenberg the majority of individuals who are persistently creative are, in all probability, highly reality based. Indeed, the ability to face and accept the real world has often been cited by personality theorists as an important condition of good mental health. However, not all researchers completely agree with these postulations. Eisenman (1997), for example, suggests that some milder forms of mental illness may contribute to the creative process. Richards (1990, p. 202), too, suggests that "it is those with relatively milder mood disorders and normalcy who may show the greatest creative advantage." Richards's (1993, 1996) research provides evidence that for both eminent and everyday creators, elevated mood was correlated with creative problem solving and an increased capacity for making unusual associations. She noted that elevated moods are often accompanied by higher degrees of risk taking, courage, and self-confidence. A study by Schuldberg (1990) lends some support to these assertions. This investigator identified three different types of individual traits that were positively associated with creative attitudes and activities: (1) unusual perceptual experiences and beliefs; (2) hypomanic traits; and (3) impulsivity and nonconformity. However, Schuldberg indicated that these traits were really of a subclinical nature (i.e., non-psychopathological). Similarly, Mraz and Runco (1994) found that problem finding but not problem solving (two central components of creative thinking) was positively associated with suicidal ideation in a sample of college students. Hence, although highly creative individuals may be more likely to exhibit some milder forms of distress or aberration, these behaviors are probably highly specific and compartmentalized and are not likely to be in the clinical range of disturbance. Nor are these individuals likely to manifest serious difficulty in their everyday functioning. In fact, according to Schuldberg, "the critical factor differentiating genius from madness may be ego strength, referring to resiliency, stress-resistance, a sense of physical and mental well-being, and facility for controlling one's primary process productions" (1990, p. 219).

Eminent creativity has also been associated with deviance, suicide, and schizophrenia (Lester, 1999; Plucker and Runco, 1999; Schuldberg and Sass, 1999). Plucker and Runco (1999) examined similarities in the definitions of creativity and deviance. Characteristics of both concepts include unconventional behavior, avoidance of entrenched ways of thinking, dissatisfaction with the status quo, taking risks, rejecting limits, being open to trying new things, and receptiveness to new ideas. However, deviance and creativity entail very different qualities and behaviors in individuals. One tends to lead to positive outcomes (creativity) and the other negative outcomes or consequences (deviance) with regard to self and others.

Some have asserted that creative individuals are at higher risk for suicide (Lester, 1999). However, according to Richards (1999), everyday creativity has been found to buffer at least some of the effects of mood disorders (the disorders often associated with suicide). The observed or reported relationship between suicide and creativity is one that usually involves the suicides of eminently creative individuals as seen, for example, in some highly gifted artists of the twentieth century (Lester, 1999). Yet even with eminent creators throughout history, suicide is much more the exception than the norm.

The relationship between creativity and schizophrenia is exceedingly difficult to understand due to the nature of this disorder. Schizophrenia involves serious manifestations of thought disorder, including poor reality testing, delusional thinking, and hallucinations. However, individuals with schizophrenia may have moments when they are highly imaginative and creative. Indeed, Schuldberg and Sass (1999, p. 503) have noted that, "The fluent generation of new and possibly useful ideas in creative intelligence . . . is difficult to distinguish conceptually from the novel productivity of thought disorder." However, since individuals with schizophrenia, particularly those of the disorganized, paranoid, or undifferentiated type (American Psychiatric Association, 1994), experience a number of other difficulties with thinking (e.g., blocking, incoherence, flight of ideas), communicating (e.g., disorganized speech, word salad, clang associations), mood (e.g., flat or inappropriate affect), and social behavior (e.g., withdrawal, wariness of others), both eminent and everyday creativity is likely to be inhibited more than facilitated.

In conclusion, Richards (1990) summarizes the relationship between creativity, mental health, and psychopathology in the following ways. First, creativity may represent a joyous and healthful fruition, or derive from problems, conflicts, personal illness, or political disruption. Second, it should not be surprising to find that—whatever its origins—creativity may promote good mental health. This health may be psychological or physical and may even involve survival. Third, however, there may still be exceptions to these healthy outcomes, involving, for instance, people who decompensate from creative insights they cannot handle. Finally, everyday creativity may be adaptive and health oriented, with more extreme features of creativity common to people who are emotionally disturbed. But even here, eminent creators are not usually the most severely ill among those carrying their particular diagnoses. Richards concludes with some insightful comments:

> Thus, as with most medicines, the prescription for individual creativity is not necessarily, "the more the better." On the other hand, in a world of escalating problems, shouldn't we somehow encourage greater numbers of people to shift in the creativity direction? One approach is to start small. A groundswell in the practice of everyday creativity, in the originality of day-to-day life, might not only enhance individual health, but create a more accepting climate for the major societal innovations we so badly need. (1990, p. 323)

BREAKING OUT OF THE BOX: CREATING MY METAPHOR

At the beginning of this chapter we described how we are often photographers in session. When we are puzzled or stuck in session as therapists, we switch hats and become photographers looking for snapshots (opportunities) that reflect connection, beauty, and hope. Although at times we need to "zoom in" to better touch the hearts and souls of our clients, at other times we need the wide-angle lens to better understand the broader stressors (financial, extended family, work, school) burdening a family.

When working with couples we also envision ourselves flying a dual-controlled kite. To effectively fly such a kite (with two separate lines and controls), one must be connected with and sensitive to the pulls and wind that each side of the kite is experiencing. Couple therapy is very similar. As a couple therapist, one needs to be connected with and sensitive to each partner. Each partner is a unique individual connected by the fabric of love, history, and pain. To be effective one needs to use both hands, hold on tight, and be sensitive to the nuances of the wind.

Now it is your turn to create your own personal metaphor. Give yourself permission to go beyond yourself as a therapist. Who else are you in session? Are you a white-water rafting guide working together with your clients to navigate the currents and potential risks of the river? Are you an orchestra conductor striving to bring out the soulful best in each musician (family member)? Or are you a sculptor, joining with the couple or family to reshape the form and texture of the system? We invite you to spend some time considering this part of your journey. Please allow yourself to relax and see where your working metaphor takes you.

Chapter 3

Creativity and Resiliency in Children, Adults, Marriages, and Families

CREATIVE INCUBATION EXERCISE #3:
A FRESH PERSPECTIVE

In our training clinic we have witnessed an interesting and often predictable pattern among our clients and therapists. Since we are bound to the semester schedule, the large majority of our cases start within a week of each other. Hence, as a collective group, we often "hit the wall" together at or around the fifth session. Each semester we find ourselves (including supervisors—as we seem to have rather short memories) frustrated with both our clients and ourselves. These are moments of self-doubt, increased anxiety, and exhaustion. We find ourselves working harder than our clients, caring more about their futures than they themselves do. Upon reflection, we understand (and remember) that we have been at this place before. It is as if we reenter the same forest from a different path, yet all paths lead to the same recognizable spot—the edge of a canyon with depths that are frightening, a rickety old rope bridge that sways in the wind. Wherever we are, it always seems that hope is a mere glimmer a great distance away. We are standing on the edge with our clients. We are all fearful of falling (or being pushed) into the abyss.

At these moments we invite ourselves to seek a new perspective. The view from this angle immobilizes all of us. Whether based upon old messages, traumas, realistic fears, or something else, we are frozen as we find ourselves trying the same thing over and over again yet expecting a different result. We are trapped in pathological hell—a point of impasse. We have become inducted into the despair of the system. It is time for a fresh perspective.

Place yourself at the edge of the canyon standing beside an individual, family, or couple. Together you have visited this place several times. As their guide, your task is threefold:

1. Ask your client(s) to take a rest by the edge of the canyon. Admit to them that you too are struggling with how to get across to the other side. Let them know that you are going on a walk but will soon return. Envision yourself as you find a variety of places to reexamine the situation. See yourself walking safely to the bottom of the canyon, looking up to the bridge, the canyon edge, and your clients. See yourself elevated in midair as you rise above the bridge, the canyon edge, and your clients. See yourself both at the other side of the canyon as well as back in the middle of the forest as you gain a variety of fresh perspectives. Make a list of what you are noticing that is different or new.
2. Now see the canyon's edge as a developmental opportunity. Everyone (including yourself) is ready to be at the edge. Many people never make it to the edge. What did it take for the couple or family to make it this far (e.g., determination, courage)? What did it take for you to make it this far?
3. Now for the fun part. Take a few minutes as you join with your clients in creating change. You are still at the canyon's edge and the bridge remains the same, yet your perspective has changed. In either written, oral, or picture form, describe how you and your clients will proceed from the canyon's edge. Create a path or trail for all to take.

CREATIVITY AND RESILIENCY

Creativity has been defined as the ability to bring something new into existence, a way of thinking, and one form of ordinary creativity as a kind of novel adaptation to one's environment. According to Runco (1994a), creativity involves a resolution of subjective tension or disequilibrium that can lead to enhanced growth and awareness. In a similar vein, the concept of resiliency generally refers to successful behavioral adaptation despite challenging or adverse circumstances. It is defined as a person's ability to deal successfully with everyday strains, acute crises and traumas, and major enduring life events (see

Chapter 4). *Resiliency* is a term used to specify the nature of adaptation and can be viewed as the process of, capacity for, or outcome of successful adaptation. Hence, resiliency "implies effective coping, meaning efforts to restore or maintain internal or external equilibrium under significant threat by means of human activities, including thought and action" (Masten, Best, and Garmezy, 1991, p. 430). Given these and similar perspectives on resiliency and creativity, there may be a closer connection between these constructs than has previously been realized.

Resiliency is commonly determined by assessing individuals' levels of social, intellectual, or physical competence (e.g., educational achievement, athletic, artistic, or mechanical ability), their ability to cope with stress, and their psychological and emotional health. These approaches are, of course, limited in what they tell us about a person's overall resiliency. For example, to date we know little about the conditions that augment resiliency, the processes involved in resiliency, the global versus compartmentalized nature of resiliency, or the stability of resiliency over long periods of time. However, creative thinking or activity may be a major facilitator of resiliency in both children and adults. In contrast, limited creativity may be associated with lower resiliency and greater vulnerability to mental, emotional, and/or relational difficulties. Creativity might also be associated with coping and adaptive behavior in terms of the ability of an individual to think more divergently about both major and minor life events, as well as to engage in higher-level problem solving with regard to everyday life situations and people (Brown, 1989; Dowd, 1989; Runco, 1991). Theoretically, for example, if a person is able to think more fluently, flexibly, originally, elaborately, and in a way that resists premature closure, then that individual would be more likely to exhibit effective coping behaviors in different social situations (Carson et al., 1994). Carson and colleagues found, for example, that such was the case in a sample of school-age children. Further, although divergent thinking or creative problem-solving abilities do not automatically result in more effective coping and greater resiliency, they may be a necessary condition for adaptive behavior. One reason for this is because these intellectual capacities allow one to consider a variety of options or alternatives to a problem or imposing stressor, as well as provide greater means for reframing (relabeling) the event or difficulty so that things are kept in perspective and hope and optimism are maintained. Thus, these capacities, along with many other aspects of creativity, are believed to be important components of successful coping, especially with regard to dealing with the more ambiguous aspects of human relationships.

The study of resiliency represents a slow but important paradigm shift in the treatment of mental and emotional disorders—a move away from the past dominant question of "How can psychological malfunction best be undone?" toward new and more fruitful questions, such as "How does wellness come about in the first place and what can be done to promote it?" Resiliency is thought to be a dynamic, context-bound phenomenon. Hence, all individuals are vulnerable in some circumstances and situations, more so at some times in life than others. Resiliency does not signify an absence of problems, a complete lack of symptoms, or good adjustment in all spheres of functioning. It entails, however, generally successful efforts to cope with life stressors and strains. The concept of resiliency also entails positive developmental outcomes in individuals despite high-risk status, as well as recovery from trauma (i.e., traumatic life experiences). Resiliency, and its counterpart, vulnerability, are influenced by a host of "risk" and "protective" factors in the lives of children, adolescents, and adults. Resilient outcomes in children are associated with the following triad of protective factors or mechanisms: (1) individual characteristics (e.g., gender; certain cognitive abilities; temperamental predispositions such as responsiveness, outgoingness, and independence); (2) a warm, secure relationship with family members; and (3) other loving adults who are involved in the life of the child and who provide support and serve as positive role models (e.g., teachers, coaches, club leaders).

Sometimes the development of a person's self-reliance and ego strength (major components of resiliency) is achieved at great personal cost (e.g., children with abusive or mentally ill parents who achieve in school and eventually their careers but who have great difficulty dealing with feelings and close personal relationships). Hence, the long-term outcomes of being resilient may not always be positive (for children or adults). That is, the mechanisms that help some individuals be resilient in their youth may hinder them as adults. Based on their longitudinal research of abused children who appeared to be resilient or invulnerable, for example, Farber and Egeland (1987) indicated that in spite of these children's apparently good coping strategies and adaptive behavior not all of these children were emotionally healthy. Thus, high-level behavioral competence is not necessarily paralleled by superior adjustment on measures of internalizing symptoms of psychopathology.

Common characteristics of resilient individuals, according to Wolin and Wolin (1993), include insight, close relationships, independence, initiative, humor and creativity, and morality. Other common characteristics of more resilient individuals are listed as follows:

1. Know-how, resourcefulness, effective problem-solving abilities, savvy or tacit knowledge
2. Information seeking
3. Strategic and decisive risk taking (vs. passivity or learned helplessness)
4. Formation and utilization of relationships for survival
5. Cognitive restructuring of painful experiences
6. Sustained altruism, optimism, and hope
7. Effective and appropriate dissociation of affect (but not pervasive and persistent blunting of affect)
8. Positive projective anticipation (e.g., fantasy, futuristic thinking, imagining alternative strategies and different outcomes for the future) that give one a greater sense of mastery over the present

Many of these characteristics of resiliency are also central features of creativity (e.g., resourcefulness, problem-solving abilities, strategic risk taking, cognitive restructuring, and positive projective identification).

Finally, with regard to the creative person, creativity experts assert that creativity is probably not a general trait but that people are more or less creative in relatively narrow areas. Amabile (1983, 1996) suggests that creativity is best conceptualized not as a personality trait or a general ability but as a behavior resulting from particular constellations of personal characteristics, cognitive abilities, and social environments. Many of the same characteristics and capacities that have been used to describe highly creative persons are also those which typify highly resilient individuals (Carson, 1999b). Furthermore, to a large extent, the processes involved in creativity and resiliency require similar integrative abilities (e.g., holding seemingly contradictory information simultaneously in one's mind; remaining open and ready to various information retrieval processes, including inner sensations, images, symbols, dreams, hunches, and fantasies).

CREATIVITY IN MARRIAGE

The marital literature is replete with descriptions of passionate marriages (Schnarch, 1997), successful marriages (DeGenova and Rice, 2002), smart marriages (www.smartmarriages.com), hot monogamy (Love, 1999), and the like. Healthy couple relationships include such characteristics as commitment, good communication, compatibility, honesty, trust, empathy, sensitivity, respect, unselfishness, forgiveness, friendship/companionship, and affection/emotional expressiveness, to name a few. Little has been written, however, about creative marriages (or couple relationships) or the role that creativity plays in these kinds of intimate relationships. Among clinicians and family life educators, some characteristics of creative marriages which are commonly discussed are that these marriages:

1. Are like a tapestry or quilt (uniform whole with diverse but complementary pieces)
2. Have a common philosophy and general purpose for being and growing together
3. Are a blend of tradition and innovative change
4. Are not too moralistic or hedonistic (i.e., too rigid or loose)
5. Balance social conformity with nonconformity (e.g., civic duty and responsibility with living their own lives, charting their own course, and at times taking unpopular positions on issues or standing against the status quo)
6. Are like true art with regard to the couple's everyday relationship
7. Live life in a balanced way, i.e., neither too seriously nor in a lax manner and often find time to engage in humor and play
8. Are based on acceptance and appreciation (not just tolerance) of individual differences
9. Maintain a congruency between feelings and behavior (as in their verbal and nonverbal communication)

It appears that many modern marriages are lacking in a number of these traits. Thus, creative marriage development may be viewed as an important societal need or goal that has the potential to lead to more satisfying and growth-promoting conjugal relationships.

As we have seen, creativity appears to be related to a person's coping abilities and overall resiliency. These abilities are important to developing and maintaining a healthy marriage. Creative problem solving as a couple is required to successfully cope with or adapt to both normative and nonnormative life events. Normative transitions include having children, going back to work after childbearing or changing jobs, adjusting to an empty nest, facing retirement, and getting older, along with fluctuations in personality and income (Silverstone and Kandel-Hyman, 1992). Nonnormative events entail unexpected loss of loved ones, serious illness, and divorce.

Because all couples experience conflicts and difficulties, learning how to problem solve in more creative ways can help keep the energy and spontaneity in a marriage. Thinking more divergently can also assist couples in seeing options or alternatives, keeping problems or issues in perspective, and preventing hurt, frustration, or anger from building up. Creative couples are also more likely to suspend judgment and question assumptions or values that may have a negative influence on their relationship (Goleman, Kaufman, and Ray, 1992).

Along with the everyday hassles and stressors married couples experience, some transitions typically require a great deal of adjustment and adaptation. Having children is a life-transforming experience that challenges couples on many levels. These include such areas as their sex life, time together, communication, financial stability, and coparenting efforts, to name a few (Kruse-Nordin, 2000). These kinds of changes require that couples be creative and planful in meeting both their individual and relationship needs.

Another common experience of many couples in today's world is divorce (DeGenova and Rice, 2002). Regardless of how creative a couple is, divorce remains a highly emotional and traumatic experience. It is normal to experience pain and loss from divorce, and even the most creative and emotionally well-adjusted individuals must work hard to transcend the losses associated with divorce. However, divorce can be a growth-producing experience. Some writers (e.g., Ahrons, 1995) believe that couples can even experience a healthy divorce, both in terms of their civility toward each other during the process and the positive ways that they can change because of divorce. Individuals who are more creative may be more likely to both see and experience the potential benefits of ending a marital relationship and freeing each other to live different lives. Creative problem solving and negotiation during the divorce process may also facilitate more of a win-win situation. In short, just as couples can learn how to have more creative marriages, they can, when necessary, learn how to have a more creative divorce as they take time to explore that which is in the best interests of all parties involved (children included). Creativity is also important in the later stages of divorce adjustment. This includes getting on with one's personal life, single parenting, remarriage, and the possible formation of a blended family with all of its new demands, expectations, changing roles, and newly acquired relationships with immediate and extended family members. Indeed, creating a new vision is a crucial aspect of a healthy divorce and establishment of a better life (Ahrons, 1995).

Another transition most married couples experience is retirement and old age. Growing into old age requires a new perspective and the ability to see oneself and one's partner differently. Retirement involves a dramatic change in personal roles, since one of the most defining characteristics of a person, his or her job or career, has ended (Silverstone and Kandel-Hyman, 1992). Married couples will see themselves and their spouses differently. Creativity is important after retirement in redefining one's purpose and role, as well as pursuing new activities, experiences, and relationships. Changes in one's physical and mental health also require a high level of adjustment. Many limitations can be compensated for, as older adults, both individually and maritally, exercise their creative thinking in searching for and implementing ways of keeping excitement, meaning, and love in their lives.

Facilitating Creativity in Marriage

Because creativity plays a unique role in marriage, it is important that couples understand how to further its development in their relationships (Page, 1997). Everyday creativity can be enhanced just as anything else a couple would care to learn. It is also important for couples to understand how creativity can be stifled in the marital relationship (Goleman, Kaufman, and Ray, 1992).

The creative process demands a great deal of freedom, a non-threatening arena, and acceptance from one's partner. The creator must not feel threatened by potential reactions to new ideas generated or creative acts attempted (Hogan, 1988). Hogan also notes that in order for creativity to occur there must be sufficient mental energy. If a married couple is continually stressed or exhausted from work, children, or even marital conflict, creativity may be prevented from developing.

Another prerequisite for creativity in marriage is passion (Leuzzi, 1999). There must be a certain degree of emotional investment in and attachment to that which is being created, be it a product, activity, or creative insight. Couples must also be willing to transcend traditional ideas, rules, and patterns in their relationship, as well as show some degree of nonconformity to the expectations and wishes of others (e.g., friends, extended family members, and even children) (Leuzzi, 1999).

Some ideas and general principles, if adhered to, may help couples enhance the creativity in their relationships. These notions have been pulled together partly from the work of Goleman, Kaufman, and Ray (1992), as well as Hogan (1988). It is important to remember that couples do not have to become high-level creative thinkers before they can become more creative in their marriage. Often, by choosing and learning how to change everyday, simple behaviors toward each other, creativity can be facilitated in the couple relationship. In this way behavior and learning may complement each other and are mutually enforcing. Given the significance of the quality of the marital relationship to family health and function, it is important that partners discover new ways of being more creative with, and toward, each other. They may want to start with the following suggestions:

1. Creativity may occur at the most unpredictable moments, but also in particular places at planned time intervals. Partners should encourage each other to think and daydream in places (or while engaging in certain activities) that are likely to facilitate creativity. For example, a person may find that he or she is most creative when in the shower, while running or playing golf, or while sitting in the park. Couples, too, may find that certain places (and times of the day or week) allow them to fantasize

about how their relationship could be more creative and to share creative experiences.

2. Recognize the judgmental voice when speaking to one's spouse. All of us tend at times to have a critical voice that can hinder creative insight and experience. It is important to recognize when a particular way of communicating is shutting down creative thinking and problem solving in a relationship.

3. Take time to play together often and allow humor its full expression in marriage. Couples today spend way too much time focusing on those things which, in the long run, have little or no real significance instead of those few areas of life and their relationship that do and fail to realize the extreme importance of being able to enjoy each other's company as they did earlier in their relationship.

4. Accept frustrations along the way. When trying to learn anything new or establish a different way of relating, frustration often occurs when goals are not immediately achieved. It is the same with augmenting creativity. Ideas and insights may not come naturally at first, and it is important for couples to be tolerant and forgiving and not give up.

5. Allow each person to freely express his or her emotions (as long as they are not hurtful or destructive). Emotional release and exploration are often precursors to creative problem solving and relational growth. Any fear of punishment, reprimand, or even passive-aggressive response is inhibiting to creativity in marriage. Jealousy of and unhealthy competition with one's mate is also deadly to the development of creativity.

6. Learn to listen with your heart and mind, for without this spouses cannot become cocreators or understand their mates as individuals who are linked to and yet separate from them.

7. Be open to new experiences and be willing to take risks as a couple. Also, focus more on efforts and the process of being creative than on outcomes or performance.

8. Finally, develop the ability to see things in a fresh way. The willingness and ability to question your own assumptions is imperative to developing creativity in a marriage.

Some other practical ways that couples can develop creativity in their marriages are listed as follows. This list may give couples some additional ideas for how they can get the creative process going in their relationships.

1. *Recognize and break routines.* This does not mean all routines, but those that could use more excitement. For example, if a couple finds that they tend to watch television and do little else most evenings during the week, they can choose one of these nights to do something out of the ordinary. This may help promote creativity by way of new activities, be they in or out of the home.
2. *Brainstorm.* Part of finding new outlets or activities to do together is letting the imagination run wild as a couple, and then being willing to act on ideas that feel exciting or sound interesting. Just start with one and others may follow.
3. *Challenge things that are accepted the way they are.* This could be anything from figuring out together a way to fix a door or something else around the house, to accepting that one person does not like going to the movies and the other does. Finding solutions to problems or changing experiences are ways that creativity may have a chance to grow and make married life more enjoyable.
4. *Look or shop for things of interest together.* Shopping for things that each person likes can, for some couples at least, be an exciting activity. For example, some couples may find and play games (i.e., board or computer games) differently than as specified by the rules, and in such ways that might spark ideas for new games they can make up and engage in together. Couples might also purchase materials (e.g., construction paper, markers, pens, glitter, etc.) and then think of ways to use them creatively to help themselves talk about issues or solve problems in their marriage (e.g., creating a money-saving system that helps them work together). One such couple created a money snake, a paper reptile that gained or lost a body segment with each allotted increment of money saved or spent by the couple. Since couples argue over money-related issues more than anything else in marriage, creating ways to talk about or deal with saving and spending can help to lessen the conflicts and worries associated with money.
5. *Show interest in and learn about each other's hobbies.* Taking time to learn about the hobbies of one's spouse will nurture positive feelings and may result in a greater commonality of inter-

ests. When couples have more shared interests and a greater understanding of and appreciation for their own unique ones, they tend to have more creative power in their relationship.

6. *Accentuate ongoing common activities.* Activities that couples commonly engage in are often taken for granted, and this does not have to be the case. Even something as simple as sitting down together for dinner can be creative. Dinner can be anywhere and can have changing themes. The same can be said for just about anything married couples do together but have gotten used to do routinely (from grocery shopping to gardening or working in the yard).

7. *Increase levels of physical exercise, both individually and together.* Admittedly, some couples will refuse to exercise together, even though creative thinking and problem solving often come when couples are engaged in something physically challenging or even demanding together. There are many outlets for physical exercise, and couples can try many of them or even invent their own.

In sum, marriage is a special relationship in which both members are ultimately part of each other's creative experience. Vital, healthy marriages, like families, provide freedom and opportunity for members to explore and develop their own creative interests and gifts, as well as avoid or remove unnecessary blocks to creative thinking and expression.

CREATIVITY IN FAMILIES

Research on family strengths and resiliency has been a tour de force in the field of family science the past two decades (Curran, 1983; Stinnett and DeFrain, 1985; McCubbin, 1999). Common characteristics associated with resilient families are commitment; cohesion; time together; positive communication patterns, problem-solving skills, and the ability to cope effectively with stress and crisis; adaptability to change; shared responsibilities; expressed appreciation, affirmation, and support for one another; a healthy lifestyle; a strong marriage; a realistic but positive outlook on life; spiritual wellness; a sense of right and wrong; rituals and traditions; acceptance of each individual's uniqueness and need for independence and privacy; balanced involvement with friends and community; forgiveness; and play, laughter, and humor. However, although these traits are exceedingly important, most of them have little to do with creativity. Furthermore, most family members overlook the importance of creative thinking and expression within the family unit.

Highly creative families encompass many of the previous traits but appear to have additional qualities not typical of perhaps the majority of families. According to Albert (1996), these families tend to have a connectedness with and deep appreciation for their family history (legacy), as well as family processes that allow knowledge and abilities to be passed across the generations. They also have a strong sense of what is important and not important (e.g., from their culture and society at large). Research by Dacey and Packer (Dacey, 1989b; Dacey and Packer, 1992) has identified several common characteristics of families of highly creative individuals:

1. A nurturing parenting style (i.e., not permissive, authoritative, or authoritarian) in which parents model a clear set of values and encourage their children to decide upon behaviors that exemplify those values
2. Play and frequent expressions of humor
3. Parental recognition of children's unique interests and abilities at a young age and the provision of a wide range of opportunities to express and develop these abilities without force (i.e., encouragement vs. pressure)
4. Parents who have a variety of intellectual interests as well as activities other than their work
5. A solid work ethic modeled in parents and encouraged in children (again, without pushing)
6. An emphasis on such internal states as honesty and imagination
7. A larger number of traumatic experiences in these families that involve grief and loss, illness and disability, or other threats to family unity and security

Perhaps in this last case, some children discover, develop, and use creativity as one way of coping with a harsh reality (e.g., inner exploration and/or outer expression).

A number of other studies have examined the family's influences on the development of creativity in children, particularly those which facilitate creative growth (Kerr and Chopp, 1999). Common characteristics include adaptability (Gardner and Moran, 1997); self-confident mothers who encouraged their children to be independent (Michel and Dudek, 1991); high levels of parental love and acceptance, high expectations of and cooperation with their children, coupled with respect for children's subjectivity and autonomy (Mendecka, 1996); an emphasis in the family on openness to experience, internal locus of control, and the ability to play with elements and concepts (Olszewski, Kulieke, and Buescher, 1987); and a high degree of both stimulation and support from parents (Csikszentmihalyi, Rathunde, and Whalen, 1993).

An earlier review of a wide body of research concerned with family influences on the development of creativity in children by Miller and Gerard (1979) revealed several interesting common and incongruous findings among studies. Sample and measurement differences were considered in their attempt to resolve discrepancies and integrate the findings. As a general rule, family size was not related to children's creativity. Social class was positively associated with children's verbal creativity, but results were mixed for studies in which nonverbal measures were used. Although birth-order findings were inconsistent, younger children who were distant from siblings in age tended to be less creative. With regard to gender differences, older girls tended to score higher on verbal tests of creativity, whereas older boys scored higher on the figural portions. According to Miller and Gerard, parents of creative children tended to be highly creative and competent themselves (both intellectually and interpersonally) and were characterized by a strong sense of personal and family security. Perhaps most interesting was that relationships between creative children and their parents tended to be "neither overly close emotionally, nor hostile and detached, but marked by respect, independence, and freedom" (p. 295). This sounds much like the "balanced" family described by Olson and colleagues (1983).

Amabile's (1983, 1996) research has shown that a number of parental attitudes expressed toward their children were related to children's creative thinking and production. These included freedom to think, learn, and grow according to their own unique developmental path; respect; moderate emotional closeness (e.g., not too overinvolved or controlling); an emphasis on values rather than rules and achievement and grades; parental independence and involvement in their own activities outside the family (balanced with involvement with their children, of course); an appreciation of creativity in all its forms; humor; and a vision for the future. Moreover, according to Amabile, highly creative children often have highly creative parents. A lack of creativity within marital, coparental, and parent-child sub-systems can also discourage children's natural curiosity and desire to be creative. Amabile (1989) lists five major parental behaviors that can inhibit the development of creativity in children:

1. Surveillance (when adults constantly hover over their children or monitor their learning, behavior, or exploration of their world, including the world of ideas)
2. Excessive use of rewards
3. Overcontrol (telling children exactly how to do things, and seeing any mistake as unacceptable or exploration a waste of time)
4. Restrictions on children's choices
5. Grandiose or unrealistically high expectations for children's accomplishments

In addition to these behaviors, failure of parents to provide rich and varied opportunities for children to play, and for family members to play together, can damper creative learning and socialization. The creative process, like play, demands a nonthreatening and nonpunitive environment (Hogan, 1988).

Torrance (1961) discussed a number of factors that seem to affect the development and expression of creative thinking in children. Negative influences on creativity include:

1. Elimination of opportunities for fantasy and imagination
2. Restrictions on curiosity, exploration, and manipulation of the environment
3. Conditions that result in fear, timidity, and unhealthy competition in their relationships with peers and adults
4. Misplaced emphasis on the mechanics of verbal communication and skills
5. Overemphasis on achievement and success

   6. Lack of opportunities for talking about ideas and ways to or resources for working out ideas

   7. Differential treatment of boys and girls

Positive influences on creativity include:

   1. Teaching and exemplifying principles and methods for generating ideas and problems

   2. Providing warm-up instructions and exercises (i.e., practicing new ways of thinking and problem solving)

   3. Rewarding creative thinking but in a particular manner (e.g., treating children's questions and ideas with respect and genuine interest and encouraging and evaluating self-initiated as well as cooperative learning so that children learn to value both their own ideas and those of others)

Before we overestimate the importance of creativity in families, it is necessary to point out that not all healthy families (or marriages) are highly creative and that creativity does not always work in the best interests of the family. For instance, some families are highly creative in their maintenance of a destructive homeostatic system. Hogan (1988) indicates that when creative processes are destructive, or when creative resources (economic or emotional) within the family are limited, family therapy can be exceedingly effective in helping set the family on a new course. "Creativity must then come from the therapist, at least for a good part of the time" (Hogan, 1988, p. 44). Hogan mentions creative hypothesizing and the use of video playback (which allows family members to observe their interactions firsthand) as two creative approaches.

OTHER WAYS OF FACILITATING CREATIVITY AND CREATIVE THINKING IN CHILDREN AND ADULTS

Simonton (1995) estimates that although many children are born with the potential to develop exceptional creativity only about 1 percent actually have the opportunity to do so. As has been discussed, parents play a major role in the development and expression of creativity in their children, as well as in the family system. Teachers and other school personnel are also in an excellent position to enhance creativity in children and adolescents, as are other key adults within and beyond the school environment.

Education about creativity and creative thinking is thought to be beneficial to both adults and children (Sternberg and Lubart, 1995). Often, simply learning more about these domains has an influence on an individual's movement toward thinking and acting more creatively. Moreover, involvement in right-brain activities such as music and art is thought to be important to the child's overall development of mental capacities and language (van der Linde, 1999). Creative activity and thinking are not only important to education but, as we have seen, are also key components of resiliency in children and adults. Creative activity involves a mental preparedness to take on new challenges, even welcoming them, as part of the process of arriving at newer and deeper understandings about oneself and one's work (Fisher and Specht, 1999; Russ, 1999). Humor and joke telling are also common elements of creative thinking and can be encouraged (Derks, 1985).

Advantages to fostering creativity in children include encouraging use of their imagination (Raines and Isbell, 1994) and supporting and extending their social development (Britsch, 1992). Another effective method of enhancing creativity is through storytelling (Phillips, 2000). Storytelling is thought to increase creativity by allowing children to use their imaginations, to explore ideas, and to learn about the meanings and feelings associated with human experiences. Other ways that creativity can be increased is through the provision of materials that encourage pretend (sociodramatic) play and make possible the free manipulation of a variety of objects. Adults can also reflect on the child's beliefs and actions with the child in a way that helps facilitate an integrated structure of mental skills (Antonietti, 1997).

Finally, according to Nickerson (1999), creativity in children and adults tends to increase when people do the following:

- build on existing skills;
- have an established purpose and intention;
- focus on or encourage acquisition of domain-specific knowledge;
- stimulate and reward curiosity and exploration in themselves and others while building on or enhancing intrinsic motivation;

- encourage confidence and a willingness to take risks;
- concentrate on self-competition and mastery;
- provide opportunities for choice and discovery;
- promote supportable beliefs about creativity;
- develop self-management and meta-cognitive abilities;
- teach and model techniques and strategies for creative performance; and
- provide or maintain balance in one's own life or the lives of others (e.g., children at home or in the classroom, or adults with family members, friendships, and work).

If even some of these principles are enacted some of the time, creativity has a greater opportunity to flourish in the lives of children and adults alike.

CONCLUSION

The importance of creativity has been emphasized in this chapter, not only in children who are learning to manage life's difficulties and challenges, but also in adults who experience stress, trauma, relational difficulties, and/or a tendency toward specific types of mental illness. Creativity may play a key role in the lives of children when it comes to coping with both daily hassles and major stressors, be they acute or prolonged. Interpersonal problem solving has been shown to increase in children as creativity is augmented. However, it has also been argued that many parents and even teachers know little about the importance of teaching creativity and creating an environment that encourages creative thinking. Teaching or facilitating creativity is not the complex or difficult task it would appear to be. Fostering creativity in children means letting them think and providing opportunities for them to imagine, invent, and improvise. Much of the developmental process of creativity includes not inhibiting creative children at play, whether it be with peers, siblings, or parents, but rather encouraging and appropriately rewarding efforts toward creative thinking, behavior, or production.

Potential benefits of enhancing creativity and creative thinking were also seen in adults. Creativity was shown to be an important component of self-actualization, one of the milestones of adult development. Indeed, the path to self-actualization would be difficult without the ingenuity needed to obtain basic needs, adapt to an ever-changing environment, and cope effectively with the inevitable stressors and hassles (both major and minor) of life. Furthermore, creativity may be central to both individual and family resiliency and therefore one's overall mental health.

There may be some connection between creativity and mental illness in adults, particularly in eminent creators. However, although many of these individuals may exhibit mild to more severe forms of psychological or emotional disorder, as a general rule, severe psychopathology tends to be an inhibitor of both ordinary and genius-level creative production. Moreover, some research supports the assertion that people with higher levels of everyday creativity are more optimally mentally healthy.

In summary, creativity serves a unique and important function in couple relationships, marriages, and families. Creativity, like variety, may be part of the "spice of life" in intimate relationships, especially given that close relationships often seem to experience periods of routine, boredom, and mundaneness. Although stability and predictability are important to marital and family relationships, equally vital is the ability of people in these relationships to invent, grow, and change in both the large and small areas of their lives.

BREAKING OUT OF THE BOX: CREATING SPICE

Therapy is often hard and serious work. People entrust their hearts, souls, and children to us. This responsibility can take its toll unless we address our self-care in a proactive (rather than reactive) manner. One such approach is to periodically add a bit of "spice" to our work. We invite you to utilize the following steps as you create spice in your personal and/or professional world.

Step 1: Imagine yourself as a fly on the wall observing your own life. Write a paragraph (from the fly's perspective) that would accurately describe a typical day or week. Be as detailed as possible.

Step 2: Now imagine that a dash of exotic and intriguing magical spice had been sprinkled over your life. The fly has become a stunning monarch butterfly, and you notice that just the right amount of spice has been added to your daily and weekly recipe. Changes have occurred. These changes may be quiet or loud, tangible or abstract. Write a paragraph or two (from the butterfly's perspective) that captures the texture and fragrance of your newly spiced life.

Step 3: Share your observations with a friend or colleague.

SECTION II:
THERAPISTS' PERCEPTIONS
OF CREATIVITY IN THEIR WORK
WITH COUPLES AND FAMILIES

Chapter 4

The Meaning, Importance, and Role of Creativity in Couples and Family Therapy

CREATIVE INCUBATION EXERCISE #4: CREATIVITY IS . . .

In the first three chapters we heard from a variety of professionals about their views of creativity. However, we have yet to ask the most important person—you! Before you start reading this chapter, for those of you who are practicing clinicians, please take a few minutes to complete the following statements and questions on the survey that was administered to the therapists in our study.

Directions: Respond to each question that follows using the scale. Circle your response 1 through 5.

5	4	3	2	1
Strongly Agree	Agree	Neutral	Disagree	Strongly Disagree

1. I am a creative individual.	1 2 3 4 5
2. Others see me as creative.	1 2 3 4 5
3. I regularly implement creative interventions in my work.	1 2 3 4 5
4. I have mastered the set of creativity skills that I use on a regular basis.	1 2 3 4 5
5. I am receptive to ideas that challenge my way of thinking.	1 2 3 4 5
6. Time constraints are not a problem for me in being creative in the workplace.	1 2 3 4 5

7. I regularly take time to learn and implement advanced creativity techniques.   1 2 3 4 5

8. I am receptive to team creativity, even if rewards are shared equally between all team members.   1 2 3 4 5

9. I have in-depth knowledge of the areas of my job that require me to be creative.   1 2 3 4 5

10. I consistently take my ideas from conception to application.   1 2 3 4 5

11. I am not limited by my position with respect to implementing creative ideas.   1 2 3 4 5

12. I am aware of my unique way of being creative and I use it on a regular basis.   1 2 3 4 5

13. I have participated in formal training (e.g., graduate course work, workshops, institute training, etc.) in the area of creativity.   1 2 3 4 5

14. I believe that a lack of creativity in couples and families is related to conflicts, difficulties, and dysfunction.   1 2 3 4 5

15. Intuition or my "gut" plays a key role in my professional use of creativity.   1 2 3 4 5

16. Creativity is important in my work as a family therapist.   1 2 3 4 5

Directions: Please provide brief and concise responses to each of the following questions.

1. What does creativity mean to you as a therapist in the context of couples and family therapy?

2. What are the top three personal qualities or characteristics of a creative family therapist?
    1.
    2.
    3.

3. List three of your most creative interventions that you have found most useful and effective in working with couples and families.
   1.
   2.
   3.

4. As a family therapist or supervisor, what keeps you from being as creative as you would like to be? Identify three barriers, blocks, inhibitors, etc.
   1.
   2.
   3.

In Chapters 4 through 7 we condense and highlight responses of therapists who participated in our study to the qualitative questions posed to them. This chapter includes what participants said about the meaning, importance, and role of creativity in couples and family therapy. These descriptions give us some unique frames for understanding the importance of creativity in clinical work. With regard to the quantitative results of the study (i.e., therapists' responses to the numerical items in the survey) we refer readers to another source (Carson et al., 2003). First, however, it is important to consider the multifaceted nature of creativity in the context of couples and family therapy.

THE MULTIFACETED NATURE OF CREATIVITY

As discussed in Chapter 1, the creative process entails an active and often intense interaction with clients that includes the therapist's training, personality characteristics, and cognitive style and capacities; clients' personalities, intellectual abilities, and presenting problems; contextual factors (e.g., socioeconomics and cultural characteristics of clients and clinicians); structural and systemic dynamics (especially in family therapy); and features of the therapeutic setting. The creative therapist is adept at integrating a wide body of information in a relatively short period of time and working collaboratively with clients to develop a flexible plan for accomplishing both short-term and long-term goals (including second-order change). We believe that creative therapists also appreciate and seek to understand that change happens, both intrapersonally and interpersonally, on a variety of levels, including the somatic/biological, cognitive, behavioral, emotional, social/relational, volitional/motivational, moral, and spiritual. Microsocietal (i.e., close friendships, residential situation) and macrosocietal (neighborhood, work, educational, ethnic, legal, economic, and political) influences must also be taken into consideration (Dacey and Lennon, 1998; Martindale, 1989). Of course, the need to target one or more of these levels of change depends on the nature of the presenting problem(s) and everything the couple or family brings with them to therapy (i.e., who they are).

If, for example, conflicting worldviews and values in a marriage are stated as initial complaints or are part of the symptom picture, then spiritual, religious, and/or moral issues may need to be a central focus of therapy. The therapist may decide to work primarily (although not necessarily exclusively) on a cognitive level, at least in the early phases of the process, in order to inform and educate. Delving deep into each partner's emotional hurt and turmoil may not be a primary objective until other issues are clarified and understood. For cases in which depression or another psychiatric disorder is known or suspected in a particular family member, the therapist must make sure that this problem is addressed early and sufficiently before much progress in couple or family relationships can be expected (including, if necessary, medication prescribed from an appropriate provider). If past trauma in the life of one person has occurred, locating where traumatic memories are stored in the body (perhaps in individual therapy) may be an important link in the therapeutic process. Or for situations in which couples come in ready and willing to work hard, the creative therapist may sense that an emotion-focused approach will be most effective. The point is, creative therapists assess early (not impulsively), make assessment a priority, and tailor their approaches to the personalities, system dynamics, and presenting difficulties with which they are confronted. They not only discern where various conflicts and relational pain in these intimate relationships are housed but also conduct the work of therapy on levels in which change is most needed and movement is most likely to occur.

SUMMARY OF QUALITATIVE FINDINGS
REGARDING THE IMPORTANCE OF CREATIVITY
IN THERAPY ACCORDING TO STUDY PARTICIPANTS

Participants in the study were asked to respond to the following question: What does creativity mean to you in the context of marriage and family therapy? There were a variety of interesting and enlightening responses, a selection of which are presented next. We have combined or eliminated responses that were redundant and, in some cases, unclear or incomplete.

Examples of the Meaning and Importance of Creativity in Couples and Family Therapy

- Creativity is the ability to work with clients in finding new ways of responding to situations in which they seem stuck, and finding new ways to allow myself to respond to their stuckness and my own. It means going outside the bounds of regular conversation . . . being able to stop the normal flow.
- Creativity to me means that I am not boxed in theory. There is not a condition in front of me but a person, couple, or family. It is the ability to go with the moment and deal spontaneously with difficult and challenging situations in a dynamic and relevant manner.
- Creativity allows one to assist a family in accessing resources beyond the expected, the traditional, the known. It means connecting to your creative "part" and then using your common sense to determine whether or not the clues it gives you can be helpful to your clients.
- Creativity is using techniques and assignments that encourage family members to expand their thinking and their behavior to resolve family conflicts or concerns in ways that had not been attempted previously. It means being flexible with respect to conceptualization of dilemmas and subsequent interventions.
- Always questioning. Seeking new ways of seeing and helping clients to see. Being like a visitor in a foreign land with all of my clients—no assumptions, expectations, in so far as I can achieve this.

- Creativity is the ability to engage in improvisation—good family therapy is good improv theater.
- Creativity is the ability to think "outside the box"—to apply known ideas to new situations and to mold or tweak them into new combinations, the ability to apply old ideas in new ways, to new situations, to new people, and the ability to reshape ideas so that they add new information to a system—hopefully new information that makes a difference.
- To be able to utilize humor, art, music, analogies, or exercises that enhance intuitive learning and insight.
- Creativity means that I can use varying kinds of materials, experiences, metaphoric images, and concepts that empower my clients to "see" the situation or get in touch with their limits and empower them to try new models of thinking to reach new understanding.
- Creativity means having the ability to draw from diverse fields of study to implement interventions in helping individuals, couples, and families.
- Being able to "color outside the lines" in order to meet people where they are. I believe, too, that creativity means being flexible enough to work with different frameworks to adapt to client needs. To color outside the lines allows the therapist to be limitless as to how to resolve problems and avoid prescriptive solutions. I like to use "literal" wording to build analogies to illustrate how the family or couple is getting in their own way. I will devise scenarios using their language to provide apt interventions.
- Creativity in the treatment process is a way of thinking. It is neither loosely controlled nor entirely orderly and logical. Rather, creativity in therapy uncovers new ideas and new meanings to extend the horizon beyond the previous level.
- Creativity means approaching each client from a new perspective, looking at their abilities and disabilities as resources for change.
- Creativity in therapy is being acutely aware of moments of possible learning and change and taking advantage of those moments.
- Creativity requires finding the essentiality of the Other and creating an ethical dialogue that brings out the most authentic and ethical behavior in the therapist and clients. It allows us to leave

feeling that we have cooperatively learned and reembedded new responses from an old situation and more adequate responses to new situations.

- Creativity is not adhering to a formula in treating clients. It is seeing and hearing what is presented as unique to this family/ couple and creating language and experiences that speak to them.
- Creativity is the use of self and therapeutic techniques in ways that stimulate the therapeutic relationship so that families can further themselves toward positive and goal-directed change.
- Creativity means being capable of joining in the relationship, conceptualizing change strategies that fit the culture and ethos of the family, and implementing those strategies.
- Creativity means literally doing something different and unexpected or counterintuitive. It is being open to multiple points of view, including turning things upside down when necessary.
- Creativity entails the ability to take risks, use my intuition as well as skills, and honor the unconscious both in and between sessions.
- Creativity in therapy involves an understanding that often people are "experience deprived," meaning that they seem to have the same experiences producing the same results over and over again. Part of my job is to provide some new, challenging experiences in the context of therapy.
- Creativity is the ability to facilitate insight and change through non-talk therapy means. It means being willing to bark like a dog, crow like a rooster, wrestle with crocodiles, or write fables for my clients. It means being able to assume different roles and be comfortable with my own definition of "professional." It means being willing to look stupid in order to find the open window and having enough confidence to make things up as I go. It means being present every minute so that each session is unique from every other.
- Creativity means being able to "see" the world from clients' eyes and providing interpretation for both the client and the "other" (i.e., situation in their lives that has brought them to therapy)—also being open to hearing the creativity in the client as they struggle to understand their own situation in life and then help the client to see their own answer.

- Creativity means being fully present in the moment to what is happening in the room on all levels, with myself and with my client(s) and allowing myself to respond spontaneously to what is called forth in the interaction. It means trusting my own intuition/responses, holding my clients as resourceful and creative beings with the ability to find their own answers with my support and guidance. It also means being flexible and open and thinking/responding outside the box while still able to hold the therapeutically appropriate boundaries and create a safe, holding environment for my clients. Creativity is the ability to help move clients and families toward second-order change. First-order change is doing the same thing over and over, just louder or longer. Creativity is jump-shifting to a new realm of thinking (cliché: a new paradigm).
- Creativity is letting my intuition bring what is most needed into play, even if none of us has heard of it before. It involves looking for ways to reframe situations so clients can engage themselves and others differently.
- Creativity has to do with my own willingness to take risks with clients and involve them in the creative process. It means helping a family find its own way, learning from each of the family members, respecting the process of therapy, and allowing for spontaneity and fun.
- Creativity is the ability to generate metaphors and verbal pictures that reduce complex ideas to terms that can be understood and implemented by clients. In addition, it is the ability to use words to motivate and to overcome resistance—words that the client and the client system can take in without feeling shamed.
- Creativity means not being required to follow the masters in theory or practice but utilizing their theories and interventions as a guide toward formulating my own methods as a therapist.
- Creativity means being uniquely responsive to the people with whom I am working and to the situation we are all in. It means thinking of ways to talk and understand such that the entire context gets considered from individual to community to societal levels. It also means paying attention to clients and utilizing their ideas in a tailor-made fashion so that our collective ideas fit them perfectly.

- Creativity is the ability to explore and be open to what is not known or "mystery" in the clinical setting. It means being able to seize the moment appropriately by adopting a creative tool.
- Creativity means looking for new, alternative, and less symptom-producing ways of reconstructing perception and experiences with regard to the internal and interpersonal realities of clients.
- Creativity means following your instincts, breaking out into original and innovative methods when conventional ones are proving ineffective. Creativity is being able to see and feel what is not being said and then act on it.
- Creativity is an ongoing challenge that impacts outcomes and is one of the key elements that makes counseling fun.

Some general themes can be noted in these responses. These include the ability to apply traditional modalities to new clients and situations in fresh ways (i.e., to break out of the mold in helping couples and families get unstuck and move forward); being able to think and act on one's feet (spontaneously and courageously in the moment) and being willing to improvise and take risks; and the capacity to connect with the creative, intuitive part of ourselves and our clients. What is demonstrated in these therapists' responses is the multifaceted nature of creativity in therapy. Creativity is a way of

- *conceptualizing* (i.e., clients' issues, needs, and difficulties) and *intuiting* (e.g., seeing, hearing, or feeling what is not being expressed in one's clients, as well as staying in tune with one's own intuitive voice);
- *acting* and *intervening* (i.e., challenging perceptions and helping to reconstruct paradigms);
- *communicating* through both verbal (i.e., metaphorically, lyrically, allegorically) and nonverbal (i.e., facial expression, body language, and other ways of listening) modes;
- *experiencing* (i.e., empathizing with clients; creating opportunities for emotional connectedness and working-through of couples and family members);
- *cooperating* (i.e., being able to elicit the creativity that lies within clients, both individually and corporately); and

- *accepting* (i.e., the mysteries and incongruities of people's pain and conflict, as well as the complexity and elusiveness of therapy itself).

The richness and variety of these responses testifies to the powerful role creativity plays in the therapeutic process.

BREAKING OUT OF THE BOX: FROM THE EYES OF BABES (AND BEYOND)

As therapists it is common to find ourselves surrounded by other therapists and helpers. Although we are diverse in many ways, we have some very similar ideas about creativity. To stretch a bit we would like you to interview three nontherapist individuals using the following format. These individuals need to include (1) a child, (2) a person who is ethnically different from yourself, and (3) a person who is at least thirty years older or younger than you. We also encourage you to spend time with both males and females. Remember, these individuals cannot be in the helping profession in any way. Have fun!

1. Please share with me who your heroes or role models are (or have been).
2. What do you like about each of these individuals? What characteristics are most appealing to you?
3. When these individuals are (were) faced with a problem, how do (did) they handle or solve the problem?
4. (Design your own question.)

Discuss with a friend or colleague the relationship between creativity and the responses of the individuals that you interviewed.

Chapter 5

Characteristics of a Creative Family Therapist

CREATIVE INCUBATION EXERCISE #5: MY CREATIVITY TIME LINE

Each one of us is a creative being. We truly believe this. Unfortunately, many of us have been told otherwise. This activity is designed to help you reflect upon several of your creative moments by revisiting a few of your personal and professional high and low points. It is our belief that creativity is an unrecognized sidekick of success and perseverance. Please take a few minutes to complete the following tasks:

1. Draw a personal/professional time line that extends from childhood to the present time. It may look something like the one that follows.

_____

childhood   adolescence   adulthood   present

2. On your time line identify several personal and professional high and low points. These are both the tough times and your accomplishments. Include a variety of both small and big examples. Do not limit yourself.
3. Under (or beside) each high and low point—identify the specific personal and/or professional strengths, qualities, and characteristics that you demonstrated. These characteristics assisted you in persevering and/or succeeding.
4. Compare this list to those provided in this chapter.

QUALITIES/CHARACTERISTICS
OF CREATIVE FAMILY THERAPISTS

With regard to the therapist as a creative person, creativity experts assert that creativity is probably not a general trait, but that individuals are more or less creative in specific areas or domains. Amabile (1983, 1989) suggests that creativity is best conceptualized as a behavior resulting from particular constellations of personal characteristics, cognitive abilities, and social environments, and not as a personality trait or a general ability. There are a variety of commonly observed characteristics of highly creative individuals. Although not all highly creative individuals possess each of these qualities and abilities, we have incorporated a number of frequently observed characteristics from various sources (see, e.g., Barron and Harrington, 1981; Dellas and Gaier, 1970; Dowd, 1989). The degree to which these characteristics are common, or even important, in highly effective therapists, is a matter of debate. However, many of the same characteristics and capacities that have been used to describe highly creative individuals are also those observed in effective psychotherapists (May, 1975; Nystul, 1993).

The processes of counseling and creativity require similar integrative abilities (e.g., holding seemingly contradictory information simultaneously in one's mind; remaining open and ready to various information retrieval processes, including inner sensations, images, symbols, dreams, hunches, and fantasies). Moreover, it is our assertion that creative therapists are more likely to take risks, be willing to fail, and combine sensitivity, open-mindedness, and divergent thinking with more traditional scientific behaviors and modes of cognizing that include rigorousness, convergence, impartiality, objectivity, and tough-mindedness. Hence, as Frey (1975) indicates, passion and reason are more integrated in creative counselors, "leading them to achieve a larger and more comprehensive perspective that transcends imposed dichotomies and thus links divergent elements that might not otherwise be united" (p. 25). A summary of these characteristics complied by Carson (1999b) is presented.

Some Common Characteristics of Highly Creative People

- Unconventionality (free spirit; unorthodox)
- Openness to both "inner" and "outer" experiences

- Takes advantage of chance, is alert to opportunities
- Ability to think and accomplish things that go beyond the logical
- Expectations of follow-through on part of oneself and others
- Empathy and superawareness of the needs of others
- Charisma
- Futuristic thinking and a strong sense of possibilities rather than impossibilities
- Flexible and skilled decision making
- Independent style, tendency to set one's own agenda
- Sensitivity
- Hardworking, persistent
- Enjoyment of frequent quiet contemplation
- Copes well with and appreciates novelty
- Finds order in chaos
- Often asks "Why?"
- Appreciation of nonverbal communication as much as verbal
- Aesthetic taste and imagination (e.g., appreciation of art, music, culture)
- A preference for complexity and yet appreciation of simplicity
- Keen attention to the social and natural world
- Motivation and the courage to risk, try new things, and surmount obstacles
- Relative absence of repression and suppression defense mechanisms
- Often a theme of remembered unhappiness, conflict, or struggle in childhood
- Enjoyment of social interactions and yet a tendency toward introversion
- Tolerance of ambiguity
- Willingness to grow and change
- A desire for recognition from others
- Emotional expressiveness
- Ability to make transformations between the figural and the verbal
- Enjoys the world of ideas
- Frequently questions social norms, truisms, and assumptions
- Allows oneself to be outrageous
- Willingness to take a stand
- Keen evaluative abilities (e.g., can accurately evaluate the strengths and weaknesses of one's own work)

- Humor and an appreciation of humor in self and others
- Fantasy proneness and richness of mental imagery
- Generally a strong internal locus of control
- Autonomy and independence of judgment
- Self-confidence
- Openness to new experiences
- A wide range of interests
- Curiosity and enthusiasm
- Vivid imagination, a sense of wonderment, and childlike playfulness

Characteristics of a Creative Family Therapist As Reported by Study Participants

When asked to list the three most prominent qualities or characteristics of a creative family therapist, our study participants provided us with a wide variety of responses. A list of all characteristics mentioned follows.

- Sense of humor
- Intuitive
- Teachable
- Able to take risks/willing to do something not done before
- Flexible and adaptable
- Thinks outside the box
- Self-awareness (i.e., how you are reacting to your clients and how you might intervene)
- Open to new ideas
- Honesty
- Curiosity
- Attentive
- Secure with oneself
- Competence in both critical and out-of-the-box thinking
- Intelligent and insightful
- Authenticity and genuineness
- Well read
- Empathic
- Good listening skills
- Able to see the big picture
- Being able to look at all sides of any new issue or idea

- Spontaneity/the ability to jump on a creative impulse at just the right moment
- Spirituality
- Experiential
- Able to establish a helping relationship with diverse clients
- A thinking style that sees the larger system and can go beyond conventional styles of therapy
- Trusting your gut
- Belief in oneself/confidence
- Adventurous
- Ability to be surprised
- Total respect for self and others
- Comfort with oneself/solid sense of self
- Unpredictable
- Originality/uniqueness
- Self-examination/humility
- Personal energy/energetic
- Ability to be truly interested in the lives of clients
- Ability/willingness to think in images, metaphors, and verbal pictures
- Able to move back and forth between abstract and concrete issues
- Can hear the utility and wisdom of clients and benefit from their ideas
- Takes the time to think about a case
- Lack of self-consciousness
- A willingness to accept/live with the consequences of creative outcomes
- Open-mindedness
- Willingness to perceive something different
- Healthy balance between belief and skepticism
- Courageous/brave
- Ability to see oneself as part of the problem or the solution
- Humble
- Quickness
- Careful recognition of boundaries
- Mental toughness
- Imaginative
- Challenging
- Being well grounded

- Innovative
- Discernment
- Able to design interventions that break patterns of interaction
- Able to adapt therapy to the unique circumstances in which clients live, work, etc.
- Personal charisma
- Uninhibited
- Ability to be artistic in one way or another
- Has a strong understanding of family systems theories and paradoxical strategies/solid grasp of the field
- Patience with people and so-called human condition
- Maturity based on professional and personal experience (living)
- Ability to soothe my anxiety and hold on to myself as an individual and as a professional
- Being able to read clients during sessions
- Having a tolerance for not knowing
- Ability to be fully present in the moment with oneself and others
- Enjoyment of people and the therapeutic process
- Goal oriented
- Keeps abreast of the cutting edge
- Unconventionality
- Being able to read between the lines
- Atheoretical
- Acting on what you see in the moment
- Perceptive
- Compassion
- Possibility thinker
- Able to make connections between things that may not seem to have any relationship
- Can be irreverent by reconsidering even sacred ideas by courageously holding them up for reexamination, thus preventing stuck thinking
- Freedom to use artistic and drama talents of clients to enhance therapy sessions, without fear
- Wisdom
- Improvisation
- Warm, caring, and joyous
- Playfulness
- Ability to open wider ranges of thinking and behavior in clients

- Willingness to accept client resistance to creativity interventions
- Having good common sense
- Persistence
- Putting the clients' goals over therapeutic control issues
- Unconditional positive regard
- Takes what we do seriously, but not ourselves seriously
- Able to change/willingness to be different
- Abstract thinking
- Emotionally stable and secure
- Good interpretive skills
- Strong sense of spirituality, both in oneself and others
- Enthusiasm
- The ability to bring together diverse elements (ideas) to generate new thinking and acting patterns
- Compassion
- Optimism
- Good sense of boundaries
- Engaging manner/excitement and drive to learn
- A willingness to engage ("do battle" with) couples and families
- Ability to see possibilities for change and the bigger picture
- Guts
- A benign sense of mischief
- Able to make mistakes
- One who demonstrates creativity in his or her personal life
- A foundation of concrete knowledge to build upon
- Really being "with" a client
- Love of learning from the situation
- Less rules oriented
- Passion for the work/job
- Unconstrained
- Wide and varied personal and professional experiences
- Having a passion for developing new possibilities and enhancing what is
- Ability to explain to co-workers and couple/family what you are doing
- Not being afraid to occasionally look foolish or silly
- Using techniques other than talking to achieve objectives
- Childlike in learning and discovery

- Personal integrity
- A curiosity about life in general
- Learning to be a calm presence
- Exhibits awareness of both emotional and rational images
- Regularly engaged in peer consultation and team work
- Able to let go when necessary

Upon close inspection, the top three most frequently reported characteristics of a creative family therapist were flexibility, risk taking/willingness to take risks, and humor/sense of humor. Others commonly indicated were intuition, openness, thinking outside the box, spontaneity, self-confidence, courage, energy/energetic, and having faith/a sense of spirituality. Indeed, therapists cannot be expected to possess all of the characteristics listed in this chapter, and perhaps not even many of them. We have argued that although creativity is definitely personality related, it is not a personality trait per se. However, since effective therapy of any kind is partially, if not largely, a function of the "person of the therapist," the characteristics outlined can be a useful guide for those hoping to become more innovative and creative in their therapeutic endeavors. Although these lists have many characteristics in common, they also include a number of unique descriptors, suggesting that the creative qualities of family therapists are both similar to and yet different from those of creative individuals in general.

In sum, we believe that creative therapy is strongly associated with personal qualities of the counselor, which often go hand in hand with counselor experience and expertise. As Heppner, Fitzgerald, and Jones (1989, p. 278) aptly point out:

> It is our hunch that more experienced, highly skilled, and creative therapists have well-differentiated road maps of the counseling process for different types of clients, and that they can process information more quickly, accurately, and in nonlinear ways. Their successful experiences may in turn bolster their therapeutic confidence, which in turn allows them greater tolerance for risk taking and ambiguity. Most likely, these counselors can also discriminate between relevant and less relevant information and, subsequently, may have more time to concentrate on finding the missing piece or to combine information in unique and helpful ways.

ENHANCING CREATIVITY IN INDIVIDUALS, COUPLES, AND FAMILIES AS PART OF THE THERAPEUTIC PROCESS

As has been argued, individual, couple, and family difficulties are often associated with deficits in creative thinking, problem solving, and/or relating (Carson, 1999b). Indeed, for many clinicians creativity is both a process and a goal of counseling or psychotherapy (Carson, 1999a). Creative interventions frequently play a unique and powerful role in helping clients get "unstuck" (i.e., the problem-solving piece). However, since therapists often want clients to move beyond mere symptom relief or conflict resolution into the arena of personal and relationship growth, creative interventions also involve an educational and preventive (buffering) component. One of the best ways to assist clients in overcoming destructive conflicts and developing new patterns is to help them discover, experience, and practice alternate (and sometimes opposite) modes of thinking, behaving, and interacting. The enhancement of creativity is definitely one of the by-products, if not central goals, of therapy. The therapeutic process is often facilitated when therapist and clients become more aware of and practice behaviors and ways of thinking that augment creativity.

Some ways that creativity can be enhanced both in and out of session are briefly examined as follows. Although we agree with Nickerson (1999) that "there is no easy, step-wise method that is guaranteed to enhance creativity to a non-trivial degree" (p. 420), the creativity literature is replete with ideas for facilitating creativity in children and adults, all of which may influence both individual and family resiliency. We provide here only a sample of suggested mental activities and behaviors.

Recently, Thomas (2000) has asked why therapists should attempt to nurture creativity in therapy. He lists three major reasons, including (a) because the processes of therapy and creativity are similar and often parallel one another in terms of flow, problem solving, and change; (b) because creativity is a part of personal growth, and the development of unique skills, abilities, and talents, that involves new discoveries about oneself and others (e.g., family members); and (c) because creativity often involves enjoyment and fun, which, in cooperation with others, can enhance interpersonal relationships. According to Thomas, creativity in therapy has four components. First, creativity, in part, can be seen as a trait of the therapist. Second, creativity is a cognitive ability that involves divergent thinking and problem solving. Third, creativity is a process that includes or results in different feelings and experiences in the lives of clients and therapist. Fourth, creativity always involves some degree of innovation and an original product, which might be family members communicating better or showing more compassion and forgiveness toward one another. Central to Thomas's way of thinking is that creativity in therapy is (after Csikszentmihalyi, 1996) a flow experience. A flow experience has the following characteristics: immediate feedback to one's actions; balance between challenge and skill; a merging of actions and awareness; an unawareness of distractions; no fear of failure; disappearance of self-consciousness; a distortion of time and place; and the realization that the therapeutic activity is an end in itself. In workshops geared toward helping therapists be more creative with families, and also enhance their own creativity, Thomas (2000) involves participants in a variety of experiences that include family storytelling, group drawing exercises, and family puppet interviews.

Csikszentmihalyi (1996) suggests that the first step toward a more creative life is to cultivate our curiosity and interests and to find our sense of flow, the enjoyment we experience when we are engaged in mental and physical challenges that completely absorb us. Based on his interviews with some of the world's most creative adults, he recommends the following:

1. Try to be surprised by something every day.
2. Try to surprise at least one person every day (i.e., by being unpredictable.)
3. Write down each day what surprised you and how you surprised others.
4. Wake up each day with a specific goal, task, or experience to look forward to (in your work, leisure time, or family life).
5. Determine what time of day and under what circumstances you are most creative and take charge of your schedule, and
6. Learn to solve problems creatively by, for example, experimenting with a number of alternative solutions or engaging in continuous experimentation and revision.

Stein (1988) lists three major techniques to stimulate creative thinking, including stimulators such as brainstorming, redefiners, and distancers. There are two major principles (deferment of judgment and quantity breeding quality) and four rules to be followed when an individual or group is brainstorming. These rules are that criticism is outlawed, that freewheeling is welcomed, that quantity is desired, and that combination and improvement are sought. Redefining a problem as a challenge, a puzzle, or an opportunity also helps prepare the mind for creative solutioning. Further, deliberately distancing oneself from a problem or situation can help one gain perspective and enhance the probability that creative problem solving will occur or that a creative solution will evolve. Metaphors and analogies can also play a central role in the creative process.

Benjamin (1984) and others (e.g., Baer, 1993; Barron, 1988) have discussed various ways to enhance creativity and divergent thinking in adults that have implications for therapists. These include, for example, providing opportunities for futuration (examining a situation from a futuristic point of view); imagery and visioning; suspending judgment, recognizing and exercising multiple options and choices; and learning to integrate thought and emotion (i.e., balancing intellectual and emotional intelligence). According to Benjamin, mastering these processes can help people produce more creative outcomes in decision making, as well as use creative thinking in planning, goal setting, and problem solving.

In conclusion, the most effective interventions sometimes include those aspects of creativity that clients have overlooked or failed to develop and integrate into their lives. Creative therapists (and therapy) can mobilize clients to discover or release their creative passions and abilities, both individually and relationally.

BREAKING OUT OF THE BOX:
FINDING MY FLOW

As stated earlier in this chapter, the first step toward a more creative life is to cultivate our curiosity. Let's take some of Csikszentmihalyi's advice. By completing and following through with the following tasks, you are making a personal commitment to finding your flow. Complete the first four questions (1 through 4) before going to sleep this evening. At the end of the day tomorrow complete the last three questions (5 through 7).

1. As I awaken tomorrow morning I will be looking forward to . . .
2. The one person that I will surprise tomorrow is . . .
3. I will surprise this person by . . .
4. I will be open to being surprised throughout the day tomorrow by doing the following . . .
5. What surprised me today was . . .
6. I surprised others today by . . .
7. Tomorrow I am going to . . .

Chapter 6

Creative Interventions in Couple and Family Therapy: Therapists' Descriptions

CREATIVE INCUBATION EXERCISE #6: CREATING OPTIONS

Ruth and Jesse were referred to you due to difficulties in their marriage. Their youngest child died in an auto accident last summer. Since this tragedy they have drifted apart and seem to connect only when in conflict. You have been working with them for a number of weeks and realize that you are at an impasse. They seem to be too frightened and hurt to reach out, forgive, and connect. Before reading the chapter, brainstorm a list of ten possible interventions utilizing the following criteria:

- At least three of the interventions must be predominately verbal
- At least three of the interventions must be predominately nonverbal or experiential
- At least three of the interventions must be your own unique ideas

THERAPISTS' DESCRIPTIONS OF CREATIVE INTERVENTIONS IN COUPLE AND FAMILY THERAPY

Therapists in our study identified as creative a number of well-known interventions with couples and families. Most commonly mentioned were the following:

1. Role-play, role reversal, and psychodrama
2. Various types and uses of sculpting and genograms

3. Family drawings and art therapy (e.g., drawing the problem or possible solutions)
4. Construction of murals and collages; stories, parables, and fairy tales that provide helpful illustrations for clients
5. Metaphors and analogies
6. Guided imagery
7. Hypnosis (e.g., after Milton Erickson)
8. Letter writing and other forms of narrative therapy
9. Gestalt interventions, such as various uses of empty chair and mirrors

Some specific examples of interventions listed by respondents we thought were lesser known and utilized by therapists in general (not in any order of importance) are included here.

Examples of Creative Interventions Listed By Study Participants

- Asking a couple or family if they would be willing to make a 5 percent change in their relationship and discussing what this might entail
- Having clients occasionally sit back to back to speak to each other (to simulate physical distance) as though they were on the phone or in a chat room
- Letting clients sometimes take the role (and chair) of the therapist, including children
- Asking the children to come up with a solution for their parents or family, and then as a family act out the solution together
- Having couples and family members (collectively) use poems, films, songs, or book titles to tell their story, express feelings, illustrate conflicts, or depict the ideal
- Having family members draw the problem or possible solutions, individually or corporately such as through family murals
- Having family members engage in a "pick your passions show-and-tell" so that they can better understand one another's interests and skills, and then discussing how to transfer these strengths and positives to other areas of their lives
- Having couples and families create a video of a happier marriage/family in their future
- Using miming to elicit ideas about mending and forgiveness

- Having couples and families design their own treatment plan as if their situation or problems were occurring with friends (e.g., "What would you suggest they do?" "What might make a real difference?")
- Having couples write a relationship vision together
- Developing a family escape plan from the issue or problem attacking the family
- When couples or families are stuck, asking to have a session in their home, if you can do a home visit
- Explaining the meaning of, then interviewing, each person's "internalized other"
- Reframing cognitive beliefs in spiritual terms or language
- Using conga drums to assess and teach couples communication: when to speak, when to listen, how to harmonize, and how to support each other
- Having couples/families videotape arguments or troubling behavior at home (or videotape them in therapy), then talk about them and have them rewrite what they would do differently if they could
- Using puppet or doll play to get children involved and explore relational patterns and dynamics
- Engaging in "benevolent sabotage," suggesting that symptoms can be used to benefit the client(s)
- Using clay symbols made by members of the family
- Having clients act as researchers to get multiple ideas when they are having difficulty coming up with what is workable
- Outdoor therapy—seeing families outdoors, such as in the wilderness or on the beach, etc.
- Walking therapy (taking walks with clients)
- Using animals (imagined by family members) to verbalize interests, wishes, desires, and show weaknesses and strengths
- Redefining family membership by including significant, non-related people in treatment (neighbors, teen friends, etc.)
- Using atonement rituals when needed by individuals and couples/families
- Creating a penny-pitching game in which children or adolescents and I pitch pennies to determine who gets to ask questions
- Physical illustration (e.g., having clients get up on the chair to achieve a higher point of view)

- Using laughter to teach clients to learn to laugh at themselves and situations
- Getting quieter rather than louder when speaking to clients who are arguing
- Taking positions of wondering with clients
- Videotaping couples or family members working on a project together in therapy, then having them watch and learn about interactional patterns/dynamics
- Asking couples/families, If your lives were a movie, how would it turn out and why?
- Playing calming music for a child to listen to in a separate room when parents have strong conflict
- Using a spinner to take turns to talk with a family with young children; children see it as a game and participate more
- Having couples identify and capture their passions for life
- Creating an "experiential template" with couples that shows how not having an experience of being loved means a person may not experience feeling loved even when the other person does love them
- Using word association pictures with partners to help them communicate feelings and needs to each other
- Using physical space to represent memories that are difficult to recall and to aid in recall
- Using magic wish bottles (bottles filled with colored water and glitter or confetti)—each family member makes a wish for something he or she would like to have different (wishes are not necessarily shared out loud, but can be)
- Using a gratitude journal when a client is angry, resentful, or resistant
- Having couples rate their relationship by giving them a graph and asking them to assign a numerical value to their relationship each day; then having them write a note beside each number that briefly explains why they gave that rating so that their record can be discussed next session
- Videotaping or audiotaping a fifteen-minute segment of the couple's dialogue and have them watch and/or listen to themselves so they can learn to talk about what they want rather than always about their problems

- Using some cliché statements intended to shock clients, such as "the divorce begins in the courtship"
- Walking out of the room when it is necessary
- Appropriate and timely use of playful bantering
- Using the "talking stick" with couples and families
- Using costumes for "dress up" in working with families, especially those with younger children
- Having stuffed animals and animal puppets around the room for family play therapy when younger children are present
- Using animal metaphors (e.g., "the frog that eats what's bugging you")
- Phone calls to the family (or certain members) from the president, a rock or rap star, etc.
- Having clients write or draw something prescribed or creating with their nondominant hand, then talk about it
- Playing a "letting the secrets out" game or grab bag with family members who are concealing things

A couple of others that caught our attention in the respondents' answers included the assignment of preparing and eating an artichoke in therapy to get to the "heart" of the problem and, one of our favorites, teaching couples the "cranky song"—a silly song either party is authorized to sing or hum from a safe distance to alert the other of possible crankiness. Indeed, many people could sing that one in operatic fashion to their mates after they have had a rough day!

Although use of music and games in couples and family therapy was mentioned by several respondents, none of them went into much detail. Today there is a host of games for use in family therapy (many we would label as highly creative) intended to help family members practice and learn how to solve problems, communicate more effectively, express feelings, talk about sensitive issues (e.g., sexuality), and deal with traumatic issues or events such as death, divorce, domestic violence, substance abuse, and serious illness or accidents (e.g., see the *Creative Therapy Store Catalog* published by Western Psychological Services, 2001). For example, games such as Family Happenings and Exploring My World help family members clarify feelings and perceptions and increase understanding by allowing them to tell stories, express wishes and fantasies, answer specific questions, and respond to sentence completion cards. Although these games are not appropriate for all families and should never dominate the therapy session or process, they can be extremely useful tools in family work.

Finally, listening to music (both in therapy and as assigned at home) can ease tension, induce specific emotional states and alter mood, and elicit memories of both painful and pleasurable life events. Music has long been considered the language of emotion, and songs are often powerful metaphors for client's experiences. Music can be used in a multitude of creative ways in treating couples and families. Therapists working with troubled or difficult adolescents in family therapy can use music to help them relax or to provide avenues of expression through their music. Disturbed couples in therapy can listen to music cherished by them earlier in the relationship or popular songs with penetrating love themes that can soothe and teach them in the present. Couples can also share with each other verbal and emotional responses to the lyrics, rhythm, or melody of a favorite song. Moreover, one person may select a song or piece of music that communicates something special to his or her partner. Couples or family members can also be encouraged to draw, move in sync, or close eyes and imagine in response to a particular piece of music. Finally, parents can learn how to guide and discipline their children in kinder and gentler ways through listening to and discussing the message of both adult and children's music. Music has also been used effectively to calm a hyperactive child or an agitated adolescent. In sum, melody and lyrics can touch the soul in a way that is often an inexplicable catalyst for change and renewal in intimate relationships.

Other Creative Interventions with Couples and Families

Veteran clinicians know that creative therapy involves experiencing as much as talking, even though technically one might define talking as a type of experience. However, by experiencing we are referring to "being" and "doing" more than dialoguing. Having corrective, therapeutic experiences is especially important in working with couples and families. In couple and family therapy, experiential interventions tend to augment partners' and family members' understanding of one another and provide a conduit for constructive expression of emotions. These approaches increase the likelihood of hooking people into the therapy process because many of them have grown tired of "hashing over their problems until they're blue in the face" and are now doing it again, only this time with a therapist. In addition, frequent directing of their interactions to one another more than to the therapist facilitates a sharing of emotions and perspectives in a safe environment, be they ever so threatening or painful. In short, experiential therapy can help couples and families be released from painful emotional gridlocks/entanglements and free their creative thinking and energy. It is our intention to briefly outline some techniques and interventions (including some emotion focused) that readers may find useful in their work as therapists, including ways to build on the inherent strengths of couples and families. These interventions often help make the "unsaid" said, understood, and felt.

It is our conviction that assessment and therapy generally go hand in hand, particularly in the early stages of the therapeutic process. Along with gaining essential information about couples and families (presenting problem, history of their relationship, pertinent family-of-origin material, etc.), we often employ some common interventions. These are ones that can easily be integrated with traditional talk therapy methods, and include the following:

Enactments, Pretending, and Role-Plays

Enactments can be immensely beneficial not only during the assessment phase of therapy (e.g., "Act out a frequently occurring problem in your relationship." "Discuss/act out a certain issue or difficulty that has come up recently at home.") but also throughout the treatment process (e.g., "Pretend there is a 'better way' to handle that problem when it comes up." "Show what you both could have done or wish you would have done differently when that issue/difficulty came up last week."). One method we have found occasionally effective is to have couples act out a beloved scene from a movie or book they have both seen or read. One married couple, whom two of our supervisees worked with recently as cotherapists, enacted a scene from *Romeo and Juliet* that, surprisingly, helped get them unstuck and moving in a new direction in their relationship.

Often it is also useful to have couples/family members switch roles so that each person sees and feels things from the other person's vantage point (role reversal). Therapists too can role-play with couples/families as one member of the relationship (or "double" for one partner during the couple role-play) in order to instruct or enlighten.

When doubling, the therapist sits or stands beside one person and either speaks for that individual to someone else or provides that individual with lead-in words or phrases to help that person express a thought or feeling. Role-plays and enactments can enhance the therapist's understanding of the dynamics of people's relationships and their conflicts, help clients see things more objectively, and provide opportunities for emotional catharsis and clarification. Role reversals have been shown to be very effective in enhancing perspective taking and empathy with one's partner, parent, or child. Family members (including children) can also be instructed to take the role of the therapist while the therapist becomes a member of the couple or family, or temporarily sits out altogether. Variations of the Gestalt empty chair can also be used as couples, for example, are told to counsel friends who are having the same problem(s) that they have.

Sculpting

Along with the traditional uses of sculpting (i.e., having each person portray their relationship in the here and now and then freeze, reflect, and share feelings and impressions), it is often helpful to have each partner/family member sculpt the ideal relationship, couple, or family. This ideal sculpture is often surprising to participants and often helps them understand what others really want or need. The therapist can also have the couple show (step by step) how they might get from the "real" to the "ideal" sculpture. Afterward the therapist can process these steps with the couple in terms of feelings, needs, wishes, choices, and desired changes in their relationship. This procedure provides a powerful visualization of possible steps or goals that can be incorporated into the treatment process. Other variations can include the therapist sculpting the couple's/family's current relationship(s), having couples sculpt their relationship as it was early in their marriage or during courtship, or, when children are present, having them sculpt their parents' relationship.

Creative Drawings, Artwork, Storytelling, and Reading Aloud

Much has been written about the ways in which these interventions can increase mutual understanding and cooperation, teach, provide insight, and help keep therapy from becoming excessively problem focused. For example, couples and families can be instructed to draw, paint, or construct something (e.g., collage) in session that illustrates their struggles or some potential solutions to them. Moreover, since couples and family members often do not fully understand or appreciate how they sound or come across to their partner until they witness it (in one sense, "experience" it), audio or video feedback can enhance individual awareness and challenge all parties to begin doing some things differently. Storytelling and story completion, just as in child therapy, can be useful interventions with couples and families. These stories can be created/instigated by the therapist or family members. Finally, we have found that having couples (and sometimes family members) read aloud can provide deeper insights and powerful emotional experiences and breakthroughs. These can be published or personal short stories, poems, song lyrics, or letters (as in narrative therapy) written to or about one's partner or family member.

Couple and Family Collage

Having couples work on their own collage, either individually or together, can be a creative and meaningful experience for them as well as enlightening for the therapist. As a corporate project, the therapist can gain a window into many of the couple's relationship dynamics, including power, decision making, patterns of communication, gender issues, and so forth. (Note: The same can be said for the use of collage with families.) When they are asked to create individual collages, both therapist and clients can gain a great deal of insight into the family and cultural backgrounds of each partner. Common materials used for making this type of collage include four large sheets of white paper, a number of magazines and newspapers, scissors, and paste or glue. The following instructions can be given to the couple as an example of a family-culture-gender collage.

> I would like you to look through these magazines and newspapers for pictures, quotes, and other artifacts that can be cut out and glued to your own sheet of paper. The material you attach should represent, as best you can, your life and character, in other words, what it is that makes you unique and what is important to you. Be sure to think about how your family of origin (the family you grew up in) has influenced you, including your basic values, beliefs, and principles. Further, I would like you to locate material that you think best represents how your gender,

ethnicity, culture, and socioeconomic status have impacted your life to date. Perhaps these things are still significant to you. When you have completed the first collage, on another sheet of paper I would like you to create a key for your collage. The key should then be used to tell each other briefly what it is about each of the things on your collage that makes it important to you now.

Cooperative family collages can also be used in the assessment and treatment phases of therapy. Family members' conflicts, defenses, and styles of interacting are revealed as they work together on the collage. One format for this type of collage is to simply ask each person to select pictures of people who are communicating/interacting and then glue them on the paper in relation to the pictures picked out by other family members (Linesch, 1999). Clients can also put words or captions underneath pictures and images that give a voice to what it is they are feeling, thinking, or communicating about oneself or to one's partner or family. As Linesch (1999) reminds us, one advantage of collage over family art therapy is that "the experience of making a collage is not bounded by the apprehension and intimidation many individuals feel about the art process itself" (pp. 230-231).

In short, these collages can serve as both process and product. The therapist can interact with the couple throughout the creation of their collages, asking for clarification, extensions, and interpretations, as well as use them as a springboard for discussion after they are completed.

Use of Commercial Films

The majority of couples and families today enjoy movies. Commercial films can and do have a powerful influence on people. The therapeutic use of films with couples and families can be employed in a variety of creative ways for teaching, modeling, and discussion purposes. Couples and families can also be assigned movies to watch as homework. Movies can be chosen by clients or the therapist in which one or more family members identifies (or might identify) strongly with a particular character or relationship. The exploration of these roles and dynamics can sometimes facilitate awareness and empathy in their own relationships. These films can either illustrate healthy couple/family relationships (e.g., *The Story of Us* [1999], *Sweet As You Are* [1997]) or ones that portray difficult, painful, or destructive relationship dynamics (e.g., *Ordinary People* [1980], *The War of the Roses* [1989], *Men Don't Leave* [1990]). Movies of a lighter, more humorous tone can also be selected (e.g., *Singles* [1992], *As Good As It Gets* [1997], *Runaway Bride* [1999]), which are less threatening but can open up a whole new arena of conversation.

Movement, Expressive, and Other Nonverbal Interventions

Nonverbal behavior, the nonverbal messages that people convey, constitutes a significant proportion of human communication (some would argue 60 to 80 percent). As Thompson notes,

> Many researchers maintain that another person's actual words contribute only 7% to the impression of being liked or disliked, while voice cues contribute 38% and facial cues contribute 55%. Nonverbal messages are usually more believable than verbal messages. When verbal and nonverbal messages contradict, most adults in the United States believe the nonverbal message. (1996, p. 81)

Hence, that old saying many of us learned while growing up that, "it's not so much what you say but how you say it," rings especially true in intimate relationships. Moreover, many couples and families seem to get confused by or stuck in their pain and difficulties far beyond the verbal level. When creatively and effectively used, nonverbal interventions, including movement and other expressive techniques, can be a powerful force in helping couples and families resolve differences and experience new depths of understanding.

These nonverbal interventions, according to Duhl, take on the form of "action metaphors." She poignantly makes this connection as follows:

> Interaction between people includes not only words but also gestures, voice tones, body movements, pace, energy exchanges, and all the private meanings given these behaviors by each member involved. Action methods and metaphors, unlike words alone, can capture all of these behaviors with impressive effect. Perhaps most important, however, is that action metaphors grasp "wholes," whereas language is analytic and linear. Action metaphors allow an individual to externalize entire images of

what is held in his or her mind in a form that the therapist or trainer can render safe and useful. . . . Lastly, action metaphors circumvent intellectual defenses that are activated through verbal representation. Language is often used to shield what is thought, felt, sensed, or known. (1999, p. 80)

As Duhl (1999) notes, language is "about," but experience "is." One of her many contributions has included various creative uses of sculpturing (e.g., the use of ropes in diagramming family boundaries). Some nonverbal techniques offered by Thompson (1996) for use in group therapy illustrate the kinds of nonverbal interventions that could be adapted for use in working with couples and family therapy. One technique is called "talking with your hands," an intervention intended to help clients identify and communicate feelings. Here, partners or family members are told to move a comfortable distance from one another and then communicate with their hands feelings of love, grief, joy, fear, anger, frustration, sadness, confusion, etc. In another technique, "eyes as windows to the soul," couples or family members are asked to sit facing someone else and look directly into that person's eyes for a certain period of time (e.g., one to five minutes). They are instructed to tell that person something important with their eyes and to also "pay close attention to what the other person is saying to you." Another creative technique involves blind "touch-talk." Here, two people are asked to close their eyes. One person then explores their partner or family member by touching his or her face, shoulders, hair, and hands. That individual performing the touching is told to communicate a message about what or how he or she feels about the partner/parent/child. The situation is then reversed, followed by a processing of the experience. Finally, pantomimes can be used to help partners or family members express feelings toward self and others that may not ordinarily be shown or verbalized. Without mocking or disrespecting one's partner or family member, each person is asked, one at a time, to stand and pantomime their impression of that person, showing that person's feelings with gestures and facial expressions. Then, that same person pantomimes how he or she feels a partner or family member feels about him or her. After everyone has a turn, these nonverbal behaviors are carefully examined.

Another popular nonverbal technique used with families/couples, an outgrowth of the family sculpture, is "family choreography"

(Papp, 1976). Although procedures can vary, family members are asked to demonstrate nonverbally a physical and visual picture of the manner in which they view their current family/couple functioning or relationships. Unlike sculpturing, which tends to be static, in family choreography clients are instructed to show, through movement, positioning, and nonverbal communicative behaviors (e.g., gestures, facial expressions), how they see and feel about their marriage/family and how they would like their relationships or the situation to be (see also Sherman and Fredman, 1986, for a detailed description). During or after the process the therapist can ask each person to share, in short verbal statements, how it feels to be in that place in the family, how he or she feels about others, what that person needs from certain people or what they would like others to understand or do differently, and so forth. A variation of choreography is to instruct family members or couples "to enact and repeat, through movement and positioning, the dysfunctional sequences of their interactions, trying harder each time to get what they want" (Sherman and Fredman, 1986, p. 80). As these authors note, if and when these repeated attempts to get one's way or make things better prove futile, the therapist can help partners or family members explore alternative solutions through further movement and positioning.

Free Association Games

Authentic responses from clients are sometimes generated when they free-associate rather than have time to screen their thoughts and feelings or allow their defenses to do so. Creative games that provide these opportunities can be exceedingly helpful to family members. The Talk About game described by Deacon (1998) is an excellent example of such an intervention. It can be used as an assessment as well as a therapeutic technique. This game is summarized by Deacon and Piercy (2001, p. 367) as follows:

> In this game, clients throw a ball or "hot potato" to one another and give the recipient a subject to talk about. The recipient of the ball must say five things in 10 seconds that relate to the subject they were given. Then the recipient throws the ball to someone else and gives that person a subject to talk about and so on. For example, the therapist might throw the ball to a parent, saying "Talk to your son." The parent says five things quickly related to

his or her son. . . . The parent then chooses someone to throw the ball to and gives that person a topic, "Talk about school."

In sum, therapists have a seemingly endless array of creative non-verbal methods and techniques at their disposal, including (and especially) those immediate and preplanned interventions that germinate from their imagination, therapeutic prowess, and human experience. However, as with any experiential interventions, these nonverbal methods must be used sensitively and appropriately given the couple/family and their presenting difficulties. They may not be the interventions of choice for certain couples or families in high-risk situations. Some contraindications for their use, as well as play therapy and other experientially oriented interventions, are summarized in the next section.

Other Creative Interventions

Some other interventions we have found particularly helpful have included the use of instructional videos (e.g., John Gray's Mars and Venus tapes; videos on some aspect of parenting child development or guidance). It is generally not difficult to instruct couples and families to watch these at home as homework assignments, followed by in-session discussion next week. Occasionally portions of videos can also be viewed as part of therapy. Individuals can also be asked to bring films (or book titles, etc.) to therapy next time that tell their story, express how they feel, illustrate conflicts in their marriage or family, or communicate hopes for the future.

Although careful not to minimize the seriousness of the difficulties or depth of their pain in couples and family relationships, it is almost always our intent in therapy to help them recall or discover existing areas of resiliency—presuming of course that the individuals involved are truly wanting to improve their relationship and not seeking something else, such as divorce counseling or an avenue or vehicle to leave the relationship or family. In the early stages of therapy with couples, this can be accomplished through the use of early recollections (e.g., first date or birth of child memories). For instance, couples can be asked the following questions: "What first attracted you to him/her?" "How did you come to fall in love?" "What are your fondest memories of your spouse and times spent with her or him?" "Would you bring some of your favorite photos of each other next session and share them with me?" In-session couple fantasies can also be very effective (e.g., "Betty, close your eyes while Sam shares with you some of his fantasies about you and his relationship with you").

The therapist can also help couples and family members concentrate on positives and not just problems (e.g., "Tell your partner/parent/child three things you really like or appreciate about him/her"), and helping these individuals remember or discover areas of strength in each other and their relationship (e.g., "I have always enjoyed her sense of humor"; "He has always been a good provider"; "We have always enjoyed the outdoors together") as well as exceptions to the problem(s) (i.e., times when they have been successful in communicating or problem solving). Rekindling feelings and memories and remembering or discovering strengths can empower couples and families with a new sense of optimism. For example, at some point in therapy (typically not in the initial sessions), having clients read or write a poem or letter to or about their partner or family member, or compose a song, can help revive loving feelings and convey caring thoughts. Gift-giving rituals and the use of objects as metaphors (e.g., sharing of items which symbolize meanings, values, feelings, losses, hopes and dreams, or highlight special memories) can also help revive loving feelings in intimate relationships. Couples and family members can be instructed to simply "bring something to therapy next week that says something about how you feel about your partner/child/parent, or tells a story about a shared experience you have had with your mate or family." Gratitude lists can accomplish similar purposes in couple and family relationships. Ideal couple and family fantasies can be effective in giving clients a means for expressing hope for change or desire for renewed passion or closeness (e.g., "One at a time and while your partner/family listens and does not interrupt, I want you to close your eyes and fantasize, aloud, how you would like your everyday life to be with each other; such as on evenings after work, weekends, holidays, and so forth"). Sentence completion exercises, either given as homework or completed in therapy, are sometimes extremely useful in helping therapists gain a greater understanding into the dynamics of couple and family relationships, as well as helping family members more fully understand one another's feelings and perspectives.

Finally, variations of therapeutic massage or touch such as biores-onance can be extremely useful in helping couples reconnect. One form of bioresonance is to have each person touch his or her partner, for thirty seconds to a minute, on certain areas of their body, includ-ing hands, feet, abdomen, chest, neck, and forehead while the partner is relaxed with eyes closed, then have each reflect, with particular at-tention to their emotions. Touch needs to be used in a careful and timely way with couples and families. However, when used appropri-ately, few interventions are more powerful in facilitating the release of positive emotions, enhancing pair-bonding, and increasing people's understanding of one another at a deeper and more meaningful level.

In sum, experiential interventions can be integral to couples and family therapy, in that experience is often a precursor to awareness and emotional healing in intimate relationships. Building on existing strengths and extrapolating from prior "successes" can also help cli-ents develop a renewed hope for change.

CREATIVE CLOSING RITUALS AND TERMINATIONS IN COUPLE AND FAMILY THERAPY

Rituals in couples and family work can serve as important markers into and exits out of a system, clarify boundaries within and around a system, and redefine the membership of a system (Imber-Black, 1989). Rituals can be useful in helping couples and families adopt new roles and release themselves from the familiar yet rigid patterns of interaction to which they cling so tenaciously (Frankel, 1993). They are particularly important and appropriate at the end of each therapy session and at the termination of therapy.

Closing and termination rituals serve several important functions. First, they allow clients to honor one another as individuals, partners, and family units by providing an opportunity for each person to ac-knowledge his or her own hard work and that of others in therapy. Second, rituals can be celebrations of the changes and accomplish-ments people have made as a couple or family. Third, rituals can serve as powerfully symbolic rites of passage out of therapy for cli-ents and back into the real world once again as independent sojourn-ers, either for a week or permanently. Finally, rituals make it possible for the therapist and clients to say goodbye in a respectful and cere-monial way, and in a way that can help all parties deal with issues of closure and loss, even if they have agreed to keep in touch with one another. Thus, although closing and termination rituals serve a rather serious purpose, they are often concocted and conducted in fun and creative ways. Following are a few examples of such rituals.

Closing Rituals in Couples and Family Therapy

At the beginning of therapy (i.e., the first or second session) it is our belief that the establishment of a ritual at the closing of each session is very important for the reasons previously stated, and for the simple fact that rituals often make it possible for clients to end the difficult and sometimes painful work of therapy on a more positive and uplifting note. Although closing rituals may be more important with families than couples, we have found them useful in counseling a variety of couples as well. Closing rituals are often cocreations between partners/family members and the therapist. However, frequently in family work children are encouraged to suggest or create the closing ritual. Even though the vast majority of families will settle upon one closing ritual they will enact after every session, sometimes families will choose to create a new ritual each time (hence, the "ritual" is the freedom to create new rituals after each session or whenever they want). This freedom can be empowering and may encourage creative thinking and risktaking.

Closing rituals for couples, for some interesting reason, are often characterized by more subdued behaviors and a relatively calm, relaxed emotional tone, although there is nothing absolute or mandatory about this. Our experience has been that couples will frequently use closing rituals to deflate or regroup after a challenging session. These rituals may include sitting in silence with one's eyes closed; stating something positive about one's partner or the relationship (e.g., "One thing I like or appreciate about you is . . ."); holding hands and looking into each other's eyes; hugging for a period of time; planning a date for the week; voicing a dream about the future; reading a favorite poem or listening to a favorite song together; writing a renewal of their vows or a statement about commitment to their relationship or marriage early in therapy that they then read at the end of every session; and so forth.

Family closing rituals, on the other hand, often seem to be much more active and peppered with emotional energy. Group huddles, cheers, hand-holding ceremonies, hugs, and newly created songs or dances are not uncommon, nor is the sharing of positive thoughts and appreciation from each person in the family to everyone else (including the therapist). Whatever closing ritual is decided upon early on, it is important that each family member is in agreement with the ritual and understands its purpose at some basic level. Interestingly, often closing rituals developed in therapy have an uncanny way of being replicated, or at least modified and enacted to some extent, at home.

Termination Rituals in Couple and Family Therapy

It is perhaps not surprising that termination in family therapy has been the least examined phase of treatment (Roberts, 1993). Yet the end of therapy can be an anxious time for couples and families (McCollum, 1993). Worries about relapse are common among clients, and it is important that therapists not overemphasize the positive in such a way that ignores or invalidates clients' concerns over the "what ifs." Indeed, sometimes termination rituals can be used to deal directly or symbolically with clients' worries over regressing, and there is much room for creative thinking and exploration in this process on the part of clients and the therapist.

Termination rituals, which often take place the last session or two of therapy (although they can begin earlier), can help reduce some of this anxiety by giving clients permission to celebrate their efforts and successes and providing an appropriate forum. Termination rituals can include something as simple as clients giving feedback to the therapist about the therapy process (and possibly to one another). Some other common and sometimes creative termination rituals can include the following: sharing food/having a meal (e.g., potluck) together in the therapy room or in clients' homes; gift giving; bringing in something (e.g., an object or picture) that symbolizes what therapy has been like for each person in the marriage or family, or one thing brought in by the couple/family that signifies their feelings for one another, thoughts about or impressions of their experiences in therapy, etc.; the creation of a poem, short story, or letter that each person brings with him or her and shares during the last session; and the co-construction of a termination ritual in the last session that allows the couple or family to characterize their current relationship(s) or express their thoughts and feelings about the progress they have made in therapy. This might be a newly created newspaper heading, title of a song, or the name of a best-selling novel. In short, termination rituals can help clients deal with feelings of loss and emancipation, remind them that it is the clients who made the changes and not the therapist, and perhaps provide them with a compass (mental map) that allows them to navigate with greater confidence and skill the unforeseen currents that lie ahead.

CONTRAINDICATIONS IN USING EXPERIENTIAL AND PLAY-ORIENTED APPROACHES

A variety of therapists (Botkin and Raimondi, 2000; Keith and Whitaker, 1981) have offered helpful lists that serve as guides to when family play therapy may be contraindicated. We have reorganized their suggestions and blended other red flags into five central assessment areas that we utilize to determine the appropriateness of creative and playful experiential methods and techniques. We believe that what couples and families need most at these moments are our respect, empathy, immediacy, and support. Creative interventions delivered during these times may result in the exact opposite of what the therapist may be attempting to create. In fact, a therapist's drive to utilize techniques at these times may be a form of self-protection if the therapist uses the technique to create a distance between himself or herself and the family/couple in an attempt to manage his or her anxiety that has been stirred up by the issues or dynamics at hand.

Power is our first and most critical assessment area. Power imbalances may take extreme (and often dangerous) forms such as family violence, oppression, and abuse (physical, sexual, and emotional). These are dynamics that require direct, open, and concise interventions. Although some of these red flags are communicated in the text of a referral, it is our experience that power imbalances are more often hidden in the fabric of couples and families initial and ongoing presentation. The fibers are held together by fear, threats, and history. At these times our intuition or gut reactions are often our best predictors that a power imbalance is present in the room.

Creative interventions require that a certain level of freedom to choose and openness of expression be present for success. These qualities are often perceived as a direct threat to those who hold the power within such families. In addition, asking family members who are in the subordinate position(s) to take such risks within a family session (or as a homework assignment) may actually result in increased levels of power control and manipulation. In extreme (but unfortunately not uncommon) cases, these techniques may be putting a family member in real danger (most often after the session).

Connectedness is our second assessment area in determining the efficacy of creative interventions with couples and families. Families that can be characterized as extremely rigid or extremely disconnected tend to have greater difficulties with the playfulness and spontaneity that many creative interventions evoke. Although we believe that a degree of anxiety is helpful (and often necessary) in session, families that are extremely rigid or inflexible experience panic when too much of their routine or order is cast to the winds. We agree with Keith and Whitaker's (1981) recommendation that these couples and families be given very modest or small doses of nonlinear and playful interventions.

"Like ships passing in the night" describes family systems marked by extreme disengagement. To be engaged with another person in a playful and hopeful manner, a small degree of connection must exist. With these couples and families there is often a series of serious historical issues, pains, and traumas that need to brought to the table and addressed before they will risk a more playful level of interaction. The distance and level of reactivity they have developed over the years has been built to serve a purpose. To expect that individuals can simply hurdle these protective barriers to engage in our techniques may be both naive and disrespectful.

Assessing sacred life events is our third area. Sacred life events include recent deaths, losses, traumas, illnesses, and tragedies. These are times when a couple or family is frightened, sad, angry, and lonely—times of normal emotional pain. Being present with the feelings and thoughts that exist in the room is a gift that we (as helpers) can offer. Techniques at such times can trivialize the significance of the experience. Allowing the emotions to be in the room *is* the healing element.

We draw from Walsh's integrative family therapy approach (Walsh and McGraw, 1996) as we implement our fourth assessment area. Individual personality dynamics (IPD) refers to individual traits, strengths, limitations, and challenges that assist in either facilitating or blocking healthy change within the system at large. In our experience IPD issues are often alive within the therapy session when we hit a therapeutic impasse. Specific IPD issues that may run counter to implementing creative interventions include current drug/alcohol abuse, the inability to meet basic needs (work, food, shelter, etc.), and the potential for self-harm. Creative interventions do not put food on the table, keep a person from wanting to escape life, or magically separate an addict from his or her substance. These are intrapsychic struggles (with obvious systemic impacts) that require concrete solutions. As basic needs are increasingly and consistently addressed, an individual will be freed up to accept and participate in more creative activities within the therapeutic process.

The therapist's level of personal anxiety in implementing creative approaches is our fifth and final assessment area. To be effective with these interventions, a therapist must be comfortable with his or her playful and spontaneous side. This requires letting go of at least some of the structure and order of a session as well as an appropriate and ethical letting go of professional inhibitions. This is difficult for many of us, especially in the earlier stages of our professional development. On good days family therapy can feel like riding a wild horse that has not been broken. The idea of introducing more unknowns (a by-product of creative interventions) may seem like adding fuel to an already out-of-control fire. If you fit this area, we encourage you to give yourself permission to move slowly as you try a wider variety of creative methods in your work with couples and families. Small steps work well for all of us, not just our clients. Finally, remember that your personality is a critical element in the use and success of any approach or technique (Keith and Whitaker, 1981).

BREAKING OUT OF THE BOX: A SESSION OF POSSIBILITIES

This chapter started with a list of ten creative interventions identified by you and was followed by a wide range of ideas from many different therapists. As you proceed with the following activity, utilize the ideas shared in this and previous chapters, your own unique ideas (such as your working metaphor created in Chapter 2) and your limitless imagination. As always, have fun!

Step 1: Design a blended family case study of a family that in-cludes a recently married couple and three children. In your first paragraph introduce the family members and why they are seeking counseling. In your second paragraph de-scribe the impasse that has arisen in counseling.

Step 2: Now allow the session to unfold as you implement a vari-ety of creative interventions. You are going to rewrite the session three times utilizing different paths based on the following criteria.

Path A: Low risk. As the therapist with this family, de-scribe how the session would proceed as you utilize inter-ventions with which you are relatively comfortable. These could include interventions or ideas that you have used in the past or have watched another therapist implement. This is labeled as a low-risk path because you are choosing op-tions that generate a low level of anxiety in yourself as a therapist.

Path B: Moderate risk. Now describe how the session would proceed as you utilize interventions with which you are relatively uncomfortable. These include interventions or ideas that are new to you. You can somewhat see your-self using these interventions with your personal style or approach. This is labeled as a moderate-risk path because you are choosing options that generate a moderate level of anxiety in yourself as a therapist.

Path C: High risk. Finally, describe how the session would proceed as you utilize interventions with which you are very uncomfortable. You *cannot* see yourself using these interventions with your personal style or approach. This is labeled as a high-risk path because you are choosing op-tions that generate a high level of anxiety in yourself as a therapist.

Step 3: Share your three paths with a friend or colleague. What did you learn about yourself? How (as a therapist) will you modulate or decrease your anxiety?

Chapter 7

Barriers and Constraints to Creativity in Family Therapy

CREATIVE INCUBATION EXERCISE #7:
BARRIERS AND BEYOND

As you may recall, you constructed your own personal box in Chapter 1. You may have even modified your box since that time. It is now time to revisit your box. This chapter highlights a number of barriers that therapists identified as interfering with their creative flow.

Although some of our barriers are out of our control, many of our barriers are self-created or (at least) self-maintained. Reflect upon the barriers that you expressed in the creation of your box, as well as those you provided in response to the question about barriers in the survey at the beginning of Chapter 4. Make a list of the barriers you experience over which you have at least a small degree of control. What are some creative ideas of how you could minimize the impact these barriers have upon your creativity as a therapist?

SOCIAL-PSYCHOLOGICAL INHIBITORS
OF CREATIVITY

Some of the same blocks to creativity are those which can hinder problem solving, personal growth, and fulfillment in life—both individually and in family systems (Baer, 1993; Barron, 1988; Carson and Runco, 1999; Flach, 1990; Rhodes, 1990). These barriers can be both real and perceived, and it is not always easy to tell the difference. However, a heightened understanding of what inhibits creative thinking and expression can be immensely beneficial to therapists as they negotiate the hills and valleys of clinical work.

Some of the social and psychologically based inhibitors to creativity are listed as follows: fear of failure; preoccupation with order and tradition; resource myopia (i.e., failure to recognize one's own strengths and those of others); overcertainty (i.e., persistence in behavior that is no longer effective; dogmatism or inflexibility); a reluctance to exert influence (desire not to appear pushy; a "don't rock the boat" attitude); a fear of play (overseriousness; desire not to appear foolish) and lack of humor or appreciation of humor; fear of letting imagination roam; and a squelching of "what if" thinking and fantasizing. Other blocks can include a tendency toward analysis to the preclusion of synthesis, movement toward premature closure, a preoccupation with private worries and insecurities, and environmental restraints (e.g., at home, school, or work). For example, premature closure can involve stereotyping individuals or groups based on insufficient knowledge of or experience with them, or drawing conclusions and making decisions before all facts or options have been carefully considered. On the other hand, creative techniques such as futuration (examining a situation from a futuristic point of view); imagery and visioning; suspending judgment; recognizing and exercising multiple options and choices; and learning to integrate thought and emotion (i.e., balancing intellectual and emotional intelligence) can facilitate clients' decision making, planning, goal setting, and problem solving (Benjamin, 1984).

INSTITUTIONAL/ORGANIZATIONAL RULES, POLICIES, AND TURFISM AS INHIBITORS OF CREATIVITY

Torrance (1961) discusses several factors that can negatively affect the development and expression of creative thinking in children and adults:

1. Elimination of opportunities for fantasy
2. Restrictions on manipulative behavior and curiosity
3. Conditions resulting in fear and timidity, in both authority figures and peer relations
4. Misplaced emphasis on certain verbal skills, especially on grammar and mechanics
5. Overemphasis on prevention and on success

6. Lack of opportunities for talking about ideas and resources for working out ideas
7. Differential treatment of boys and girls or men and women

Although this list was not constructed for a therapeutic audience, the relevance of these factors to couples and family treatment is noteworthy.

Ricchiuto (1997) notes that, with regard to conflict resolution in group settings (i.e., work or educational environments), "Differences become conflicts when we have not become creative enough to invent new and useful ways to meet or exceed our different needs" (p. 11). However, differences between individuals or groups can spark new and useful ideas and stimulate richer options and alternatives. Therapists should model such interchanges in their own places of employment. Unfortunately, despite our (supposed) insight into human nature and the psyche, as well as our understanding of group behavior, we are just as likely as other people to succumb to the same pettiness and unhealthy comparisons and competition that block creative involvement and production. In fact, sometimes due to our excessively high and unrealistic expectations of ourselves and others, as well as our obsessive-compulsive tendencies, our capacity to both invent and find creative solutions with co-workers becomes even more difficult. In creative groups, however, "differences take the group beyond individual capabilities to new levels of possibility" (Ricchiuto, 1997, p. 11). In contrast, uncreative groups, organizations, and companies polarize and paralyze people from completing even the most simple task.

Ricchiuto (1997, pp. 21-22) lists five creative myths that inhibit our ability as individuals or groups to be more creative. Really these serve as excuses much of the time.

1. Creative people are experts in the field (i.e., brighter than us).
2. They have the money to be creative.
3. They have a lot of freedom within which to work.
4. Their ideas just come to them out of nowhere.
5. They are spontaneous—no Franklin Planners.

Of course, he goes on to refute each of these myths, despite the fact that they may contain grains of truth. Organizational hazards in the idea garden, according to Ricchiuto, include:

1. Idea bottlenecks (i.e., requiring that ideas pass through too many chains of command)
2. Being bound by quality slogans (e.g., "Do it right the first time" or "Efficiency is everything")
3. Getting the short end of the stick (i.e., not being acknowledged for creative ideas and even having others take the credit)
4. Team player guilt (punishment from the group for not being a team player because you have different ideas, questions, or proposed solutions)
5. Rewarding conformity more than independent thought and innovation
6. Little or no time away from work to play with ideas with your colleagues and build relationships based on trust and respect
7. Airtight, inflexible job descriptions
8. Organizational patriarchy (i.e., power, information, responsibility and reward haves and have-nots)

One might add individual or group turfism to this list ("This is our job or area of expertise, not yours, and we're not going to share and work together with you"). Creative organizations or "cultures," on the other hand, encourage original thinking and empower people to make some independent decisions in their work environment, both as individuals and small groups or divisions. Hence, we might safely assert that creativity is unleashed in organizations, including therapeutic milieus, that have discovered the true power of partnerships. Partnership-based organizations entail shared responsibilities, resources, rights, and risks. Perhaps Ricchiuto (1997, p. 101) is correct in saying that "in a partnership, the gap is closed through education, empowerment, and equity." This is not to imply that agencies, organizations, and companies should (or could) operate in the absence of a hierarchy of roles and differentiation of responsibilities. But, are these entities based more on patriarchy than partnership? To what extent does the structure block the expression of creative problem finding and problem solving? These are the crucial questions and ones that pertain to potential barriers to creativity in the work of therapists and others involved in the business of helping people.

RESPONSES FROM STUDY PARTICIPANTS
REGARDING BARRIERS TO CREATIVITY
IN THERAPY

Results from the study participants (summarized in the next section) indicated that by far the most common barriers/blocks/inhibitions to "being as creative as you would like to be" in therapy were time constraints. Most frequently reported was simply not having enough time to contemplate, learn about, and implement more creative techniques and interventions. Also embedded in this response were complaints about having too many cases and administrative or other duties, as well as too much paperwork. The next most common barrier was surprising, in that it had to do with client resistance/rigidity with regard to the therapist's creative interventions or directives and a general lack of response or willingness of clients to participate when the therapist attempted to be more innovative or do something creative. The third most frequent barrier reported was dealing with managed care/ HMOs/insurance companies. Complaints were numerous and included everything from a lack of coverage of client sessions and frustrations over getting reimbursed to excessive paperwork and time on the phone. The fourth most common block to creative therapy centered around the limitations of the person of therapist, namely personal inhibitions and self-doubts, not trusting the self to be more creative, and a lack of confidence. Other common responses included fatigue/lack of energy; institutional, agency, or work setting restrictions (e.g., rigid supervisors or overcautious administrators); a lack of money and resources (e.g., to order more creative materials, have the space for more creative interventions, or attend workshops and conferences that would enhance knowledge of creative interventions); a fear of liability from clients and/or breeches of ethical practice; laziness, habit, or stuck in a rut with oneself or because of one's prior training; a fear of failure or a negative outcome with clients if one were to be more innovative and creative; and a lack of contact with other therapists that would allow for the sharing of creative ideas and techniques. A capsulized list of participants' responses follows.

Barriers and Constraints to Being a More Creative Family Therapist As Listed by Study Participants

- Restraints of managed care/insurance companies/HMOs, etc.
- Managed care paperwork (and the lowered rates for service which make it imperative that I see many more clients than I would prefer to see)
- Time restraints (i.e., not enough time to sit and ponder my cases, to be more creative, or do more creative thinking and process ideas, etc.)
- Restrictive parameters of licensure
- Fear of overstepping ethical boundaries
- Institutional structures
- Legal issues of liability (e.g., by using what might be seen as unorthodox methods)
- Anxiety/fear of failure
- Fear that the intervention will be unintentionally harmful
- Fear of being misunderstood, even radical, in the eyes of some clients
- Unwillingness on the part of clients to take risks and try something new
- Personal inhibitions
- My own limitations and self-doubts
- Distractions of my own inner dialogue
- Too much pain in client(s)
- Diagnosis/*Diagnostic and Statistical Manual of Mental Disorders* (DSM-IV)
- Potential risk to the client
- Experience with or knowledge of particular issue(s)
- Regularly being able to integrate new meaning
- Laziness/just get in a rut
- The size of my office (not big enough to do a lot of movement or sculpting, etc.)
- Lack of time to do outside reading or attend conferences that would help me be more creative
- Working in a large hospital where there are many restrictions
- Temporary lack of insight
- Mostly my own neurotic impulses
- Preconceptions
- Lack of sense of humor on the part of the client

- Not enough time allotted for sessions
- Long hours (seeing families in the evening after all day of consultation)
- Initial training—the way one first learns to do therapy is difficult to set aside even when something better comes along
- Client rigidity/resistance/unwillingness to tolerate uncertainty
- Parents who restrict creativity of children in therapy
- Lack of understanding from colleagues
- Finances/lack of resources (e.g., many ideas take money and time to implement, particularly if they reflect a significant change to daily business)
- Lack of contact with other therapists/minimal interaction with and stimulation from colleagues/lack of a community of creative therapists
- Concrete clients
- The difficulty moving from abstract to usable ideas
- The amount of paperwork I need/am required to do
- Personal courage to press on until the creative moment works through to completion
- Outside noise that can be inhibiting
- Fear of doing something different that may not be understood by the agency (especially as a new therapist)
- Issues that arise in my own life with family, spouse, children, and friends
- Being sometimes too certain, and therefore, using the same old moves (but at the same time being respectful of boundaries and propriety)
- Lack of energy/fatigue
- Routine
- Lack of self-confidence
- Not trusting myself or the environment in which I work
- Self-criticism, judgment
- Concern that I may be reading the situation with clients incorrectly
- Not being able to earn the clients' trust, especially in short-term therapy
- Lack of clinical research to justify creative modalities (which makes me reluctant to try new interventions)
- Not enough training on creative techniques

- Forgetting and going on automatic pilot
- Supervisors that direct how I use my time or what I can do in therapy
- Thoughts of self as a noncreative person
- Depression that takes place when I see the immensity of issues out there and the lack of resources to make a (real) change
- Difficulty sometimes joining/connecting with (or warming up to) the couple or family
- Lack of imagination in the moment
- Boredom in session
- The image of what some people perceive of a therapist
- Lack of time to establish a strong therapeutic alliance (given the frequency of short-term therapy)
- Fear of running against the tide of current practice in the field
- Being overwhelmed and preoccupied with administrative and/ or faculty-related tasks
- A belief that I already know what needs to be done
- A sense that the couple or family will not play along
- Seriousness—taking therapy or myself too seriously, or believing that therapy is usually serious (or should be), either of which can prevent one from seeing alternative ways to proceed
- Fear that the client(s) will tell everything I did and said to others (who will likely misunderstand the purpose of the intervention)
- A belief that I need to impart the "answer"
- Inability to anticipate the outcome
- Lack of fresh ideas/fuzzy thinking on my part
- Not having seen something demonstrated before
- Not having truly listened to the clients
- Perfectionism/my own impatience

This list sheds light on potential blocks to creativity in therapy that are both individually as well as organizationally or institutionally based. If the therapist (and clients) do not detect and successfully remove or learn to adjust to and work within the context of these barriers, the process of change and growth in couples and family work will likely suffer. On the other hand, therapy itself can be one of many venues that provides adults and children with opportunities for creative self-expression, as well as cooperative exploration of ideas and solutions to life's difficulties. Although not all barriers can be eliminated or even necessarily modified, creative therapists are always searching for ways to make the difficult better and the seemingly impossible possible by changing their own thinking about and approach to these so-called barriers. In working in this manner, they may help their clients do the same.

BREAKING OUT OF THE BOX: DESIGNING A CREATIVE RITUAL

You have been holding on to your box for some time now. We appreciate your patience. It is now time to make some decisions. More specifically, what do you want to do with your box and the many messages (positive, negative, and neutral) that it represents? This activity (which can easily be adapted to families) invites you to design a ritual that honors your box, recognizes realistic barriers, and facilitates a transition to move beyond the restrictive nature of some of the messages involved. As always, use the following steps as guidelines that can be modified to best fit your needs.

Step 1: Update your box as needed. Reflect upon the list of barriers mentioned in this chapter. Do any of these barriers apply to you? How would you represent these barriers on (or in) your box?

Step 2: Brainstorm as many ideas as possible about what you could do with your box. For example, some of our students have created rituals to let go of or banish their box or parts of their box. This has included everything from mock burials to trips to the local municipal dump. Other individuals have put their box in a special place in their home or office as a reminder of their progress and future hopes. Another individual reconstructed his box so what was on the inside was now on the outside and vice versa. Take your time with this list. There is no hurry.

Step 3: Once you have a list that feels right to you, make your decision and put it into action.

Step 4: Share your reactions and insights with a friend or colleague (or in your journal).

SECTION III:
CREATIVE INTERVENTIONS IN INDIVIDUAL, COUPLE, AND FAMILY THERAPY AND SUPERVISION

Chapter 8

Creative Interventions in Ten Contemporary Schools of Thought, Part I: Psychodynamic, Intergenerational, Cognitive Behavioral, and Emotion Focused

CREATIVE INCUBATION EXERCISE #8: HERDING CATS

Understanding and exploring our hearts and souls is like herding cats. They seem to have a mind and intent all their own with little regard to what we are wanting or needing in the moment. While in session our feelings and emotions often enter and exit the room (much like our family cats) as we are touched by the stories, pain, and trauma of the couples and families that have trusted us with their most tender parts. Although at times we are drawn toward our clients in a need to comfort and take away their pain, at other times we are compelled to detach or run to the nearest quiet spot available. These unconscious dances are often initiated by the old rhythms that stem and live within each of us from our family of origin. These feelings of anxiety and vulnerability are normal reactions to both past relational voids and our current striving for finding balance in love and intimacy.

Step 1: Reflect upon at least three outstanding unhappy or painful memories within your family as a child or adolescent and/ or your most significant adult relationships. Identify and list the feelings you experienced at the height of these interactions.

Step 2: Now list three to five key dynamics/struggles that when exhibited in session with clients will trigger the feelings and memories you just identified above.

Step 3: Contemplate how your life experiences can either decrease your effectiveness in session or enhance your creativity and connection with clients.

INTRODUCTION

Some creative interventions inherent to ten popular approaches to couple and family therapy are summarized in this chapter. We first summarize the basic tenets of each approach. This overview is followed by some highlights and illustrations of creative techniques and interventions we have found especially effective in our therapy with clients. Some of these interventions have also been chosen on the basis of a number of years of observing and supervising our trainees who work with individuals, couples, and families. At least three techniques or interventions central to or evolving from each school of thought are briefly discussed. Although a number of these methods are integral to each particular approach, we describe some modifications and offshoots of these interventions. A few of them are original creations of ourselves and our trainees. Many of these interventions can be tailored for use with adults (and in some cases children) in individual therapy, especially for therapists who conduct all of their work with clients from a systems perspective. A bit more space will be given to describing the psychodynamic approaches that follow, given their time-honored roots and diversity of perspectives.

PSYCHODYNAMIC APPROACHES

A psychodynamic framework includes any approach "that focuses on the interactions of mind, body, and environment, with specific emphasis on the interplay among an individual's internal (intrapsychic) experiences, conflicts, structures, functions, and processes" (Reiner, 1997, p. 135). This perspective assumes that subliminal mental activity and motivation are paramount to human behavior and that early experiences, especially with parents or parental figures, have a profound influence on later functioning and relationships. Hence, psychodynamic theories have a strong developmental and family orientation. Most schools of psychotherapy derived from this perspective are based on Freudian theory as well as the writings of clinicians whose work is grounded in self psychology and object relations theories (e.g., Heinz Kohut, Margaret Mahler, D. W. Winnicott, and W. R. D. Fairbairn). Some names often associated with a psychodynamic approach to couple and family therapy include Nathan Ackerman, Lyman Wynne, Ivan Boszormenyi-Nagy, Theodore Lidz, and to some extent Murray Bowen and James Framo. Contemporary proponents of object relations family therapy include Jill Scharff and David Scharff (1987) and Samuel Slipp (1988).

As will be seen, creative thinking is an inherent aspect of psychodynamic psychotherapy, and the possibilities for creative interventions in working from these perspectives are seemingly endless. Before we engage in such considerations, however, an overview of the foundations of a psychodynamically oriented approach to working with couples and families needs to be provided. This overview includes key concepts and processes.

Roots of Dysfunction in Couple and Family Relationships

Individual difficulties, as well as dysfunction in couple and family relationships, can have several major underlying causes. First, they are influenced by unresolved intrapsychic conflicts resulting largely from childhood experiences (e.g., problems with one's parent or parents) and/or failure to work through childhood complexes. These unresolved conflicts, operating mostly outside of a person's awareness, continue to attach themselves to current objects (e.g., family members or other significant people) and situations.

Second, dysfunction and conflict can be caused by an excessive or unhealthy use of the defense mechanisms (e.g., denial, rationalization, suppression) that give rise, for example, to unresolved anxiety, anger, guilt, or shame.

Third, relational problems can be affected by a person's failure to successfully work or progress through the various psychosexual stages of development outlined by Freud (oral, anal, phallic, latent, genital), which in turn can have a negative influence on personality development (e.g., anal fixation associated with rigidity, stubbornness, and greediness as an adult; unsuccessful resolution of the oedipal complex during the phallic stage in early childhood resulting in a confused gender identity). Personality traits of various family members, especially the parents, can have a profound influence on the healthy or pathological functioning of one or more family members, or the family as a whole (e.g., symbiotic survival patterns and intersubjective fusion; pseudomutuality; scapegoating; etc.).

Fourth, since all family (and nonfamily) interactions are conceptualized in terms of object relations, difficulties and conflicts are associated with internalizations, introjections, and projections derived from particular objects and the person's relationship with these objects. The residues of internalized objects and organization of introjects form the core sense of self (a coherent and cohesive sense of self, being essential for deep and meaningful human relationships). A child's emerging sense of self can become organized, for example, around narcissistic needs, infantile dependence, or defensive conflicts (e.g., due to a failure of individuation) and result in many types of child psychopathology (e.g., aggression, grandiosity, or inferiority/inadequacy). Examples of individuals without a clear sense of identity include those with a borrowed identity, or "as-if" personality. Severe forms of individual psychopathology include various personality disorders, schizophrenia, and delusional disorder.

With regard to couple relationships (including marriage), these intimate relationships are enhanced or contaminated by the pathogenic introjects that each partner brings to it from the past (e.g., failure to detach from one's family of origin and develop a clear and separate identity). This is why often in mate selection, opposites attract (but later often repel). Projection and introjection are often played out on both sides of the marital interaction. Thus, marital discord is considered an acting out of internal conflicts within an interpersonal context. Moreover, partners are frequently attracted to each other by their shared developmental failures (Skynner, 1976). From a psychodynamic perspective, individual problems or marital difficulties can easily be projected onto one or more of the children.

Clinical Aspects of a Psychodynamic Approach

As Nichols and Schwartz (2001) remind us, "For all of the complexity of psychoanalytic theory, psychoanalytic technique is relatively simple—not easy, but simple. There are four basic techniques:

listening, empathy, interpretation, and analytic neutrality" (pp. 217-218). Central to these four techniques are a number of key elements to working with couples and families. First and foremost is the establishment of a therapeutic alliance. The relationship between therapist and clients is paramount to the therapeutic process, itself a transformative agent, and the clinician is, in one sense, very much the method of psychotherapy. Second, the therapist must be keenly aware of and able to manage transference and countertransference processes. In working with couples and families, transference must be seen as transgenerational. Using transference in couple and family therapy may involve interventions geared toward helping clients experience and carefully examine dynamics in the client-therapist relationship that are associated with other significant object relations (e.g., spouse, parent, child). Third, the therapist must learn to deal with the concept and the reality of client resistance. In family therapy, resistance may come from individuals, subsystems, or the family as a whole. However, from a psychodynamic perspective resistance is seen less as an obstacle to treatment (although it can be) and more as a way in which individuals in the family reveal the nature of their difficulties and conflicts. Hence, it is not so much a problem to be overcome as a behavior and attitude that can be channeled and used in the process of therapy. This takes a good measure of creativity and skill on the part of the therapist. Fourth, as indicated by Nichols and Schwartz (2001), interpretation is the primary form of communication the therapist uses to elucidate the unconscious meaning in fears, conflicts, narcissistic wounding, projections, introjections, and other intrapsychic phenomena. The purpose of interpretation is to make the unconscious conscious, which is called insight. Change in clients occurs through the uncovering of unconscious needs, thoughts, feelings, wishes, desires, motivations, and so forth, through interventions that lead to insight, awareness, understanding, conflict resolution, and emotional "working through" to create, ultimately, both intrapsychic and interpersonal change.

In sum, some of the major goals of therapy from a psychodynamic perspective include increased insight, psychosexual maturity, strengthening of ego functioning, reduction or elimination of interlocking psychopathologies, and more satisfying object relations. The meeting of these goals requires the neutralization and integration of anxiety, aggressive impulses, and/or childhood complexes such that family members can interact with one another from a position of ego strength and integrity rather than impulse and intrapsychic conflict. The therapist makes interpretations of family dynamics and individual personality and behavior patterns. The work of the therapist involves reorganizing, reshaping, redirecting, and reconstituting each family member's relationship between his or her own sense of self (based on critical introjections drawn from past and present, immediate and extended family relationships) and the parental images that represent these critical object relationships. Actions of the therapist also involve mirroring, monitoring the process of emotional gridlock, supporting efforts toward differentiation (seen especially in couples work), and dealing with clients' psychological defenses and other subconscious or unconscious processes, including motivations, anxieties, wishes, fantasies, and various other blind spots in awareness. Interventions associated with or evolving from psychodynamic approaches have included psychodrama, individual and family play therapy, use of various forms of imagery, and a host of expressive therapies (i.e., art, projective drawings, journaling and other forms of writing).

Contributions of psychodynamic approaches to the field of couple and family therapy are numerous. First, these approaches acknowledge the unique contributions of individuals to relationship difficulties and family pathology. Second, they shed light on the ways in which subliminal processes can influence couple and family relationships. Third, they provide clues as to how to deal with resistance toward change in these intimate relationships. Finally, they stress the importance of patterns and dynamics in parent-child and intergenerational relationships. However, some limitations of psychodynamic approaches may include the following:

1. Focusing too much on the individual within the family rather than systemic influences and processes and de-emphasizing the role of family structure in creating and maintaining relationship conflicts and difficulties
2. Interpreting family dysfunction as lying largely within the unconscious of individual family members rather than seeing the causes of these problems as being primarily consciously motivated and controlled
3. Placing more emphasis on the past than the present

4. Overemphasizing pathology more than wellness and existing areas of strength and resiliency in individuals as well as couple and family relationships

Examples of Psychodynamically Oriented Creative Interventions

One of the early interventions in couples and family work, which requires a great deal of creative skill and insight on the part of therapist, involves hypothesizing with and about clients' patterns and defenses (one way of making interpretations) and listening to the themes of the unconscious (Scharff, 1992; Scharff and Scharff, 1987). One assumption made by object relations therapists is that unconscious themes lie behind clients' spoken words. These themes are a window into the inner lives of clients which reveal what it is that needs to be addressed or healed. Patterns of interaction often point to what is being defended against in couple and family relationships. By helping clients identify these themes and patterns, the stage is set for a reemergence of missing parts of each individual's unconscious into a more integrated whole. Here, the goal of therapy is not to rid the individual, couple, or family of all symptoms but, according to Scharff and Scharff, to use symptoms as leverage in helping clients master developmental stresses more effectively both now and in the future.

A number of creative and useful interventions have evolved from various psychodynamic perspectives. Some are briefly described as follows.

Questions Involving, "What's Missing for You in Your Family or Relationship with Your Partner?"

According to Scharff and Scharff (1987), this type of questioning helps clients fill in what is missing rather than risk undoing what they already have going for them. This is because often in couple and family therapy clients are as careful about and protective of not losing what they still have as they are in pain over what is not working in their relationships. These questions and their responses can also be directed to and from clients in the form of an open-ended sentence which the therapist initiates such as, "What I want (or most need) from you in our relationship is . . ." "What's missing for you" types of statements or questions are appropriate, given that individuals in intimate relationships are often dealing with issues of attachment, hurt, rejection, grief, loss, shame, guilt, self-worth, and sometimes narcissistic wounding from the past or present. Questions or statements expressed in the first person (i.e., "I" rather than "you" statements) are more likely to take the focus off "who did what to whom" (keeping partners and family members off the defensive) and convey responsibility for one's thinking, feeling, and behavior. Couples and family members can also be asked to say what they think their partner, parent, or child would say in response to the question, "What's missing for you?" This can be a useful estimate of the degree of perspective taking and attributional understanding in these emotionally charged intimate relationships. Finally, rather than having clients use words, they can be asked to "show" their partner or family member(s), such as through pantomime, facial expression, or other body language, what they need, desire, or are missing. Others can then be directed to interpret (thorough verbal or nonverbal means) these messages, as well as to convey what *they* wish to communicate more from the heart than the head.

Sentence Completion Games or Tasks

The psychotherapy literature contains a number of variations of sentence completion measures, games, and tasks that can be used in creative and effective ways with clients, both for assessment and treatment purposes. For example, Sherman and Fredman (1986) describe several, including exercises involving family-of-origin kinds of statements ("Mom always said . . ." "Dad always said . . ." regarding money, sex, religion, work, leisure, family, etc.) and self and family-oriented types of statements (e.g., "If I weren't so angry I . . ." "If we were closer I would . . ." "One way I punish you is . . ."). One series of sentence completion materials we have found extremely useful in couples and family work as well as individual therapy are Brown and Unger's (1992) *Sentence Completion Series*. This set includes eight different forms: adult, adolescent, family, marriage, parenting, work, illness, and aging. These forms can be used for the purpose of assessment (i.e., take home or complete in session early in therapy) or in a variety of creative ways as part of the treatment process. For example, partners can share their completed sentence with each other one by one (or selectively as directed by the therapist) in session, with each partner reflecting his or her thoughts and feelings in response to the other. These include such statements as "We get along best . . ."; "My expectations of marriage . . ."; "Without my spouse . . ."; "I want my spouse to understand . . ."; "Sharing feelings . . ."; and "What we most need as a couple . . ." The family form also has a great deal to offer, and often children and parents are surprised by other family members' responses (e.g., "Our family always . . ."; "It's hardest to get along . . ."; "The ideal family . . ."; "What brings us together . . ."; "An unspoken family rule . . ."). Similarly, the parenting version includes such helpful statements as: "The way I was parented . . ."; "A good parent . . ."; "Working together as parents . . ."; "As a parent I worry most about . . ."; "The most effective discipline . . ."; and "As a parent I enjoy . . ."

Seeing Myself in the Other and the Other in Me Explorations

As mentioned, projective identification is a central concept of most psychodynamic theories. According to Scharff and Scharff (1987), it is the basis of all intimate relationships, that part of ourselves (both good and bad) which we see in others, and that part of others which we see in ourselves. Projective identification is the unconscious connection that both allows people to feel bonded and in sync with one another and to have difficulty accepting and relating to another person. It is often a neglected dynamic in couple and family therapy.

One simple procedure we have used to explore projective identifications is to ask family members to write down five personal aspects seen in each member (separately) and five traits of others that are recognized in the self. These can be viewed as positive, negative, or neutral. The quantity and content of each person's responses can tell them and the therapist much about their connections and identifications with one another (as well as boundaries, resistance, and subsystem alliances, etc.). These lists can be expanded to include certain extended family members in both couple and family therapy (i.e., husband's and wife's parents). The construction and sharing of these commonalities can be risky but enlightening and growth promoting. Diagnostically, use of this technique can flesh out specific areas of anxiety and conflict that need to be addressed in therapy.

One intervention that gets to the heart of projective identification issues is Karl Tomm's (1987a,b,c) "internalized other" interviewing technique. In this procedure, couples and family members are told not to role-play the other but to speak from that person's inner experience. Clients can be asked to close their eyes, relax, and imagine that they are that other person. For example, in one session, Pete was asked to become Jolene, and Jolene, Pete. The therapist then asked Pete, "Jolene, how do you feel about coming to this interview today?" and asked Jolene the reverse. A series of questions can then be used to probe feelings, perceptions, wishes, fears, and so forth (e.g., "Pete, tell me what it was like growing up in your family"; "Jolene, what was the happiest time of your life?"). Afterward, clients are asked to offer feelings about and impressions of their partner's (or family member's) embodiment of them. This can be an extremely effective diagnostic tool for therapists and enlightening experience for clients.

Various Uses of the Inner Advisor or Hidden Observer

Psychodynamic theorists have long talked about that hidden part of our psyche sometimes referred to as the hidden observer. What others might call our intuitive voice, this component of our intellect seems to alternate between our conscious and subconscious minds. At times we are in tune with and listen carefully to our hidden observer. However, both therapists and clients (as discussed previously in the section on intuition) are often completely unaware that our hidden observer is speaking to us (sometimes literally and sometimes in the language of the unconscious), or if we sense that it is, we fail to trust in or understand the message. In our work we have occasionally found it useful to encourage and assist clients in allowing their inner advisors or observers to speak, either to us or to one another. Hence, an inner journey is facilitated. We also help them externalize their hidden observers in ways that they can then listen to and converse with them. It is as though the client is making a visit to the sage. For example, after explaining (in lay terms and on the clients' level) the concept of the hidden observer or inner advisor and being assured that clients have bought in (which most seem to), the following interventions can be used in helping clients give a voice to this part of themselves. The first exercise is described by Sherman and Fredman (1986, pp. 58-62).

Use of the inner advisor, as described by Sherman and Fredman (1986), is a form of guided imagery in which, after helping clients relax, the therapist can employ various methods to bring clients to their inner observer. Through this process, unlabeled ideas and feelings can be brought into conscious awareness:

> One method is for the therapist to choose a scene that she believes indicates the client's conflict, fear, or desire for change. She requests that the client project himself into that scene and describe it aloud. The therapist then picks up on something or someone alive in that scene other than the client. The client is asked to get in touch with that "alive" being to be used as an inner advisor. She has the inner advisor reframe the pain or problem unto itself and away from the client, seeking his agreement to do so. Then the client is requested to return to his usual state from his relaxed state. (Sherman and Fredman, 1986, p. 59)

Another method, a version of which we have used, involves asking clients one by one to imagine going into a room where there is a very wise being who knows the client inside and out, knows the problem(s), and understands everything about all personalities and preceding events. Next, clients enter the imaginary room, either as an individual or corporately as a couple or family, and converse with the wise being who tells them what to do. This imagined visit is then processed with the therapist and one another. A creative extension of this technique with couples and families is to have two or more individuals visit their inner advisor at the same time and then allow their advisors to speak openly and plainly to one another. In sum, use of this intervention "encourages self-reflection, creative living, and trust in one's own resources. It is a relatively non-threatening technique since the client can imagine whatever s/he chooses without any pressure" (Sherman and Fredman, 1986, p. 61). This procedure can help clients break free of the prisons of their own belief systems.

Other psychodynamic-related interventions include a number of creative uses of the empty chair and other Gestalt techniques discussed by Thompson (1996), Jacobs (1992), Sherman and Fredman (1986), and a host of other authors. We have found that both planned and spontaneous uses of the empty chair integrate well with the other experiential techniques discussed in this book.

INTERGENERATIONAL APPROACHES

Intergenerational approaches to couple and family therapy are multifaceted. These perspectives, perhaps best represented by Murray Bowen (1978) and James Framo (1982) and popularized by such writers as Hovestadt and Fine (1987), have become a cornerstone of the family therapy field. In a nutshell, these approaches emphasize the significance and power of family patterns (beliefs, values, attitudes, behaviors, ways of thinking and viewing the world, etc.) that tend to get passed on from generation to generation. These family patterns can contribute to both health and dysfunction in individuals and in couple and family relationships. By definition, these patterns are difficult (though not impossible) to break or change. This is partly because present relationships with extended family members on both sides of a couple's relationship tend to support preexisting patterns and expectations. Hence, our family of origin has both a past and present influence on marital and parenting behavior and the quality of these interactions over time.

Some common intergenerational themes in couple and family work include the following: unresolved conflicts and difficulties with individuals in one's family of origin which are playing out in one's marriage, family of procreation, or reconstituted family system; and unresolved system dynamics (e.g., fusion/differentiation of self issues that involve, for example, emotional stuck-togetherness or gridlock and the need for some emotional cutoff, invisible loyalties, ongoing control behavior, triangling, and projection of family-of-origin dynamics onto one's spouse and children). Treatment from an intergenerational framework may involve the inclusion of one or more family-of-origin members in some of the therapy sessions. Often, direct corrective experiences with one's family of origin in the here and now can have profound therapeutic effects on one's present marital and family relationships. When this is not possible or feasible, unresolved issues with one's family of origin can still be dealt with in therapy. This is partially accomplished through improved differentiation of the self and the creation of healthy boundaries between clients' immediate family and family of origin (Bowen, 1978). According to Framo (1982), intrapsychic problems resulting from one's family of origin may also need to be addressed (e.g., unresolved anxiety, guilt, or shame issues).

A variety of techniques have been proposed for working with couples and families on intergenerational issues and for assessment purposes. These include, for example, the family floor plan (see Sherman and Fredman, 1986), Satir's (1983, 1988) life fact chronology, and, as implemented in Imago Relationship Therapy (Hendrix, 1988; Luquet, 1996), unique methods for helping couples deal with developmental wounding experiences (i.e., of their own childhoods) and connecting these experiences with current relationship dynamics. However, we believe that genograms offer therapists one of the most creative and potentially helpful possibilities. For a detailed understanding of genograms, as well as the basics of constructing genograms, we refer you to *Intergenerational Assessment of Individuals, Couples, and Families: Focused Genograms* by DeMaria, Weeks, and Hof (1999). These authors provide wonderful and concrete examples and explanations. Three different types and uses of genograms are briefly described as follows.

Spirituality/Religious Genograms

In therapist training, as well as when working with individuals, couples, and families, we have found that the facilitation of spiritual/religious genograms are particularly helpful. According to Wiggins Frame,

> The primary purpose of the religious/spiritual genogram is to enable clients to become more aware of and sensitive to the religious or spiritual histories, beliefs, and experiences that shaped their families of origin and to gain insight into how these patterns affect other issues in the couple or family unit. (2000, p. 70)

In these explorations with families, we define (for ourselves only) spirituality as including both the way in which people connect and disconnect. We are hoping to help each individual better understand how he or she fosters and creates meaning in his or her life (connection) and the mechanisms he or she may have learned and is currently using to disengage from meaning (disconnection). After constructing the basic genogram, we utilize the following questions adapted from Haug (1998) and Wiggins Frame (2000) as a guide to gathering family information specific to religious and/or spiritual histories. These questions allow a conversation to unfold that extends from the past to the present and future.

1. What language or terms are you comfortable using to convey your spiritual/religious beliefs?

2. How important was religious practice or affiliation in your family? What religious affiliations exist within your family of origin today?

3. What was the importance of religion in your extended family? How did it influence family members' beliefs (about human nature, life's meanings, etc.), feelings (such as hopelessness, caring, fear, guilt, etc.), and behaviors (in relationships inside or outside the family, religious practices, etc.)?

4. How have religious/spiritual beliefs influenced self-esteem, marriage, parenting, sexuality, and familial responsibilities and loyalties? What did/does your religious/spiritual tradition say about gender (being male or female), ethnicity and difference, sexual orientation, etc.?

5. How does your family celebrate rituals of connection: family meals, rising and retiring, coming and going, going out and going away, couple rituals, etc.?

6. How has your family observed rituals of celebration and community: special-person rituals (birthdays, Mother's Day, Father's Day), Thanksgiving, Christmas, Chanukah, community and religious rituals, rituals of passage (weddings and funerals), etc.?

7. What additional religious/spiritual rituals did you participate in as a child or adolescent? How important were these experiences to you and your family? Which practices have you maintained and which have you discontinued?

8. What do you see as the core spirit-empowering messages embedded in your family's religious/spiritual beliefs and practices?

9. Who in your extended family was particularly spiritual/religious and how did it show in their way of life (thoughts, feelings, behaviors)?

10. In what ways was spirituality or religion ever a source of strength and/or a cause of conflict in the family? Explain.

11. What about your family's or specific family members' spirituality or religion did you personally experience as empowering or constraining?

12. What positive or negative messages did you get publicly or implicitly about other spiritual or religious beliefs and practices?
13. Do you maintain a particular religious affiliation—if yes, how actively involved are you and how does this translate into daily practice and lifestyle choices?
14. What does spirituality mean to you? Put a few key words next to your name on your genogram.
15. How has your family's spiritual or religious heritage influenced your personal philosophy and behavior?
16. Have you seriously considered alternative beliefs and their consequences for your life? Explain.
17. What if anything about your spirituality or religion do you experience as confining or tyrannical, and what do you experience as life enhancing or liberating?
18. How free are you to challenge unhelpful beliefs and choose more empowering alternatives? Explain.
19. How willing are you to act on your beliefs? Give examples.
20. How does your religious/spiritual history connect with your current distress or concerns? What new solutions would you like to seek in light of these discoveries?

Family Play Genograms

The second, and in our view one of the most enjoyable, focused genogram to create with a family is the family play genogram. We utilize a process by Botkin and Raimondi (2000) that has been adapted from Boorma's (1999) work. Boorma states that the therapeutic value of the family play genogram is that it "has the potential to tap into the unconscious process of each family member using symbolic representation, revealing and making accessible previously unknown interpersonal dynamics" (1999, pp. 1-2). Systemic change is possible as these dynamics become conscious. The first step in developing a family play genogram is to construct the basic genogram on a large piece of paper. We utilize butcher paper and tape two four-foot sections together. It is important to create a physical space that allows all family members both the psychological and physical space necessary to fully participate. Once the genogram is drawn (in some detail) on the paper, each family member is directed to choose a miniature (from our play therapy room) that represents his or her thoughts and feelings about each person in the family, including himself or herself. As each family member simultaneously chooses and places the miniatures on the genogram, the therapist observes and makes a note of all individual choices, as well as the family process that unfolds during the development of the genogram. We often encourage family members to bring the relationships to life by choosing additional miniatures that represent the relationship dynamics (e.g., strengths, connections, cutoffs, and conflicts) within their family and extended family. Upon completion of the family play genogram two photographs are taken, one for the file and one for the family. Finally, the family is invited to process and discuss both the content of its genogram and the process of creating the genogram together. A variation that has worked well is to then invite the family to move to the sand tray and create a second world that depicts how they would like their family and relationships to be. This addition provides the family with a visual representation of their hopes or goals for therapy.

Feelings Genograms

The third genogram that we find facilitative is the emotions (or feelings) genogram. This intervention is particularly helpful with families or couples that are restricted in their range of emotional expression. DeMaria, Weeks, and Hof (1999, p. 107) offer the following questions (as well as others) to assist families as they construct their feelings/emotions genogram.

1. What were the dominant feelings for each member of your family?
2. What was the predominant feeling in your family? Who set the mood?
3. Which feelings were expressed most often, most intensely?
4. Which feelings were not allowed? How were members punished when an unallowable feeling was expressed?
5. What happened to the unexpressed feelings in the family?
6. Who knew or did not know about how others felt?
7. What happened to you when you expressed the taboo feeling or feelings?
8. How did you learn how to deal with these so-called unacceptable feelings?

9. Did others try to tell you how you should feel?
10. Did you ever see anyone lose control over his or her feelings?
11. If corporal punishment was used in your family, what feelings did parents express? What feelings were allowable for children?
12. Do you find yourself having feelings that you cannot explain but that seem like feelings you have had in the past?

To more fully engage children in the process of creating the emotions genogram the therapist can invite them to draw the feelings associated with each family member or use the feelings faces (a chart of comic-style faces with associated feelings) to better identify an emotion. Cutouts of the feelings faces (sad, anxious, confused, etc.) can be easily developed to have on hand to assist clients with this project.

COGNITIVE-BEHAVIORAL INTERVENTIONS

Today, cognitive and behavioral approaches to therapy are often blended (Fenell and Weinhold, 1997). This perspective emphasizes that behavior and emotions are largely contingent upon thinking (cognition) and beliefs. At the same time, however, thinking, behavior, and emotions are mutually reinforcing. That is, emotional responses and behaviors are intertwined with and supportive of a person's thought patterns and worldview as much as one's thinking and beliefs about reality influence one's choices, actions, and feelings. Clients become conditioned to the irrational beliefs that they practice and to their typical ways of responding to life events both emotionally and behaviorally.

According to Fenell and Weinhold (1997), goals of therapy in cognitive-behavioral treatment include:

1. Practicing and acquiring new skills and behaviors (e.g., communication and social skills, conflict resolution strategies, stress management, etc.)
2. Learning to become assertive and ask clearly and directly for what one wants and needs
3. Learning to become more independent, responsible, self-directed, self-accepting, accepting and tolerant of others, flexible, open to change, and willing to take risks

4. Becoming more able to give and receive both positive and negative feedback

5. Unlearning old ways of thinking and behaving and learning new ways of conceptualizing difficulties and possible solutions (including being able to recognize and challenge self-destructive behaviors and thoughts)

6. Getting clients in touch with their worst fears and helping them modify or change them (e.g., by putting them in proper perspective) to an appropriate and balanced level of intensity and manageability

One way of conceptualizing the cognitive component is according to Albert Ellis's (1989) Rational-Emotive Therapy (RET) model. This approach involves helping clients understand the connection between (1), activating events, (2) irrational, self-defeating beliefs about the event(s), and (3) the consequences of the belief about the event(s). Problem resolution then comes through disputing client's beliefs about the irrational activating event(s), replacing these irrational beliefs with more reality-based rational beliefs, and realizing and reinforcing the positive outcomes (effects) of this disputation and replacement in one's thinking.

Some common cognitive-behavioral interventions include

- Cognitive restructuring (e.g., shame attacking; thought stopping; disputing irrational beliefs such as unhealthy absolutes revolving around "shoulds" and "musts" and replacing them with more rational, reality-based thinking;
- Helping clients learn to take life less seriously;
- Teaching mental imagery and relaxation;
- Interjecting communication skills (and problem-solving) training in therapy;
- Using humor, paradox, and exaggeration to challenge clients' irrational beliefs;
- Helping clients learn and practice new ways of interacting with loved ones through modeling and behavioral rehearsal; and
- Assigning behaviorally oriented homework and contracting (e.g., contingency contracts) in individual, couple, and family work.

Some examples of creative uses of cognitive-behavioral interventions are briefly described as follows.

Rational Emotive Behavior Therapy (REBT) Techniques

Thompson (1996) describes a number of REBT interventions in individual counseling that, with a slight twist, have the capacity to be adapted to couple and family therapy. For example, irrational beliefs and cognitive distortions (see Handly and Neff, 1985) that are supporting relational difficulties or undermining progress (i.e., perfectionism, rejection, negative focus, refusing the positives, fictional fantasies, shoulds and oughts, various forms of self-blame) can be challenged by different types of rational self-talk or other talk. Ordinarily in REBT it is the therapist who does the confronting or challenging, at least initially. However, a creative use of REBT in working with couples and families can involve having each person challenge his or her own self-defeating beliefs, or have others challenge them, in cooperation with a partner or family members. For example, "Bill, convince (prove to) your parents and siblings that you have never been successful at anything. . . . Now, I want each one of you to challenge Bill's belief that he has never been successful at anything" (i.e., present solid evidence to the contrary).

Clients can also be taught specific problem-solving techniques using cognitive-behavioral therapy by helping them become aware of the close connection between thinking, feelings, and behavior. This can be accomplished through helping individuals connect thoughts with words (e.g., self-talk that creates sadness, anxiety, etc.), analyze or critique errors in one's thinking (e.g., overgeneralizing, all-or-nothing thinking, disqualifying the positive, personalization, magnification or minimization, etc.), keep a written record of these automatic thoughts and their corresponding feelings for a period of time and then brainstorm goals with family members that can help change unwanted behavior or distressing feelings. These goals should be agreed upon and supported by family members and should be specific, self-motivating, achievable, realistic, and trackable (Thompson, 1996). When an atmosphere of basic civility is created in therapy, alternative interpretations of one person's thoughts, feelings, and behavior by other members of the family (or partnership) become increasingly powerful. Couples and family members can be asked to make a list of five experiences they wish to have or create with one another (each one specific and measurable). Then, at the beginning of each "vision," they can substitute the words, "we choose" (e.g., "We choose to have a family meeting on the first Monday evening of every month"; "We choose to have dinner together one night a week"; "We choose to provide one helping behavior a day to someone in our family").

Often in systems-based therapy the focus of blame needs to be defused and the center of responsibility shifted from "him, her, or they" to "I." This is equally true for those who tend to criticize or attack as well as see themselves more as passive victims. Various methods of cognitive restructuring can help clients make this shift. For example, the following can be one way of helping someone in the family or marriage shift the center of responsibility. First, have one person think of something that really made him or her angry or resentful, such as an incident or someone else's behavior that tends to be ongoing. Second, have this person describe in writing the incident or behavior as if that other person (or persons) were completely responsible for making this individual angry, sad, fearful, etc. Blame him or her and clearly make it all that person's fault. Third, have the client rewrite the incident (or describe the behavior in a new way) as if he or she were totally (solely) responsible for the problem. This person is asked to take full account of what he or she could have done so that the entire problem would have never occurred. Finally, although this person may feel a sense of unreality about one or both points of view, have this individual carefully reexamine them to see if and to what degree his or her view of reality has been challenged. Without allowing anyone in the family to be placed in the identified patient role, perhaps this exercise can be conducted with everyone who is directly involved with the creation and maintenance of the problem. Guidelines can be set up by the therapist that provide opportunities for each person to reflect on and offer feedback to others regarding issues of blame and self-responsibility.

Helping clients overcome their fears of or resistance to change is also, in many cases, a central component of therapy (Huber and Baruth, 1989). The irrational beliefs and self-defeating behaviors that keep couples and families stuck can be challenged in direct but caring ways. Some common examples of resistance that can keep clients from taking risks or being responsible for change (Grieger, 1986; Thompson, 1996) include fear of discomfort, disclosure, shame, failure, or disapproval by others; feelings of powerlessness and hopelessness; discouragement; self-punishment; and fear of change itself. One technique for helping clients challenge their own and one another's beliefs and substitute them with rational thinking is to adapt Beck and Emery's (1985) "A-FROG" procedure. This is a five-step process that can help clients think and behave more rationally. The A-FROG method includes the following questions that can be directed to clients by the therapist or, with the therapist's assistance, from one family member to another:

> A: Is my current thinking and behavior keeping me *alive* and helping me thrive?
> F: Do I *feel* better as a result?
> R: Is my thinking based in *reality*?
> O: Does my thinking (and behavior) help me get along with *others* in my family and be the best person I can be toward them?
> G: Does my thinking (and behavior) help me get my needs met and reach my *goals*?

Communication Skills Training

Someone once noted that, "Therapy is education too late." Therapy with couples and families often involves an education and skills training component, either formally or informally. This can include everything from assertiveness training to parent education to couple communication enhancement. Sometimes even the most sophisticated clients need and can benefit from what we as therapists might see as the simplest kinds of training. For example, therapists can be uniquely creative in teaching and modeling various aspects of effective communication (i.e., "I" messages, active listening, paraphrasing, clarifying and verbalizing conflicting messages) through role-play and role reversal, showing film clips (e.g., "wrong" and "right" ways of communicating), and helping clients decipher nonverbal aspects of communication through pantomime, sculpturing, practicing attending skills, and numerous other modalities (see Sherman and Fredman, 1986; Thompson, 1996).

Behaviorally Oriented Homework

The techniques previously described are but a few of the kinds of interventions that therapists operating from a REBT perspective can employ. Creative therapists will explore innovative ways to help people examine their own, and one another's, belief systems that trigger distressful emotions, support dysfunctional behavior, and block progress toward healthy and rewarding relationships. Keeping in mind that therapy is not solely a one hour in-session phenomenon, behaviorally oriented homework assignments can provide clients with additional ammunition between sessions, aimed at distinguishing destructive interactions and encouraging positive interchanges. Examples of such assignments for couples can include caring days (Stuart, 1980) or love days (Jacobson and Margolin, 1979), where clients are instructed to engage in and record specific acts of kindness and helpfulness toward one another for an entire day regardless of whether they want to or feel like doing so. This part of therapy can involve identifying, in detail, the needs and wants of oneself and one's partner and committing oneself to provide for some of these needs and wants in surprising and potentially creative ways (e.g., "Exactly what would you like your partner to do to show that he or she cares for you?"). Initially, clients may need some specific guidance from the therapist in making items on their list specific, positive, relatively short in number, doable, and not related to any current conflicts. However, in a short time they should begin to generate their own. Clients can also be instructed to record their emotional and behavioral reactions to their partner's actions and, when appropriate, to share these with one's mate. The idea here is that change often happens, simply but powerfully, in small steps and that the best way to eliminate undesirable behavior and interactions (or increase the likelihood of their extinction) is to both perform and reward actions in relation to one's partner that are inconsistent or incompatible with the undesired behaviors. As negative behaviors are gradually replaced by positive ones, new hope is often instilled in relationships and destructive patterns have a chance to be replaced by constructive ways of relating. Creative therapists will know how and when to use their "expert power" in getting clients started and holding them accountable for their choices and behaviors with regard to these caring or love days. Variations of this intervention, of course, are to assign couples a fun afternoon or date night (or equivalent) away from the children, even if they have little or no money to spend (e.g., have a candlelit dinner at home together). Simply teaching clients how to give compliments to their spouse or family members can be incredibly reinforcing. Personally, we have found that talking about the meaning and importance of civility and helping couples develop a portrait of what this might look like in their everyday relationships can be therapeutic. Moreover, one should *never* underestimate the power of a (genuine) compliment. Compliments can involve how a person looks ("Your eyes have always knocked me out"), acts ("It really makes me feel great when you help out around the house"), personality traits ("Your sense of humor brightens up my day"), or abilities ("You are a terrific mom/dad/mechanic/skier"). With partners who are a bit more safe and secure in their relationship, tasks such as "hug-'till-relaxed" (Schnarch, 1997), therapeutic touch, or massage can be prescribed for so many minutes a day or times per week. It has been our experience that sometimes the most straightforward and seemingly noncreative homework assignments can be the catalyst that breaks the ice and turns clients in a new direction.

EMOTION-FOCUSED INTERVENTIONS

Emotion-focused approaches are based largely on the writings of Susan Johnson and Leslie Greenberg (Greenberg and Johnson, 1988; Johnson and Greenberg, 1994; Johnson, 1996). Although their work has primarily concentrated on therapy with couples, we believe that many of the principles of emotion-focused therapy (EFT) are adaptable to individual and family treatment. Essentially, this approach emphasizes the crucial importance of human emotions and emotional engagement in helping clients problem solve and increase their level of satisfaction and stability in their relationship (Johnson, 1998). Relationship distress and conflict are often maintained by emotional responses that support rigid, self-reinforcing patterns of interaction. Understanding couple difficulties from an EFT approach can be summed up in a quote from Johnson

> Partners are viewed as being "stuck" in certain ways of regulating, processing, and organizing their emotional responses to each other, which then constrict the interactions between them and prevent the development of a secure bond. In turn, constricted interactional patterns then evoke and maintain absorbing states of negative affect. (1998, p. 451)

The goal of EFT, then, is to help couples expand the emotional responses that prime their interactions, and to structure interactions that facilitate secure bonding and emotional engagement. Hence, this approach draws heavily from attachment theory (Bowlby, 1969, 1988).

Clinicians working from an EFT framework focus on both self (intrapsychic) and system (interpersonal) realities in helping clients understand how each reflects and generates the other, with emotion being the primary link between self and system. For significant and long-lasting change to occur, "the therapist needs to help the couple construct new corrective emotional experiences, which subsequently will organize new relationship events" (Johnson, 1998, p. 453). As each partner is allowed and encouraged to reexperience genuine emotions in therapy surrounding real problems, the therapist helps the couple concentrate on the issues of vulnerability and/or fears that are believed to underlie their emotional processes and reactions (Crane, 1996). One assumption underlying EFT is that insight, skill building, or negotiation will not be as effective as an emotion-focused approach. Johnson summarizes the nine steps of change in EFT as follows:

> (1) assessment; (2) identifying the destructive interactional cycle that maintains attachment insecurity and marital distress; (3) discovering the unacknowledged feelings underlying interactional positions; (4) reframing the problem in terms of the cycle and unmet attachment needs; (5) promoting the owning of needs and of new, expanded aspects of self and experience; (6) promoting acceptance of these aspects of self and experience by the other; (7) facilitating the expression of needs and wants; (8) fostering collaboration in regard to problematic issues; and (9) consolidating new positions and new cycles of attachment behavior. (1998, p. 454)

Upon careful examination, although emphasis in EFT is placed on the role of emotions in attachment relationships, in our opinion the approach itself is fairly cognitive-behavioral in orientation, and experiential interventions in the strict sense are not commonplace. Although a major goal of EFT is to activate powerful emotions in therapy, the focal point is on helping spouses challenge their interpretation of their partners' behavior. As Crane (1996) notes, this is because it is the meaning associated with the observation of one's partner's behavior that drives emotional reactions. Thus, "couples are brought to a high level of emotion, and the dysfunctional beliefs about themselves and their partners are directly challenged. It is through this process that couples learn more appropriate ways of thinking about themselves and their partner" (Crane, 1996, pp. 32-33).

Given the many contributions of EFT, opportunities for creative-experiential interventions that help clients have emotionally corrective experiences that assist in breaking rigid interactional cycles are seemingly boundless. The following interventions highlight such possibilities.

Escalating and Clarifying Emotions in a Safe Environment

Couples who present for therapy are usually caught in a tangled web of emotions. However, human emotions, like language, often have both a surface structure and a deep structure (sometimes referred to as core emotions). Clients know what the surface-level emotions are all about, for these are frequently experienced and encountered. However, the underlying core emotions of these overt emotional expressions are often disguised, undifferentiated, unattended to, or disowned (Johnson, 1998). For example, hurt, guilt/shame, and feelings of rejection or being unloved (or unlovable) may be the roots of anger, defensiveness, and contempt. The fear of experiencing further hurt (or psychological abuse or neglect) from one's spouse can cause one to withdraw or be defensive, critical, or contemptuous—all of which are corrosive agents in couple relationships (Gottman, 1999; Gottman and Silver, 2000). Fear and anxiety are also frequent emotions that underlie these kinds of behaviors (e.g., fear of being abandoned by one's spouse, of other possible losses, or of experiencing some type of abuse or retribution). Fear, hurt, sadness, and rejection are attachment-related emotions that need to be fleshed out in couple therapy. In EFT, clients are not only allowed but encouraged to express their full range of emotions (in nonabusive ways) so that they can be clarified and understood by their partners. Often these emotions need to be exaggerated and amplified in order to be understood. Therapists can employ a variety of creative interventions aimed at helping each spouse give a voice to his or her emotions, such as through colorizing, animalizing, or pictorializing these emotions, drawing them, or writing about them. In our view, in therapy each person in the relationship often needs to be allowed to experience the full impact of the emotional realities of his or her mate before some degree of movement and emotional working through can occur. The receiver is then encouraged to share how these emotional expressions of his or her spouse have touched or affected him or her. Often in EFT, clients are directed and redirected to talk to and share with each other rather than the therapist ("Susan, tell Hank what you are feeling right now"; "Susan, your sadness touches me right here in my _____" (i.e., this part of my body).

Once emotions have had the chance to be expressed and the connection between surface and deeper-level emotions has been clarified, a basis is established for identifying the interactional cycles that maintain attachment insecurity and relationship distress. This discovery of unacknowledged feelings underlying interactional positions and provision of new corrective emotional experiences is often a first step toward attitudinal and behavioral change. As the therapist reframes the problem in terms of clients' unmet attachment needs, each person can be assisted in sharing his or her needs and wants with the partner in a way that is civil and reality based. The clinician can use "softenings" to facilitate this process.

The Use of Softenings

Problematic interactional styles that maintain attachment insecurity and emotional distress are deescalated by a process Johnson and Greenberg (1994; Greenberg and Johnson, 1988) refer to as softenings. Softenings are experiences in therapy that allow family members to reconnect, particularly as they assess and begin to understand emotions such as hurt, sadness, or fear that often underlie their anger or distress (Johnson, 1996). For example, when a critical, blaming spouse shows some degree of humility and vulnerability and asks for closeness or comfort from the other spouse who theretofore has remained distant, that person is exhibiting softening behavior (Nichols and Schwartz, 2001). Therapists need to be creative and sometimes provocative in helping clients find their own unique ways of softening (e.g., "Jim, imagine for a minute that each time you blamed Sara for something or were critical of her that you took away one day from her life but that each time you were vulnerable and caring that you added one more day. Now, with that in mind, close your eyes and say something to her that will give one day to her"). When interactional patterns begin to shift, it then becomes possible for clients to enjoy new bonding experiences.

Fostering Collaboration and Facilitating New Attachment Behaviors

According to an EFT approach, change in and between clients is most likely to happen when corrective emotional experiences in therapy are provided, destructive interactional cycles are understood, and problems are reframed in light of these dynamics. It is a bit like emptying the old oil in one's car before new oil can be added. In this case the new oil is the re-creation of a new type of attachment relationship with one another. Here, couples need guidance and assistance with promoting behaviors that will continue to reinforce feelings of security, protection, closeness, and contact in the relationship. This process involves discovering and implementing pragmatic solutions to ongoing problems and issues, such as what quality time spent together means (and how much each day or week) and how this translates into meeting each person's needs (and at least some of his or her wants), as well as agreed-upon corporate needs of the relationship. In this regard, homework can be assigned and couple contracts cocreated in much the same way that behaviorally oriented (and cognitive-behavioral) therapists might do with clients (e.g., "We will average one date with each other per week in any given month, regardless of child, work, or monetary considerations. Over this period, we will meet each other in the middle so that each of us will be able to experience, or approximate, the 'ideal date.'"). However, clinicians working from an EFT perspective would stress that clients continually adhere to what they have learned from and experienced in therapy—creating safe emotional engagement, owning and voicing their own needs and wants while acknowledging those of their partners, and taking responsibility for their part in maintaining a healthy and satisfying relationship.

BREAKING OUT OF THE BOX:
CREATING SHIFTS

Reflect back to the lists you created in the incubation exercise at the beginning of the chapter. It is now time to take action as both a human being and as a therapist. With your key struggles/dynamics in mind, create a case scenario in which you and your own family (or partner) are the clients. You and your loved ones are fortunate to be assigned to a therapist by the name of Sigmund Murray Albert Johnson (or Smaj). At your therapist's disposal are an endless array of creative interventions (some described in this chapter) to use with your family or couple relationship. Allow your imagination to flow as you describe (in detail) a radical shift occurring in a single session.

Chapter 9

Creative Interventions in Ten Contemporary Schools of Thought, Part II: Structural, Strategic, Milan Systemic, Solution-Focused, Internal Family Systems, and Narrative Approaches

CREATIVE INCUBATION EXERCISE #9: THE FIVE ELEMENTS OF A SESSION

Most of us were drawn to this field because we genuinely wanted to make a difference in people's lives. The intervention phase of treatment is both exciting and challenging. In training we often talk about points of intervention when working with individuals, couples, and families. Because clinicians typically have conversations about subsystems (marital, parental, sibling) and treatment issues (marital discord, parenting competence, child acting out), we invite you to look at your sessions with the following five elements in mind as a possible guiding force to how you might intervene within a session. So, the question is, "Where is your point of intervention?"

> Element 1: The individuals (clients, adults, children, therapist, etc.)
> Element 2: The relationships (marital, child, adult, etc.)
> Element 3: The setting (environment, atmosphere, office/home, etc.)
> Element 4: The structure (organization, order, expectations, etc.)
> Element 5: The timing (session length, duration, pace, frequency, etc.)

As you read the stories of other therapists throughout this chapter, reflect upon which elements their interventions address. We will revisit the five elements at the end of the chapter.

STRUCTURAL INTERVENTIONS

Structural family therapy (Minuchin, 1974; Minuchin and Fishman, 1981) incorporates systems theory concepts, principles, and practices into an exceedingly useful approach. This entails the assessment, working, and termination phases of treatment. From a structural perspective, family dysfunction is typically the result of an inflexible family structure that prevents the system from adapting to both normal developmental transitions (individual and familial) and situational changes (e.g., crises or trauma). Difficulties can involve a pathology of boundaries, alliances, triadic relationships, or hierarchy (Walsh and McGraw, 1996). Hence, relationships need to be restructured.

This framework includes such concepts and processes as joining with and being accommodating to clients; a structural diagnosis of each person's understanding of the family's composition and his or her relationship to it, including an assessment of the family's hierarchy, current level of functioning, implicit and explicit rules, and potential for both first- and second-order change; goal setting and clarification of goals with the family; and evaluation of boundary making and boundary marking (e.g., rigid, diffuse, or clear) in one's work with the family and an analysis of ways in which family members need to restructure themselves in terms of subsystem boundaries and relationships (i.e., change the degree of disengagement or enmeshment). An example of boundary making might entail the therapist resisting triangling or temporarily siding with one person while refusing to align with other family members (joining in an alliance or coalition). The therapist may also unbalance relationships in the family or manipulate mood by temporarily affiliating more with some family members than others.

Clinicians working from a structural perspective employ a number of interventions in their work with clients. These interventions include but are in no way limited to the following:

1. Various forms of role-play (including reverse role-playing) and focusing; enactment; framing, reframing, and deframing (with regard to the family's structure or presenting problems)
2. Manipulating space in the therapy setting
3. Assigning straightforward and sometimes paradoxical tasks
4. Redirecting communication channels with clients when necessary
5. Intensifying clients' concerns and escalating stress when necessary (such as overemphasizing the seriousness of a problem and motivating clients by heightening their anxiety)
6. Providing constant support and guidance for couples and families

The therapist's use of self is also central to the structural model. This includes the therapist's ongoing use of affect and actions, such as selective self-disclosure geared toward motivating clients to act and to grow. Some specific examples of structural interventions that require a great deal of creativity, movement, and often spontaneity on the part of the therapist are briefly described as follows.

Repositioning Clients and Yourself As the Therapist

Experienced therapists know that where clients sit and how they position themselves in relation to one another (space, body angle), both in the first and subsequent sessions, says much about the family structure and relationships. This includes dynamics associated with rigid or diffuse boundaries, power, hierarchy, emotional distance and disengagement, subsystem alliances and enmeshment, and the like. Structural family therapy has long emphasized the need for physical repositioning of clients and sometimes the therapist in order to create or strengthen relational subsystems, challenge alliances, support generational boundaries (i.e., adult/parental), and disrupt existing hierarchies and power bases. For example, a daughter who sits close to her mother as her father is several feet away may be asked to move on the other side of her father as he and his wife are directed to sit next to each other. Partners in therapy may be asked to sit in chairs facing each other so that eye contact can be established and their communication can be more direct (or back to back so that they must listen to their partner without the benefit of body language). The therapist may decide to sit next to the identified patient in the family or ask someone else to sit by this person in an effort to separate him or her from this destructive role. Or the therapist may ally the parental subsystem by temporarily sitting beside them, supporting their role as parents and responsible adults in a tough-love situation with a teenager. A disruptive or uninvolved client may be given the freedom to take a break for a few minutes while the therapist interacts with other family members. Sometimes, all of the children may be asked to go to the play room or waiting room for the remainder of the session so the therapist can get the parents talking about issues that have remained unmentioned. One or both partners may be asked to stand on a chair or sit on the floor so that they can view things and people from a different perspective. The oldest child in a single-parent family may be asked to sit by his or her brothers and sisters and away from the parent in order to help this child disengage from a parental role and remind the parent that this person is a child (or adolescent) and not a coparent or surrogate spouse. Empty chairs representing nonpresent extended family members may be placed across the room in a first step toward detriangling a spouse's parents by establishing a clear boundary between the family of procreation and family of origin. Many structural therapists, no doubt, are active choreographers. As such, they have realized the profound power of repositioning. Although these interventions may seem elementary, in reality they require a great deal of creative thinking, immediacy, and sometimes courage and persistence on the part of the clinician.

The Use of Complementarity Challenges

In our work we have found that most couples and families can understand the basic principles of the Golden Rule (Do unto others as you would have them do unto you), karma (in order to get you have to give something), and the basic ideas of "win-win," "win-lose," and "lose-lose." Structural family therapists often direct discussions in therapy from linear to circular perspectives by emphasizing the importance of complementarity in relationships (Nichols and Schwartz, 2001). Often this requires that clients have a basic understanding of circular causality, which (along with other rudimentary systems theory concepts) may need to be explained initially by the therapist. Clients must become aware of how their behavior feeds into someone else's, either positively or negatively, and how this has ripple effects into the whole of the family or the interactional nature of the couple relationship. Hence, as Nichols and Schwartz aptly illustrate:

> The mother who complains that her son is naughty is taught to consider what she's doing to stimulate or maintain his behavior. . . . The wife who nags her husband to spend more time with her must learn to make increased involvement more attractive. The husband who complains that his wife never listens to him may have to listen to her more, before she's willing to reciprocate. (2001, p. 257)

Although at times direct challenges may need to be directed toward certain family members or the family as a whole (e.g., "I think there are other things happening in your family that do not support your interpretation that your son is causing all the problems"), creative therapists may also find backdoor ways of implementing complementarity challenges, such as using analogies to help the family understand the interrelatedness of people's actions. If, for example, the family enjoys sports, an analogy involving teams can be used to explain how the actions of one or more team members serve as both cause and effect in regard to everyone involved. Even simple analogies, such as a pilot and those in the control tower, or a person's (or family's) care of a pet (loving and responsible as opposed to neglectful or critical) and how this affects the dyadic relationship between owner and animal, may be effective. Analogies can serve as a bridge to helping family members understand their own problem maintenance and potential restructuring of their ways of relating.

Challenging the Client's Current View of Reality, Including the "Symptom"

Clients presenting for therapy are typically set in their interpretation of the problem(s) or symptoms they are experiencing and tend to have rigid cognitive perceptions of themselves and of reality in general (Fenell and Weinhold, 1997). The structural family therapist "will challenge those realities, not to convince the family that they are wrong but to show them there are other ways to be right. . . . When the family accepts a different way of thinking about the situation, structural change becomes more likely" (Fenell and Weinhold, 1997, pp. 163-164). A great deal of creativity in thought and action is needed to help clients acquire alternative realities about particular difficulties and situations. For example, a woman who has chosen to go back to college or graduate school may be perceived as being less dedicated to her husband and children and is, hence, putting the family at risk. However, the creative therapist can assist family members in understanding things from a different point of view (e.g., mother's needs and motivation to succeed) and in imagining the potential benefits of her going back to school in both the short and long run (e.g., increased financial security for the family down the road and a happier, more satisfied wife and mother in the meantime). Even things perceived as being more difficult for particular family members can be modified. For instance, the teenage daughter may begin to realize that there are some sideline benefits for her. (For example, the daughter may say, "I know I am going to have to take up more slack while Mom is in school, so maybe it's time I learned to be a little less selfish and a little more responsible now that I'm seventeen and getting ready to graduate from high school next year. Anyway, I know when I have helped out more around the house in the past, both Mom and Dad have treated me more like a grown-up and given me a bit more freedom.") The husband, too, may realize that he has some things to gain. ("When she is challenged and more fulfilled in her life, our relationship seems to be happier even if we have less time together.") Moreover, creativity is required in helping clients gain a new perspective on their presenting problems. Often, symptoms need to be relabeled, expanded, exaggerated, de-emphasized, replaced, or otherwise altered (Aponte and Van Deusen, 1981) before progress can be made. Perhaps it is true that clients can only be assisted in thinking outside their own boxes to the extent that the clinician is able to think outside of his or her own. Knowing when and how to use one's expert power in challenging clients' rigidly held beliefs at particular times in therapy is central to a structural approach. ("All of my training and experience in working with families is convincing me the reason Amy is acting out is because she does not feel that she has access to you as her mother and father.") At other times, however, the creative therapist will know or sense when to use the art of gentle persuasion and diplomacy. ("Just suppose that there was another way of looking at this situation. What might it be? Pretend you knew the answer to this question. Let's explore the possibilities.")

STRATEGIC FAMILY THERAPY AND MRI BRIEF THERAPY/COMMUNICATIONS APPROACHES

Since strategic family therapy (SFT) is based to a large degree on the contributions of various individuals at the Mental Research Institute (MRI) in Palo Alto, California, which emphasized a brief therapy/communications approach to treating couples and families, some interventions inherent to these two approaches will be discussed together here. SFT was officially launched in the 1970s by Jay Haley and Cloe Madanes. However, Haley's association with the now-famous affiliates of the MRI (Gregory Bateson, Milton Erickson, Don Jackson, John Weakland, Richard Fisch, Carlos Sluzki, Virginia Satir, Paul Watzlawick, and their colleagues) is evident in much of his work, including that with Madanes. The focus of SFT is on the interactional patterns in couple and family relationships that maintain problematic behavior. These patterns involve, for example, alliances, various types of communication (both healthy and deviant or dysfunctional), and power dynamics (Nichols and Schwartz, 2001). Specific goals of therapy are identified early in the process, and problem-oriented strategies are utilized to disrupt unhealthy patterns and help family members develop new ways of behaving toward one another. SFT and the communications approach are rooted in family systems theory (homeostasis, circular causality, etc.) and various theories and models of human communication. Although strategic therapists in particular take on a lot of responsibility for clients' movements in therapy, identifying inroads and possible solutions and pinpointing how clients' attempted solutions have become part of the symptom picture, they do not believe in engineering solutions. Planful change is cocreated with clients, and insight is de-emphasized.

Strategic family therapy has several areas of distinctiveness. These include specifying explicit and concrete goals for therapy with clients, an emphasis on second-order change, the use of straightforward directives in accomplishing goals, attention to the various types of communication in couple and family relationships (e.g., double bind, vague, metaphorical and symbolic), reframing (relabeling) of relationship difficulties and options, and the employment of paradoxical strategies intended to decrease resistance and bring about change (e.g., symptom prescription, restraining change). SFT is generally a brief approach to working with couples and families, and strategic therapists tend to be active, directive, pragmatic, and very much in control of the therapy session. The therapist seeks to create a supportive but challenging relationship with clients. This requires a great deal of flexibility, spontaneity, and creativity on the part of the clinician (Walsh and McGraw, 1996).

The 180-Degree Shift

One intervention generated by therapists associated with the MRI has been commonly referred to as the 180-degree shift (Fisch, Weakland, and Segal, 1982). In this approach, clients are instructed or encouraged to completely turn away from their attempted solutions to the problem and try something entirely new—often something that is the opposite of what they have been doing. Obviously, this runs counterintuitive to the couple or family's paradigm and customary way of approaching the problem, and the therapist must often engage in creative reframing to both prepare clients for a bold move and support them throughout the process. In this situation the purpose of reframing is not to educate or produce insight but to induce compliance (Nichols and Schwartz, 2001). Hence, the overprotective parent is asked to back off and give an adolescent more freedom of choice and independence. The jealous husband is told to support his wife in her attempts to make new friends at work and in the neighborhood, be they male or female. Parents who are trying to pressure their sixteen-year-old daughter to stop dating someone so unsuitable are instructed not necessarily to change their rules or cease from enforcing them, but rather to refrain from lecturing her and belittling the young man, to listen more carefully to their daughter and treat her with greater respect, to enforce their rules in a radically different way (e.g., lead rather than push), to share their perspectives and concerns from the heart more than from the head, and to futurize with her about the hopes and dreams she has for herself. Talk therapy alone may not be enough to get families turned in a new direction. These issues may need to be seen, felt, renegotiated, and practiced through a series of creative enactments, role-plays, or imagined scenarios before they have sticking power.

Use of Metaphors

Selection and use of metaphors, although not unique to strategic family therapy, has long been one of its trademarks. There are a variety of metaphors at the therapist's disposal. For example, individuals, partners, and family members "can describe themselves, each other, or certain dynamics as colors, styles of music, household objects, foods, shapes, modes of transportation, sounds, book titles, toys, games, or articles of clothing" (Deacon and Piercy, 2001, p. 368). The therapist can then ask why clients chose their metaphors and what they symbolize. Metaphors generally work especially well with children and often put clients at ease. Moreover, the information generated can be extremely useful to clinicians as they come to understand the themes behind the metaphors and help family members make connections.

Satir's Sensory-Based Communication

Few therapists have been able to work more fervently and successfully in the moment with couples and families than Virginia Satir. Satir had almost a magical way of engaging people's senses (physiological and emotional) and, in so doing, identifying central patterns and themes, helping clients focus more on health and possibilities than on pathology, providing hope, and empowering clients toward change. From a Satirian perspective, although clients are always the script-writers, the therapist is the master director/choreographer. Creative therapy is being able to both track and stimulate clients' movement back and forth from feeling states to visual processing to somatic awareness to relational dynamics. Although much of Satir's influence on couples and families was no doubt the result of her keen and unique engagement of self as therapist, she also employed a number of creative interventions. One that we especially like is her use of sensory-based communication. This type of communication is different in that it leads to experiential insights in addition to cognitive ones. For example, some questions used in this type of intervention follow:

- "If you listen only to the tone of your son's voice, what do you hear?"
- "When you criticize yourself inside your head, whose voice do you hear?"

- "Now that you know where your mother's hurt is inside her, what would you like to say to that part of her?"
- "Tell your father, where in your body is your fear located? Visualize it and give it a name. What is it called?"

These types of questions and statements help clients integrate self and sometimes lost parts of the self with family system dynamics.

Pretending to Do Something Else Instead

Haley (1984) uses "ordeal therapy" as a paradoxical maneuver to motivate clients toward symptom reduction or removal. In this method, noxious directives prescribed by the therapist are paired with symptoms displayed at home which, after time, make clients' symptoms more trouble than they are worth. However, as Madanes (1981) notes, since clients are often more willing to carry out novel assignments or tasks if they are framed in the context of playing or pretending, we prefer to pair symptoms with more pleasant (and hopefully constructive) experiences in the family or couple relationship, even if they are made up on the spot and have an element of buffoonery. One way of doing this is through pretend-oriented homework assignments. Some examples of implementing this directive, which may perhaps be enacted first in session, are as follows:

1. "Next time you start having a fight at home, for ten whole minutes pretend that you are a 'super couple' with capes on your backs who are able to leap tall buildings in a single bound and solve all your difficulties. Now, here is a cape for each of you to put on when you start your next argument."
2. "When your preschooler begins to throw a temper tantrum, pretend that you are being attacked by an invisible fly and need the child's help to swat and kill it and then ask him to give you a hug and kiss to feel better. This may help him feel more grown-up."
3. "Pretend that the two of you are secretaries of state from two major nations working together to solve a crisis the next time your teenager rebels against you and present a united rather than divided front. Imagine what skills of negotiation and partnership you would need to employ, and do this each and every time that chaos breaks out these next two weeks before I see you again."

Again, roles for pretending (and their prescribed duration) will need to be established and agreed upon in session before they are carried out at home. Although these kinds of tasks may seem silly and simplistic to clients when they are first given them, these interventions are based on two proven principles: (1) one of the best ways to decrease or eliminate an undesired behavior is to do the opposite (i.e., an incompatible behavior) and (2) play introduces some level of humor, which is often empowering and helps people put things back in perspective (i.e., realize that there is a nonserious side to life and many issues), if even temporarily.

MILAN SYSTEMIC INTERVENTIONS

Systemic family therapy is based on the work of Mara Selvini Palazzoli, Luigi Boscolo, Gianfranco Cecchin, Giuliana Prata, and their colleagues in Milan, Italy. This approach, which leans heavily on family systems theory, views presenting problems as serving a particular function in the family system. Cognitive processes (e.g., ideas, beliefs, perceptions, wishes) of family members form a map that needs to be understood and challenged in therapy. This map, or familial view of reality, guides their behavior. All families also have games that illustrate patterns and interactive organization. These games are regulated by certain rules that family members have adopted (implicit and explicit). Family games can be benign or pathological. As Walsh and McGraw (1996, p. 78) indicate, an overarching goal of the therapy team is to "have the family discover, interrupt, and eventually change the rules of their game (i.e., the relational dynamic underlying the family dysfunction)."

Therapy sessions, according to the Milan approach, are often conducted several weeks apart (e.g., a month) for longer periods of time (two or more hours) by a therapy team. In accurately assessing and diagnosing difficulties, the therapists engage in various types of hypothesizing. A good part of therapy, according to systemic therapists, is hypothesis testing in which possible explanations for family problems are entertained along with possible ways to bring about positive change. Also central to this approach is the use of circular questioning in which therapists use circularity to acquire information about the family. There are a variety of types of circular questions. These generally take the form of the therapist(s) asking one family member to comment on what he or she thinks that another person in the family would feel or perceive about a change related to someone else in the family. The therapist might also act as if the change happened or was the case (e.g., "Judy, how do you think your brother Sam would feel if your father started spending more time with him?" "Bob, how will things change for your wife when your daughter Judy leaves for college this fall?"). Finally, systemic therapists make use of positive connotation (similar to reframing), prescriptions surrounding ritual and ceremony intended to alter family games, and various uses of paradox and counterparadox (e.g., prescribing to the family no change in a particular area of their lives for now since things seem to be working for them). Some interventions are discussed in the next section.

Circular (and Hypothetical) Questioning

Circular questions can facilitate psychological movement in client systems throughout the course of therapy. This type of questioning stresses the importance of mutual responsibility and interdependence. The therapist's skillful and artful use of circular questions can increase family members' understanding and perspective taking, reframe perceptions and challenge biases, and help clients contemplate the future from multiple frameworks. Clients are put in a place where they have to take an outside view of things (i.e., a metaposition where they have to think divergently or outside the box). These questions are often triggered or guided by a hunch the therapist has (i.e., often intuitive) or a hypothesis he or she wants to test. Hypothesis testing thus becomes a dynamic, evolving part of the process of systemic family therapy. Circular questions often have to do with closeness or distance in relationships, perceptions of problems or conflicts ("How serious does he see the problem on a scale of one to ten?"), and time (past events or future predictions, such as "If this continues, what do you think will happen?").

Some examples of circular questions follow.

- "If you were to leave, what would he do?"
- "John, how do you think Susan feels when William speaks that way to her?"
- "Alice, I wonder what would happen if you stopped getting on Pete's case about his drinking and left it alone for a while?"

- "When you get angry to cover up your hurt or vulnerability, how does your wife/parent/child interpret that?"
- "What will your life and those of the children be like three years from now if you are no longer married?"
- "Who in the family is most upset about Tom's behavior? Who would be next?"
- "Which two members in the family are the closest? Next? Most distant?"
- "If the conflict between you and your wife were to decrease, do you think Peter's acting out at school and home would increase or decrease?"
- "Jennifer, if this problem were to go away, what would your mom say the next problem would be? How about you?"

Creating and Implementing Family Rituals

Family rituals are highly repetitive and stylized types of interactions governed by unspoken rules (Berg-Cross, 2000). As such they make family life predictable. Rituals can be stabilizing, growth-promoting behaviors that help families remain cohesive and maintain a unique identity, or they can support homeostatic dysfunction. Although most rituals seem to evolve by happenstance, underneath they are purposeful although not always consciously planned activities (Berg-Cross, 2000).

Prescribing rituals and ceremonies is a central component of systemic and, to some extent, strategic family therapy. These prescriptions are intended to alter family games and patterns. Rituals, ceremonies, and counter family games help family members discover, interrupt, and eventually change the rules of the games that keep them stuck. They can also help create greater awareness of the meaning of their symptoms, keeping in mind that a repetitive symptomatic pattern of interaction also typically functions as a ritual form of behavior (Sherman and Fredman, 1986). Creative use of rituals can be employed that will engage the whole family in a series of actions that run counter to rigid family rules and myths (Nichols and Schwartz, 2001). For example, clients can be told to take a vacation from their problems for at least three days and nights this week (or every other day between now and their next session). Here, straightforward directives can be used to assign family members specific roles and the entire family detailed "dos and don'ts" (e.g., "do tell stories and talk about the events of the day each evening at dinner; don't criticize, complain, or argue during dinner or at any time during your family vacation, day or night"). Rituals can also be prescribed that will exaggerate family symptoms (in this case having a paradoxical effect). Members of the family, for instance, could be instructed to worry about a particular family member (e.g., the identified patient) as hard as they can from 7 to 8 p.m. every night this week, while the patient is told to worry about everyone else (and maybe their worrying) during this time frame. For ten minutes after this period each night, the patient and his or her family members must then express their gratitude to one another for caring enough to worry so much. Eventually, family members may learn that they have it within their power to rewrite their own rules that have come to dictate how they interact.

Modified Uses of Paradox

Although paradoxical techniques are still commonly used by some systemic, structural, and strategic therapists, other clinicians, because of the deception involved in their use, "have abandoned them or present them humorously and are honest about their intent" (Nichols and Schwartz, 2001, p. 361). This sentence sums up our position. Paradoxical approaches, in our view, should be reserved for unique and exceptional situations in therapy (e.g., excessive and persistent client resistance, power playing, or manipulation) and are sometimes last-ditch interventions when direct approaches have been unsuccessful or ineffective (e.g., when treating some types of sexual dysfunction in relationships). In most cases we do not recommend paradoxical techniques in the strict sense of, for example, prescribing symptoms, predicting relapse, or restraining change. However, family therapy has ample room for the creative use of hyperbole, temporary exaggeration of symptoms, and out-positioning (i.e., channeling the family's resistance toward therapeutic ends). For instance, in the previous example of the exaggerated family ritual where family members were told to worry excessively about one another, we would be up front with our clients about the apparent ridiculousness of the assignment but encourage them in a playful sort of way to just play along for a week or two on this. Families could also be asked to act on the directive playfully and in pretend fashion in session, then follow this scenario with a discussion and application to their own situation. Simply put, our motive is not some hidden agenda or power-laden approach to implementing a paradoxical intervention in hopes that we could outmanipulate the family so they would change.

Another example would be when certain individuals need to out-position others in the family (or other) system. In order to put a stop to the invasive or manipulative efforts of extended family members in their lives after repeated attempts at doing so, one couple was instructed to, for a period of time, accentuate rather than resist the very dynamics involved in his family's controlling behavior. The man, who worked for his father on the family ranch, was told to make a list of twenty more things he and his wife would like his father and mother to do for them above and beyond what they already try to do (with some requests being outlandish). When this list was presented one Sunday afternoon with initial seriousness on the part of the clients, the rancher's parents were soon overwhelmed after they got to about the eighth item on the list, saying that they "just didn't know if they could take on all those new responsibilities for the couple." Although things did not change overnight, soon a new picture of the situation began to emerge for the rancher's parents—not out of frustration or because of direct confrontation (which had failed in the past), but with the help of some gentle, humor-oriented use of paradox.

SOLUTION-FOCUSED INTERVENTIONS

Solution-focused therapy, developed by Steve de Shazer and popularized by Bill O'Hanlon, Insoo Kim Berg, and others, is a brief approach to working with individuals, couples, and families. As the name suggests, this therapy focuses on solutions more than problems in couple and family relationships and on existing strengths more than areas of deficit. Presenting difficulties (referred to as complaints) are taken at face value. Solution-focused therapy is based on the assumption that attempted solutions of clients often become as problematic as the presenting problems themselves and thus feed into the larger symptom picture. This perspective emphasizes first-order change, in that the primary objective of therapy is to address the client's immediate concerns. Hence, goal formation is a central aspect of the first session or two, and these goals must be specific, measurable, attainable, and challenging.

Unique components of solution-focused therapy include the following:

- The use of scaling to estimate the degree of problem difficulty, shifts in emotional states, and accomplished steps toward change
- Regular discussion of exceptions to the problem (e.g., At what times and under what circumstances is the problem not there?)
- A focus on existing strengths in their relationships as a couple or family
- An emphasis on normalizing clients' struggles and difficulties
- Frequent compliments and assignment of homework
- Use of the miracle question (i.e., "Suppose that one night while you were sleeping a miracle happened and this problem was solved. How would you know? What would be different? How would others know?")

Some other specific interventions outlined by O'Hanlon and Beadle (1997), which we have found particularly useful and which have much room for creative modification and application with couples and families, include the following.

Change the Viewing with Clients

O'Hanlon and Beadle (1997) describe several methods for helping clients change their views of themselves and the problem. These include:

1. Assuming and focusing on past and present times without the problem (exceptions)
2. Deframing, which challenges and introduces doubts into old beliefs that are not helping, such as those centering on self-blame, invalidation, and rigid self-images
3. Depathologizing clients by changing labels (e.g., "Maybe you hadn't heard, 'borderlines' are now known as 'interfaces,' and that changes everything") and beating them to the punch by

describing the problem in a less dysfunctional and more solu-
tion-oriented way before clients have a chance to pathologize
themselves or their difficulties

4. Framing current difficulties as an individual or family developmental stage (one way of normalizing problems)

5. Externalizing the problem and using metaphors and stories to
help clients understand and have permission to be struggling

6. Providing new frames of reference, such as through using action
descriptions rather than labels ("So there have been a lot of
times lately when you've had trouble falling asleep," rather than
"I see you have a sleep disorder" or "Oh, you're an insomniac,
huh?") and providing useful alternate views that fit the facts of
the situation ("So you have bought into the cultural idea that
people have to look a certain way or be at a certain weight before they can feel good about themselves and be accepted by
others?")

Mapping Problems and Goals in Therapy

O'Hanlon and Beadle (1997) have several creative ideas for assessment, goal setting, and charting the course of therapy. Some of
these include:

- Use multiple choice questions and statements in gathering information ("Does that mean that you need some more freedom
and space in your marriage, that you just don't like some of the
things he does, or that you would like to leave him?")

- Presuppose goal achievement that creates expected or desired
outcomes ("What will your relationship with her be like when
you begin to feel better and not so depressed?" "As you and your
teenager get a better handle on her difficulties at school, in what
ways will you begin to enjoy each other more as mother and
daughter?")

- Whenever possible and appropriate, use nonmedical everyday
language with clients in describing presenting problems (e.g.,
"difficulties," "struggles," "concerns," "feeling bad") and goals
of therapy rather than clinical labels and terminology (e.g., bipolar disorder, anorexia) or problem/symptom talk with clients

- When even smaller goals seem too big, focus on trends and desired directions for change ("So we'll know we are making progress when the trust between the two of you feels a bit stronger and the fear is beginning to fade?")

Helping Clients Connect with Internal and External Resources

O'Hanlon and Beadle (1997) have a number of suggestions for helping clients find and utilize their existing strengths and resources. Some of these are:

- Using examples of the clients' own histories to evoke inner experiences of resourcefulness and competence ("You said you had closer friendships in the past. Tell me more about how those grew from a mustard seed and what made them grow close.")
- Discovering what has worked for clients in similar situations or others with these kinds of difficulties ("You said you talked with a therapist about this once before. What happened in that situation that helped you get a handle on the problem?")
- Finding and transferring competence ("You have been a highly successful business owner for twenty years and have made it through many ups and downs. How can you use some of those same skills in saving your marriage from bankruptcy and helping it flourish again?")
- Asking who else in the community could help (e.g., exploring resources and supports with clients, be they clubs, organizations, religious institutions, self-help groups, etc.)
- Exploring why the problem has not gotten worse by asking clients to explain to you what has kept them from going deeper into their problems ("Despite your highly charged emotional relationship, what has kept the two of you from becoming physically violent with each other all these years?")

Solution-focused approaches, although not a panacea, give clinicians practical starting and maneuvering points throughout the course of therapy. They allow therapists limitless opportunities for creative modifications and extensions while building on existing strengths of clients, instilling hope, depathologizing problems, and helping them feel OK about being fully human.

INTERNAL FAMILY SYSTEMS INTERVENTIONS

Internal family systems (IFS) therapy, developed by Richard Schwartz, includes a blend of concepts and principles derived from certain family systems-oriented approaches (i.e., structural, strategic, and Bowenian), psychodynamic theories, and narrative family therapy. This approach focuses on subpersonalities or parts within family members (similar to the notions of ego states, internal objects, schemas, or roles). What makes parts unique is that they are actual components of one's personality that often become polarized or compartmentalized within the individual, in other words, fragmented from the self. This fragmentation can create internal pain and conflict within individual family members that have ripple effects into the health and functioning of the family as a whole. Moreover, certain parts within individuals can become isolated, estranged, or protected from others in the family, or in conflict with one or more of their parts.

According to Schwartz (1995), there are three categories of roles that parts commonly adopt when a person has been hurt or traumatized in life. These are really groups of parts that include: (1) exiles (those parts that contain the pain, fear, and sadness from past painful experiences); (2) managers (group of parts that tries to keep the exiles locked away and out of consciousness so that further hurt or vulnerability is avoided); and (3) firefighters (groups of parts that put out the fires of feeling that emerge when exiles threaten to take over if managers fail, often by dousing them with excessive eating, drinking, food, work, and other self-abusing activities). Hence, the major goal of therapy is to help family members get in tune with the language and function of their various parts or groups of parts (be they those listed previously or others identified and named) and be able to give a particular part or parts a voice that will help family members better understand one another and their difficulties. The idea is that it is easier (and less threatening) for each family member to begin changing a small part of himself or herself rather than change one's whole personality (which is not possible, necessary, or recommended). In this way, as Nichols and Schwartz (1998, p. 429) note: "Father is transformed from a raging tyrant to being a good man struggling with his angry part. The view of Mother is likewise changed by this multiplicity perspective of personality, which is more benevolent and holds more potential for change than the idea that people have unitary or fixed personalities." Other goals of IFS therapy include helping family members track the pattern of parts' interactions across people and inviting each person to focus on his or her own parts rather than trying to change someone else's parts.

In our view, the richness of this approach lies much more in the area of theory and assessment than in a detailed description of therapeutic interventions. In fact, Schwartz (1995) himself emphasizes that IFS therapy is not a set of techniques but rather a framework for understanding people. However, some specific applications can nevertheless be gleaned from Schwartz's writings. According to Nichols and Schwartz (2001), "Since there are a variety of ways to uncover and work with parts, therapists have used the model with a wide range of methods, including psychodrama, dance therapy, art therapy, and play therapy with children" (p. 429). Some specific methods are briefly outlined as follows.

Identifying Parts of Individual Family Members and Giving Them a Voice

A voice can be given to people's parts through a variety of means. Children can draw pictures, color, or use dolls or puppets to illustrate one or more of their parts. Couples can sculpt certain parts of themselves that have difficulty relating to each other. Therapists can also ask clients direct questions as they explore and identify key parts of themselves (e.g., "While you are discussing the problem, will you give me permission to comment on certain parts of you both that make it difficult for you to trust and connect with each other?").

Having Clients Converse with Parts of Themselves and Others

Therapists can also get a dialogue going between a person and a particular part of himself or herself that needs to be addressed. For example, after helping the client name the part and identify where it is located in the body, a conversation can be initiated between the person and that part, as well as other parts of the person that fight or keep the hurt, fearful part from being expressed (i.e., having a voice). The following segment of a session may help illustrate this intervention. The therapist is working with a couple in which an unhappy wife is afraid of standing up to her negligent (and sometimes dominating) husband, who tends to get caught up in his work and own leisure activities, for fear that he might leave her if she did.

THERAPIST: Tell me, where in your body is your fear located? Where do you feel it the most?

WIFE: Right here in my throat.

THERAPIST: Can you give your fear a name?

WIFE: What do you mean?

THERAPIST: Call it something.

WIFE: OK, I'll call it The Choker because I feel like it suffocates me every time I want to speak out to my husband about my feelings and his behavior.

THERAPIST: How do you feel about The Choker right now?

WIFE: I feel like telling it to get lost once and for all.

THERAPIST: Rather than telling The Choker to get lost, I'm wondering if you can give it a voice. Will you work with me on this?

WIFE: Yes, I think so.

THERAPIST: OK, good. But first I want you to do something else. Identify the part of your husband that you are having the most difficulty with and that causes you pain. What would you call that part?

WIFE: I'd call it Mr. Distracted.

THERAPIST: Where is it located in your husband?

WIFE: Right in the center of his forehead.

THERAPIST: Very good. Now, I want The Choker to talk to Mr. Distracted. Choker, what do you want or need to say to Mr. Distracted?

WIFE: I want you to stop being so self-absorbed and start listening to me as a person and paying a little more attention to me.

THERAPIST: (to husband, looking directly at his forehead) Mr. Distracted, please respond to The Choker.

An enlightening dialogue ensued between these parts of the clients, with the therapist keeping things focused and moving forward. In a short time the couple began to realize that not everything about their relationship that had gone bad, but a portion of it (supported by certain parts) needed to be addressed and remedied. This procedure kept the dialogue between husband and wife from becoming overgeneralized, catastrophized, and too personal. In one sense it is one way of externalizing the problem through an internalization process. As is evident from this brief scenario, there are many possible variations to a parts conversation. Often a conversation needs to take place among two or more parts within one person before, or in addition to, the instigation of a dialogue between various parts of individuals within the family or couple relationship. The IFS model can also be used to objectify and reify feelings of clients (e.g., "Give Mr. Fear a voice. What does he want to say to The Dominator?").

Using Guided Imagery and the Empty Chair in Parts Conversations

Sometimes in therapy, rather than initiating a direct conversation among people's parts, it may be useful to use other (perhaps less confrontational) methods. For instance, guided imagery can be used to take a client to a safe and pleasant place (e.g., a forest or the beach) where identified parts (either of one's own or between family members) can meet, dialogue, and hopefully heal and become more unified with the self. The empty chair can also be used in both individual and couples/family therapy to externalize a part of the self and converse with it (or a part of someone else). This may prove to be less threatening, especially in situations in which the risks of sharing or confronting are greater.

NARRATIVE INTERVENTIONS

Narrative Family Therapy (NFT) is based on a postmodern, constructionist worldview. According to this perspective, reality is constructed in conversation among people, and as such is time, context, and culture bound. Therapy, hence, is a co-constructed enterprise between therapist and clients. Founded in the early 1990s by Michael White and David Epston, narrative therapy has become one of the more popular approaches to working with couples and families. From a NFT framework, families in treatment often see their problems as if they were a concrete, stable entity (e.g., "Ours is a problem marriage; Billy is a delinquent; Mary is depressed"). One objective of NFT is to reshape clients' experiences by modifying the language they use to describe them.

Couples and families develop a dominant story about their lives and difficulties which permeates their view of each other and their understanding of reality. Thus, clients become saturated with problem descriptions (problem-saturated narratives) of their life together and fail to see and appreciate strengths of one another, good times they occasionally have, or times when the problems do not manifest themselves (exceptions). Clients need to be assisted in revitalizing subjugated (untold) stories (e.g., ones pointing to areas of resiliency and happy or more peaceful times in their relationship) that have been ignored or pushed underground. Therapy also involves helping them write (construct) new stories (narratives) that help redefine their lives and externalize their problems from themselves. In other words, they cease to define themselves and each other as "the problem" by viewing it as an external entity that can be resolved or managed. Through the process of identifying times when they successfully controlled or dealt with the problem, eventually new stories are developed that contain a new interpretation of the meaning of events in their lives, both past and present. Sometimes problem-focused stories are reinforced by dominant cultural discourses (e.g., related to weight and appearance, gender-based double standards, money, status, race, etc.) that need to be deconstructed throughout the course of therapy. Both courage and creativity are required for clients to separate themselves from the dominant cultural narratives they have internalized and prepare themselves for alternative life stories.

Narrative therapy is solution focused in that it helps families both recall previous successes at dealing with problems, develop new life stories and themes as problem solvers, and understand and appreciate the unique outcomes associated with old and perhaps forgotten successes as well as new narratives. Landscape-of-action questions (ones that focus on both the recent and more distant history of exceptions or unique outcomes) and landscape-of-meaning questions (ones that encourage clients to review and articulate the commitments that drive them to perform these alternate preferences or counterplots) are used to help clients deconstruct and coconstruct their realities (White, 1993). Externalization is used to separate individuals from their symptoms and problems, often by objectifying and naming the problem so that the family feels more empowered to work together against it. Clients are encouraged to tell and retell their newly constructed stories to significant people in their lives. In this way, newly authored stories will gain greater prominence and power, and formerly dominant stories will gradually lose their grip.

Finally, the role of the therapist from a NFT perspective is one of consultant and confidant, and much effort is spent on empowering clients by treating them with great respect and dignity, listening to their stories and viewpoints, de-emphasizing blame, and encouraging openness and honesty among all parties through verbal and written feedback. Narrative therapists will also sometimes use a reflecting team to observe the process of therapy and comment on the progress and behavior of both therapist and clients. Moreover, therapeutic certificates are sometimes awarded in an effort to help clients feel good about successes made or problems resolved. Some techniques inherent to this approach are briefly described as follows.

Letter Writing

Letters are one way of constructing new stories with clients. Narrative therapists often communicate to clients in writing, typically constructing letters or notes to them between sessions. Clients are also asked to write letters to one another that might describe their efforts to resolve difficulties and reauthor their lives. These letters might also include comments verifying successes made and statements that encourage family members to continue searching, striving, learning, and growing. A client might also be asked to write himself or herself a letter that identifies and validates personal positive attributes, and then read it to his or her family members in session. Another variation of letter writing is to have the client compose a tape-recorded message about his or her successes, hopes, and possibilities and play it back so others can listen to it (Thompson, 1996). White and Epston (1990) describe several different types of letters that can be used in therapy, such as letters of invitation, prediction, and reference. Another method employed by narrative therapists entails writing collaborative case notes with clients near the end of the session.

Ways of Externalizing the Problem and Looking for Exceptions

Similar to solution-focused therapy, a major goal of narrative therapy is to help clients externalize (and often personify) problems so that they can speak to them. Another goal is to identify exceptions to the problem or unique outcomes in their lives (sometimes referred to as "sparkling events"). These events can be historical, current, or even future oriented (i.e., what clients believe they have the capacity to do differently). Unique outcomes can also include a search for talents and abilities of individuals that are buried or veiled by a life problem. The therapist can use these discoveries to challenge clients' dominant stories and enhance newly created stories. One approach to externalizing and discussing unique outcomes is to ask exploratory questions that serve an evaluative purpose.

Examples of these types of questions include:

- "What has the problem talked you into?"
- "What does the problem have you doing that goes against your better judgment?"
- "How has the problem affected your life and influenced your thoughts, feelings, and actions?"
- "How were you recruited into these ways of thinking/feeling/interacting with regard to yourself or your relationship?"
- "If you could give your pain a voice, what would it say right now?"
- "What patterns in your relationship have been dominated by the problem, and which haven't?"
- "What is the effect of the problem for you and those close to you?"
- "What are some examples of teamwork in your marriage that remain outside of these patterns?"
- "If you could give this teamwork a name, what would it be?"

Questions can also be posed that address future possibilities, such as, "If you were to write a newspaper headline that described your life now, what would it read? What would it say six months from now?" These types of questions help therapist and clients map how the problem has managed to disrupt or dominate the system, versus how much they have been able to control it, so that people can pull together in a united front against the problem and regain control over it rather than it over them (Nichols and Schwartz, 2001).

Using the Metaphor of Teamwork in Narrative Therapy

Sween (2000) has recently outlined an approach for emphasizing teamwork in couple therapy that, in our view, could also be extended to working with clients. Since many couples come to therapy readily identifying their partner as the problem, asking about their teamwork at the beginning of therapy "can help each partner feel heard, shift the location of the problem, align the couple toward the desired outcome, and create a structure that can be returned to throughout the course of therapy" (p. 76). Partners are first reminded that, because they are two different people, conflict is inevitable in intimate relationships and that what is important is how they face or deal with that conflict. They are then asked two questions: (1) "When your teamwork is really good, what is that like?" and (2) "When your teamwork is really bad, what is that like?" A follow-up question is posed after each of these questions that asks whether there is a phrase, a memory, or a metaphor that really captures the feelings of the good and the bad. Sween provides an excellent list of examples from clients of teamwork at its best ("riding on a motorcycle across the dunes") and teamwork at its worst ("being in the mosh pit"). He notes that clients' responses can function like emblems, phrases into which multiple layers of meaning are compressed. By creating shorthand expressions for feelings and experiences, often clients are able to choose a different pattern of behaving or relating without having to be wrong or the one who has to once again sacrifice.

The metaphor of teamwork provides a convenient way to address difficulties without accusing the other person. According to Sween (2000), by asking about both aspects of a couple's teamwork, painful accounts of life experiences are allowed to be heard. This process creates greater receptiveness and provides a means for couples to acknowledge pain without becoming immersed in it. It also helps couples view their relationship from a different perspective and encourages them to work together against their common difficulties rather than against each other as the problem. This makes cooperation more likely. In addition, using the metaphor of teamwork helps normalize the couple's situation by placing them in the ranks of all other couples who struggle with conflict. Then, in the later stages of therapy, Sween

(2000) recommends referring back to some of the original metaphors to see what has changed, "weaving together as many threads as possible around the couple's metaphors of teamwork" (p. 80).

Mobilizing Interpersonal Support for Clients' Preferred Stories

The ultimate goal of NFT is to replace clients' dominant stories with alternatively constructed preferred stories. However, this can rarely if ever be done without the support of relatives, friends, colleagues, and others in the community. Narrative therapy emphasizes the need of clients to share their newly acquired self-knowledge and relational progress with others. In doing this, new stories are metaphorically performed in public, partly in an effort to recruit others in understanding, appreciating, and supporting clients' progress and newly held position of their lives. Social support is important in helping to stabilize and promote endurance of clients' self-descriptions and capacities for affirming themselves. In accomplishing this objective, therapists and clients must carefully target potential supports and brainstorm workable plans for recruitment. These actions can take the form of phone calls, letters, e-mail, planned gatherings, and volunteer involvement in people's lives in ways that are mutually beneficial and not based solely on the needs and wants of clients. However, realistic expectations must be put in place, as others are often not nearly as excited about our progress as we are or quick to give us their support and affirmation. Hence, one aspect of creative therapy in this regard entails the preparation of clients for the possible lack of response and encouragement on the part of some whom they contact. Some rejection must also be anticipated but not internalized as such. On the other hand, these realistic expectations and potential outcomes must be balanced with a sense of optimism, persistence, and strong belief in oneself. Clients must carry with them the power of positive expectancy while at the same time not setting themselves up for disappointment. Balancing these two dynamics is an ongoing creative endeavor.

BREAKING OUT OF THE BOX:
ELEMENTAL CHANGES

At the beginning of Chapter 6 we introduced you to Ruth and Jesse who were having difficulties in their marriage after the death of their youngest child. Utilizing the five elements, or points of interventions, discussed at the beginning of this chapter, design one possible creative intervention for each element. For example, one means to support Ruth and Jesse in their grief may be to have a session or two beside their child's grave or the site of the accident (Element 3: The setting). Another example would be to invite (with everyone's permission) another couple that has experienced a similar loss and are further along in their grief process to join Jesse and Ruth in session. This might facilitate a sense of hope within their marriage (Element 2: The relationships) as well as individually in their personal feelings of loss and despair (Element 1: The individuals).

Chapter 10

The Importance of Creativity
in Supervision

CREATIVE INCUBATION EXERCISE #10:
COMPETENCE-BASED REFLECTIONS

We enjoy (and believe in) utilizing a competence-based/solution-focused approach to supervision. The following questions have been modified for use with supervisees, particularly as a means toward identifying and specifying professional training goals. Take a few minutes and answer each question before reading the chapter.

1. How have your clinical skills improved over the past six months? Be specific.
2. Imagine that when you wake up tomorrow morning you have become the therapist that you desire to be. Describe what you and others would see. How would you be different? Be specific.
3. On a scale from 1 to 10 (with 1 being that you are just getting started and 10 being that you have made and consistently maintained the change) rate how you see yourself generally at this point in time.

In this chapter we explore the role of creativity in clinical supervision. Power dynamics and their relation to creativity in the supervision process are discussed, as well as techniques for empowering supervisees and helping them become more creative in their work as therapists. The importance of isomorphism (i.e., parallel dynamics between supervision and therapy), personality characteristics, and contextual factors to effective supervision are also examined. A detailed case study illustrates one creative intervention the authors used when cosupervising two trainees who were involved as cotherapists with one married couple. For our purposes in this chapter the terms *therapist, counselor,* and *clinician* are used interchangeably, as are *supervisee* and *trainee,* even though they are technically different.

WHY IS SUPERVISION IMPORTANT?

Supervision is the most significant feature of training therapists. It has been defined as "an intensive interpersonally focused relationship in which one person is designated to facilitate the development of therapeutic competence in the other person" (Loganbill, Hardy, and Delworth, 1982, p. 4). Components of supervision include education, consultation, and counseling (Bernard and Goodyear, 1992). Although the supervision literature places considerable emphasis on teaching and learning as goals of supervision, other important goals of supervision are to facilitate a sense of confidence and competence in the counselors in training and to help them develop their own unique styles and approaches to therapy. We would add to this list the encouragement of creative thinking and action.

Both beginning and advanced practicum students indicate a continual need for positive support and feedback from supervisors about their work with clients (Borders, 1986). Feelings of apprehensiveness and fearfulness in therapists in training are expected. When effective, however, the process of supervision increases supervisees' feelings of personal and professional efficacy. Sawatzky, Jevne, and Clark (1994) found, for example, that supervisees moved from dissonance to self-trust if they felt continually affirmed in the supervisory process. Thus, a creativity-based approach to supervision may provide a useful framework for augmenting effective relationship interactions in supervision and adequately preparing therapists.

CREATIVITY IN CLINICAL SUPERVISION

The literature on creativity in clinical supervision is sorely limited, even though, in our view, creativity plays a paramount role in general psychotherapy, as well as marriage and family therapy supervision (Carson and Becker, 2000; Laughlin, 2000). Many of the seeds of the trainees' creativity are sown in supervision, most notably during and shortly after their academic training. Supervision can have a measurable effect on a supervisee's own creativity and creative abilities as a clinician. This is the time when therapists in training are perhaps most open to new ideas, developing their own theoretical orientation and honing their skills. Creative supervision empowers budding therapists to develop their own unique style and approach to working with individuals, couples, and families. As supervisees observe creative thinking and action in peers and supervisors, as well as learn from clients, they begin to invent their own creative stories and implement their own interventions. If supervision is a catalyst to creativity development, then the professional practice of counseling is where creativity grows and matures.

Doing the work of therapy requires the therapist to adapt many of the structured lessons learned in supervision and other areas of academic training in order to customize the interventions to the clients in the room. How this is done differs from one therapist to another, but a common thread connecting truly artistic therapists is the creative process used to assist those who come to us for help. For instance, Marshall (1999) describes five overlapping factors that help make group supervision a creative and growth-promoting experience for all involved. These are (1) mutual acceptance and support, (2) play, (3) tolerance and enjoyment of primary process, (4) resolution of intragroup conflict, and (5) gained competence.

Laughlin (2000) provided insight into improvisation in supervision (family therapy supervision in particular) by exploring the world of improvisational jazz and examining areas of congruency between these two professional endeavors. The purpose of her study was to investigate how a supervisor fosters the enigmatic skill of improvisation. Laughlin's research was based on two assumptions: first, "doing therapy, like playing improvisational music, is a skill not learned by technique alone or in a direct didactic manner" (p. 56) and second, most supervisors want their supervisees to acquire skills that make use of their creative skills and thinking (including their imagination) and enable them to work flexibly and improvisationally with clients. She analyzed tapes of supervision sessions and derived six categories that corresponded with improvisation in therapy. These were: (1) orienting toward improvisation, (2) staying in conversation, (3) being noncontrolling, (4) avoiding pigeonholing, (5) tolerating uncertainty, and (6) finding freedom within limits. These areas overlap in the supervision process and contribute to the creativity of both the supervisee and supervisor. As trainees gradually develop a framework of their own, they begin to improvise in their sessions, enacting un-planned and novel interventions in their work with couples and fami-lies. In short, "Just as improvisation is the key to creativity, the self is the instrument of improvisation. As such, creativity is not something that one either does or does not have, but something to which we learn to awaken within ourselves" (Laughlin, 2000, p. 58).

A creativity-based approach to supervision, then, is one of the keys to empowering those we supervise. Before this can occur, however, issues of power and control in the supervisor-supervisee relationship must first be discussed. The way in which power dynamics and hier-archy play out in the supervisor-supervisee relationship can have a profound effect on the trainee's personal and professional develop-ment, as well as her or his effectiveness as a therapist. As will be seen, a creativity-based approach diffuses unhealthy power differentials while maintaining essential hierarchy in the relationship.

SUPERVISION AND POWER DYNAMICS

Holloway (1987) stressed the importance of the supervisor-supervisee relationship in supervision. Supervision is commonly de-scribed as a process in which an experienced professional offers sup-port and provides both professional and personal input into the training of a supervisee (Bernard, 1979; Blocher, 1983; Bordin, 1983; Good-year and Bradley, 1983; Loganbill, Hardy, and Delworth, 1982). How-ever, creative supervisors also allow themselves to be influenced by their supervisees and the process. Within the supervisory relation-ship, power issues and dynamics often need to be addressed (Hollo-way et al., 1989; Nelson, 1997). Strong (1968) discussed dimensions of power and concluded that supervisees are influenced by supervi-sors to the extent that supervisors are perceived by supervisees as having expertness, attractive personalities, and trustworthiness. Thus, supervisors must first establish themselves as credible and approach-able before they can have a positive impact on supervisees. Accord-ing to Holloway (1995, 1997), social bonding or involvement is a major determinant of how social power gets played out in the supervisory process.

Distributions of power have also been discussed in relation to role model approaches of supervision. According to this perspective, the primary types of roles supervisors fill are those of teacher, counselor, and consultant (Bernard, 1979; Goodyear and Bradley, 1983; Hess, 1980). Each of these roles suggests a certain distribution of power between supervisors and student supervisees (Holloway, 1984).

When supervisors assume the roles of teachers, they are obviously focusing on educating and informing the supervisee. Coll (1986) argued that the process of education can keep students in passive roles whereby the professor (or supervisor) is dominant in the relationship by virtue of role. Even the process of graduate education often rewards students for compliance, acceptance, and obedience. Although increasing knowledge of supervisees is important and can be empowering, the power differential between supervisor and supervisee can foster feelings of ineptness. These feelings can lead supervisees to discount their knowledge, fail to develop effective counseling skills, or be unable to apply their knowledge and skills in a timely and appropriate manner with clients.

When supervisors adopt the role of counselor they are concentrating on the personal growth of supervisees. The focus is on what distresses supervisees about clients and what might be done about it. If the problem is not collaboratively defined and comes only from supervisors, supervisors are again exercising power over supervisees.

Consultant is the third role supervisors can adopt. One function of the consultant is to work collaboratively with the supervisee in discussing and identifying possible interventions and solutions with clients. Bradley (1989) indicated that consulting supervisors are specialists and that their position and level of expertise can easily create a power differential with supervisees. The role of consultant can also be construed as intimidating by supervisees if not carefully orchestrated.

According to Bernard and Goodyear (1992), evaluation is imperative in supervision in order to safeguard the clients' welfare; thus, by definition, supervision is an unequal process. The fact that supervision is evaluative can cause great discomfort in trainees, as well as contribute to feelings of inferiority. Role flexibility on the part of supervisors is essential to effective supervision. Supervisors can acquire a greater variety and flexibility of roles as they gain more experience (Stoltenberg and Delworth, 1988). There is little doubt that the changing roles of supervisors are linked to power dynamics in the supervisory relationship.

Rutan (1992) suggests that the supervision experience, like that of therapy, requires that all parties are able to function on cognitive, emotional, and behavioral levels. Supervisors are expected to be teachers, mentors, role models, and sometimes empathic disciplinarians in relation to supervisees. These many roles and levels of relationship can result in paradoxes and confusing power dynamics in supervision. As has been mentioned, by definition the supervisory relationship is hierarchical. However, what is important is whether that hierarchy is damaging to the relationship (e.g., authoritarianism and one-upmanship as opposed to treating each other with respect and, in a humanitarian sense, as coequals). When the supervisory relationship is based on authoritarian dynamics, there is danger that supervisees may replicate these dynamics in session with their clients. The authoritarian power dynamic in supervision (often fueled by the supervisor's inflated ego or underlying feelings of incompetence) can also create a sense of learned helplessness in supervisees, which is then mirrored in the counseling room.

Dealing with Power Issues in Supervision

McWhirter (1994) discussed the first step to empowerment as power analysis. The supervisor and supervisee might identify together how established familial patterns have discouraged the trainee from communicating honestly with others. For example, when one supervisee was a child, he learned that honest expression of feelings resulted in being shut off from the family. This fear was later exhibited in counseling with his clients. If emotional resistance arises within the counselor-client context, it may also play out in the counselor-supervisor relationship. In order for a supervisee to share deep issues such as familial patterns and emotions, supervision needs to occur in a safe environment. Sawatzky, Jeune, and Clark (1994) studied the issue of safety in the supervisory relationship and found that supervisees felt more secure if supervisors were trustworthy and offered acceptance, confidence, and permission to experiment in a supportive way. Indeed, creating a sense of safety and freedom to be oneself is an integral component of empowerment.

In addition to assessing power dynamics, it is essential that supervisees become aware of how their own behavior interacts with these dynamics (McWhirter, 1994). Supervisors can facilitate supervisees' ability to analyze their own behavior in terms of consequences. Referring to the previous example, the supervisor might process what consequences a lack of honesty has for both clients and the supervisee. Supervisors can also facilitate how the supervisees' behaviors operate in terms of adaptivity or maladaptivity and effectiveness or ineffectiveness relative to their ultimate goals. By conducting a power analysis directly in supervision sessions and determining the basis of power, supervisees are more likely to experience feelings of relief and feel empowered at that moment. A supervisor might simply ask, "How do you see our relationship in terms of power and how does that affect how we work together?" This processing will benefit supervisees further if, after the experience, supervisors engage in the role of teachers and process what supervisees learned by doing this exercise. In short, often supervisees feel more empowered by simply having the opportunity to discuss power dynamics.

Effective supervision also involves facilitating key skills of supervisees, such as the use of immediacy, that can help reduce the power differential in the relationship. McWhirter (1994) discussed the use of imagery in the counseling setting as an empowering technique because it gives the client control in the session. This same type of technique can be used in supervisory sessions to empower supervisees to share honestly, develop competence, and overcome feelings of inadequacy. Supervisees can be asked to close their eyes and imagine what it would be like if they were to be totally honest with the client. Another effective strategy might be to have supervisees imagine what it would be like to be totally honest with their thoughts and feelings in supervisory sessions. Images can then be processed immediately in the session between the supervisors and supervisees.

A similar technique is to have supervisees daydream about how they would like to be in session with clients or in supervision and then share this with their supervisors. Takata (1987) suggested that daydreaming opens up new perspectives and alters expectations and goals. During the daydream, supervisees can develop feelings of confidence as they vision themselves being successful as counselors. Both imagery and daydreaming techniques can help supervisees change feelings of inadequacy to feelings of self-trust and confidence in both their counseling sessions and supervision sessions. Using these kinds of approaches helps create a learning environment in which supervisees do self-work in supervision sessions rather than simply discussing ideas. Learning by doing also tends to increase authenticity in the supervisor-supervisee relationship (Takata, 1987).

Supervisees often feel vulnerable when entering the supervision process. Supervisors can sometimes empower supervisees by assuming the role of counselor, not in order to treat but simply to assist. Supervisors must focus on not only what distresses supervisees about the situation but also how the environment creates or maintains that distress. For example, counselors in training often perceive videotaping a counseling session as a means of evaluation. We all know that this can be very unnerving. Supervisors who wish to empower supervisees need to take the risk of becoming vulnerable themselves. For instance, one way of dealing with the stress of videotaping might be to videotape supervisory sessions and to have supervisees provide feedback to the supervisor about her or his interactions with the supervisee. Another approach might be for supervisors to videotape counseling sessions and share their own processes with supervisees. As McWhirter (1994) indicated, "to empower others, we must give up aspects of our own power, such as control and immunity from criticism" (p. 18). Sometimes supervisors can act more like a student with the student (Freire, 1971). Moreover, instead of always assuming the expert role, supervisors can ask supervisees for solutions to problems or issues in the supervisory relationship and give feedback on the supervision they are receiving. A creative tool to facilitate this discussion is role reversal.

THE DYNAMIC OF ISOMORPHISM

Therapist-client and supervisor-supervisee relationships share many things in common. Just as change is most likely to occur in interactions between therapist and family members that involve mutual respect, trust, honesty, genuineness, acceptance (nonjudgmental attitudes), and often a sense of humor, creative playfulness, and creative activity, the same holds true in the supervisor-supervisee relationship. These kinds of relationships increase the likelihood that both clients and supervisees will feel empowered and focus more on possibilities than problems and existing strengths more than pathology. In addition, just as psychotherapists need to have a solid theory base (or bases) from which to conduct their work, it is important that clinical supervisors have a theoretical road map that provides them with a clear sense of direction in their supervision of other therapists or trainees. It is not unusual that supervisors' evolving philosophy of supervision parallels or springs from the theoretical schools of thought that guide their therapy.

Isomorphism technically refers to the replication of similar patterns across the client-therapist-supervisor system (Liddle, Breunlin, and Schwartz, 1988). Some examples of isomorphism may initially prove useful. First, in the therapist-client relationship there is a "sameness" and equality as people but a hierarchy still exists; likewise, supervisors and supervisees move back and forth between two levels of relating. It is our belief that effective supervisors maintain a healthy degree of distance and role as expert while at the same time interacting with supervisees on a transparent and often raw human level. Of course, this will vary to some degree depending on the personality and clinical experience of the supervisor and supervisee, as well the supervisor's philosophy of supervision. Similar roles therapists perform with clients and supervisors with supervisees include observer, encourager, coplanner, codiagnostician, partner, teacher, facilitator, consultant, and evaluator. For example, just as therapists and clients cooperatively designate and sometimes cocreate goals for improvement and change, so do supervisors and supervisees. However, at times it is appropriate and necessary for goals or expectations to be suggested (sometimes strongly) by therapists to their clients and supervisors to their supervisees. Second, therapy and supervision entail both support and challenge. Constructive input and feedback to clients and supervisees, although sometimes painful or unwelcome, is as essential as the "stroking" and positive reinforcement are to the process. Effective therapists and supervisors find creative and palatable means for helping clients and supervisees face difficult realities and imagine alternative ways of thinking, behaving, and interacting. Third, background information and developmental history (both individual and family) is often important in counseling and supervision. This process may involve some fairly extensive data gathering in one's work as a therapist and supervisor. In line with this way of thinking, supervision (like therapy) is personalized, with the process evolving to meet the needs of clients and supervisees. In supervision the self-development of the supervisee is as important as his or her professional development, although supervisors set definite boundaries with supervisees and perform limited roles (as will be discussed later) with regard to their supervisees' personal development. Fourth, both counseling and supervision entail mutual responsibilities toward growth and change, and in effective helping relationships often all individuals involved are positively influenced. However, just as therapist and client responsibilities differ, so do those of supervisors and supervisees. All individuals involved in counseling and supervision are responsible only for their half of the journey toward growth and change, and it is sometimes important that these responsibilities be openly discussed. Fifth, just as counselors have professional and ethical standards from which they work with clients, so do supervisors with supervisees. These extend far beyond just doing no harm but include adherence to all of the ethical codes dictated by the profession. Finally, in supervision two members of the psychotherapy profession form a relationship for the purpose of further development of the therapist's professional identity, acquisition and integration of theory and skills, and a more complete understanding of oneself and others involved in the helping and facilitative process. Moreover, supervisors (like therapists with their clients) must be keenly aware of and sensitive to the contextual issues (or differences) inherent in their relationship with supervisees.

SENSITIVITY TO PERSONALITY CHARACTERISTICS AND CULTURAL/CONTEXTUAL FACTORS

Although we as humans have a common bond that transcends time, place, and culture (as Harry Stack Sullivan once said, "We are all more human than otherwise"), the importance of contextual variables (e.g., race, ethnicity, social class, gender, developmental level/maturation, disability, family of origin, personality, values and spirituality, etc.) in supervision, as in therapy, can never be overestimated. As middle-aged Caucasian males who grew up in fairly affluent families, neighborhoods, and cities, the authors are cognizant of the power base that has been assigned to us and from which others perceive that we live and conduct our work. Working with others from vastly different cultural backgrounds than ours, including our colleagues in India (e.g., see Carson and Chowdhury, 2000), has done much to broaden our limited perspectives. However, whether the perceptions of others about us are accurate or warranted (or their accompanying feelings or biases) is not the main issue. Our chief goal and concern in conducting supervision is to do everything possible to build trust, respect, and understanding between ourselves and our supervisees, as well as to respect, honor, and address any gaps between us that might inhibit their development as therapists.

This process cannot be forced but rather must be carefully cultivated through open, honest, and transparent dialogue. Moreover, it is primarily *our* responsibility and not that of our supervisees to model and set the tone for this mutual understanding. Supervisees too have a responsibility, but they must be gently (and sometimes assertively) led rather than pushed. Hopefully the result over time will be a reciprocal appreciation of the richness and uniqueness of our individual characteristics, family and ethnic/cultural heritage, and life experiences. Naturally this will occur more with some supervisees than others. However, in all supervisor-supervisee relationships there should be an acceptance of and respect for individual differences and cultural diversity, given that these are a large part of what makes the world an intriguing and wonderful place. An atmosphere must also be created in which differences of opinion and perspective are not only allowed but encouraged in the supervision process.

Moreover, a keen awareness of personality characteristics and goodness or poorness of fit dynamics between supervisors and supervisees is critical. All of us seem to naturally fit better with some individuals rather than others in both personal and professional relationships, and empowering supervisors encourage their trainees to think and talk openly about these issues in supervision—both in terms of their relationship with clients and their supervisor. In addition, although all of us have "disabilities," recognizing that special assistance, equipment, or services may be needed by some supervisees in order to maximize their learning and professional development is essential.

METHODS IN SUPERVISION THAT CAN IGNITE THE CREATIVITY OF SUPERVISEES

In our view, supervision that is congruent with systemic, humanistic, and psychodynamic principles has many benefits. Paramount are such practices as nondirective listening, making accurate and appropriate interpretations about the supervisee and his or her behavior and performance as a therapist, regulating parallel process dynamics, tracking supervisee affect and responses to both clients and supervisor, and building a therapeutic and learning alliance with the supervisee (Bernard and Goodyear, 1992; Fleming and Benedek, 1966; Reiner, 1997). Our approach also focuses on teaching rather than treating the supervisee. Of central importance here is the relationship that is cultivated over time between supervisor and supervisee, itself an agent of influence and change, as well as the supervisor's use of self in the supervision process and life of the supervisee. It is also imperative that supervisees continually assess the extent to which their own life experiences, and past or present family relationships, are impacting on their work with couples and families. Part of the role of the supervisor is to help supervisees assess and deal with these processes in the best interests of their clients. As supervisors working from a structural perspective, we employ a number of methods in our work with supervisees. These methods include:

1. Role-play (including reverse role-playing) and enactment; framing, reframing, and deframing (with regard to the supervisee's interpretation of the family's structure or problems)
2. Assigning straight and sometimes paradoxical tasks
3. Redirecting communication channels with the supervisee when necessary, such as in terms of peer or cotherapy input in the supervision process
4. Intensifying supervisee concerns and escalating stress when necessary, such as through overemphasizing the seriousness of a problem and motivating them by heightening their anxiety
5. Providing constant support and guidance for the supervisee in order to help them feel confident in their work with families (Aponte, 1994; Todd, 1997)

Similar to a psychodynamic approach to working with supervisees, the supervisor's use of self is central to the structural model. This includes the supervisor's affect and actions, including selective self-disclosure, geared toward motivating the supervisee to act and to grow (Todd, 1997).

A number of complementary modalities to conducting supervision can be implemented when working from psychodynamic and structural approaches. These include a great deal of listening and discussion in the context of planned meetings, protocol, and terminations (Reiner, 1997), coupled with live supervision (that can include phone-ins and midsession consultation breaks and take place in an individual or group format), use of videotapes in analyzing, for example, interactional patterns and sequences in therapy sessions, and individual and team case consultation (Todd, 1997). Other methods such as interpersonal process recall (IPR) (Kagen and Krathwohl, 1967) and assigning the supervisee readings or films to review fit well with these approaches.

Like many supervisors (as well as therapists), we utilize methods inherent in a number of other schools of thought. These include symbolic-experiential (Duhl, 1983; Whitaker and Bumberry, 1988) approaches that emphasize such interventions as mentoring and coaching of the supervisee, "experience before explanation," the primacy of affect that includes emotional experiences and connections in family therapy, interventions such as role-playing, sculpturing, and bioresonance (a form of therapeutic touch), art and family play therapy, humor and metaphor, and careful examination of supervisee responses to in vivo or videotaped counseling or supervision sessions. We also make use of some methods and interventions gleaned from strategic, systemic, and communications perspectives, including straightforward directives with supervisees, showing/demonstrating, use of hypothetical and circular questioning, and at times restraining techniques and variations of therapeutic double bind (Piercy and Wetchler, 1996; Todd, 1997; Watzlawick, 1978). Finally, on occasion we employ solution-focused methods with supervisees, including looking for exceptions, focusing more on alternatives and possibilities than on problems, scaling, asking miracle questions, and complimenting (de Shazer, 1985). Whatever methods we employ, we have learned that our work with supervisees should always be guided, yet never bound, by an overarching philosophy that lights our path along the fascinating journey of supervision.

CASE STUDY

The following case study illustrates our approach to supervision. We provide an example of one creative intervention we used with two of our supervisees that happened to be very effective and, after the fact, enlightening to all of us.

Marilyn and Ron Jacobs presented as a typical couple struggling in their sixth year of marriage. They complained of communication problems and emotional distance, describing their relationship as comfortable, yet lacking passion. They were seeking therapy in hopes of rekindling their marriage. Cheryl and Amber were assigned to work with this couple as a component of their clinical training in marriage and family therapy. Over the course of the first two sessions, Cheryl and Amber successfully joined with Marilyn and Ron in identifying and clarifying treatment goals. In supervision, they were able to clearly articulate the interpersonal and intrapsychic dynamics that constituted their assessment of the couple's strengths and challenges (structural diagnosis). It appeared as though Cheryl and Amber were successfully working together as cotherapists in supporting Ron and Marilyn's relationship. It was predicted that this would be a relatively simple and brief therapeutic process. Appearances can be, and often are, deceiving.

Seduced by the ease with which this case began, we were all quickly awakened during the fourth session. As supervisors, we were watching the session live from an observation room. The dynamic unfolded quickly. Marilyn and Ron described a recent argument during which "things got out of control." Ron had struck Marilyn. The distance that existed between them felt like a canyon. Ron was on one side trying to regain control by means of excuses and verbal domination. Marilyn was on the other side frightened, timid, and victimized. Ron and Marilyn had reached emotional gridlock. As the conflict and tension between them became more present, Amber and Cheryl's relationship as cotherapists was called into play. Unfortunately, the co-therapists' relationship quickly reflected that of their clients (parallel process). Cheryl unconsciously countered each of Ron's power-seeking moves with a grander move (countertransference dynamic). As Amber attempted to assert her role in session, she was struck down by Cheryl's need to be the one in control. The session ended with Cheryl dictating what should transpire over the course of the week. Amber quietly bade the couple farewell.

The dynamic solidified during group supervision following the session. The more Amber attempted to voice her concerns, the more vocal Cheryl's need for control became. The more their dynamic was discussed, the louder it became. As cosupervisors we were being invited to replicate the dynamic on a third level. We found ourselves competing for the right to impart our knowledge to those whom we were supervising. By the end of supervision, we were keenly aware that Amber was silently sitting in her chair while Cheryl sat on the edge of her seat vehemently defending each of her actions (tracking supervisee affect and responses). They had joined the Jacobses in emotional gridlock and we, as supervisors, were not far behind. They were asked to meet as cotherapists and discuss their struggle prior to their next session. They agreed. We decided to do the same.

The fifth session was a prime example of first-order change in supervision. Amber and Cheryl had met briefly since the previous session. They spoke professionally with each other and divided up the tasks for the next session. They avoided addressing the heart of their conflict as cotherapists (resistance and denial). The session progressed in an orderly and controlled fashion. Although several directives were sent into the session encouraging Cheryl and Amber to address the emotional dynamics of the couples' relationship, they colluded with the couple in keeping the session cognitive and emotionally safe. The session was void of passion, mirroring the Jacobs's marriage. In tracking Cheryl and Amber's affect and responses to the couple, we decided as supervisors that it was time to intensify our supervisees' concerns and elevate their anxiety in the next group supervision session.

In hopes of facilitating second-order change within their relationship as cotherapists, the directives that were not carried out in session were structured into supervision. Four chairs were arranged in the middle of the supervision room. Cheryl and Amber were directed to sit across from each other while we served as cosupervisors (restructuring boundaries and hierarchies and clarifying personal agendas). The parallel was clear to them. The direction we would take together was not. Our role as supervisors was critical. Our task was to demonstrate how they could get unstuck with this couple by first getting unstuck with each other (teaching and modeling rather than treating). We were about to ask them to take a leap of faith and self-confront. Amber and Cheryl were given one simple directive: "You are each to say something to the other that you are frightened to say" (redirecting communication channels; increasing insight and awareness). The room became silent. The group had anticipated a role-play, not a real interaction. The anxiety of these supervisees was communicated in their deafening silence. We were on the right track. Cheryl courageously went first. She looked Amber in the eye and said, "I need to be in control when I am in session. I don't feel this way when I am working alone. I never seem to know where you are going in session, and it scares me. I trust myself, but I do not trust you." Amber replied, "Your knowledge and self-confidence intimidate me. I am always second-guessing myself in session with you. I don't have this problem when I am alone in session either. I come out of our sessions feeling inadequate and incompetent."

They had each taken a leap of faith. It was time to have them self-confront. Cheryl and Amber were then given a second directive, "Tell each other how what you have just shared is less about your cotherapist and more about your own personal struggle" (focus on self and co-therapy relationship). The floodgates opened. They shared openly about how their own private pasts supported their individual beliefs. As they individually became more differentiated and their work together in session thrived, so did Ron and Marilyn's marriage. Amber's self-confidence and therapeutic voice grew louder with each session as she embraced self-validation as opposed to measuring herself against her cotherapist. Cheryl's willingness to self-confront and self-soothe, while trusting her cotherapist (guidance and support), allowed her to transform the energy she used to control into an uncanny ability to observe the therapeutic process around her. Their openness built a bridge over the canyon that kept them separate. As Amber and Cheryl continued to approach each other on the bridge, we soon became insignificant—perhaps the one true indicator of effective supervision.

CONCLUSION

The process of supervision demands that supervisees be open to engaging in the learning process (Rutan, 1992). Learning and growth are more likely to occur if supervisees are encouraged to derive their own meanings and interpretations in the supervision process and state them freely. Supervisors who are able to provide a safe emotional environment, and who are vulnerable, spontaneous, and creative in their relationships with supervisees, will be able to engage in various roles with them that are encouraging and empowering. Some of the benefits of a creativity-based approach are that supervisees gain a sense of relief about power differentials, develop a sense of trust in themselves and in their supervisor, acquire more confidence in utilizing skills such as immediacy, are more likely to experiment with new therapeutic modalities and develop their own unique approach to working with clients, are less distressed over videotaping and being evaluated, and tend to feel more knowledgeable and competent.

BREAKING OUT OF THE BOX:
MY COMMITMENT TO MY FUTURE

Congratulations! You have successfully completed a variety of suggestions and challenges. It is now time to make a commitment toward your continuing growth as a creative and dynamic therapist. We know that small change is the critical foundation to lasting and meaningful change (similar to our clients' process). Reflect back to the scale you designed at the beginning of this chapter (incubation exercise question number 3) as you respond to the following questions.

1. As you become even more effective and creative as a therapist (moving up the scale), what specific changes will you notice in your work with clients?
2. As a means of making a contract with yourself, we encourage you to complete the following declarations.
   (a) I will take the continuing steps toward my ongoing success by focusing on . . .
   (b) I agree to honor my strengths, abilities, and creative potential by . . .
   (c) I will celebrate small successes by . . .

Epilogue

Creative ideas and interventions generally do not develop in a vacuum but grow out of a field that is theoretically and empirically sound. It is our conviction that the most creative and effective therapists grasp, appreciate, and utilize well-grounded ideas and approaches in the psychotherapy literature and make them uniquely their own in their work with clients, rather than reach for the latest fads and gimmicks. These clinicians are able to use as a springboard that which has been researched and clinically tested over time while always being cautious not to become stuck in or bound by the very ideas and methods that have arisen from the rich literature in our profession.

One thing is sure: therapy has always been a creative enterprise. We hope this book has set the stage for you, the reader, in being able to chart new waters in your own journey with clients. This book represents but a beginning of what it means to appreciate the importance and role of creativity as therapists. In the end, what we have really wanted to do is to invite you to embrace both the construct of creativity and the creativity that lies within you, and in so doing experience a greater connection with your clients, effectiveness in your work, and satisfaction in your efforts to help others.

References

Ackerman, D. (1999). *Deep play*. New York: Random House.

Adler, A. (1968). *The practice and theory of individual psychology*. New York: Humanities Press.

Ahrons, C. (1995). *The good divorce: Keeping your family together when your marriage comes apart*. New York: HarperCollins.

Albert, R.S. (1996). Some reasons why creativity often fails to make it past puberty and into the real world. *New Directions in Child Development, 72*, 43-56.

Aldwin, C.M. (1994). *Stress, coping, and development: An integrated perspective*. New York: The Guilford Press.

Amabile, T. (1983). *The social psychology of creativity*. New York: Springer-Verlag.

Amabile, T. (1987). The motivation to be creative. In S.G. Isaksen (Ed.), *Frontiers of creativity research* (pp. 223-254). Buffalo, NY: Bearly Limited.

Amabile, T. (1989). *Growing up creative*. New York: Crown.

Amabile, T.M. (1996). *Creativity in context*. Boulder, CO: Westview Press.

Amabile, T.M. (1997). Entrepreneurial creativity through motivational synergy. *Journal of Creative Behavior, 31*(1), 18-26.

American Psychiatric Association (1994). *Diagnostic and statistical manual of mental disorders* (Fourth edition). Washington, DC: American Psychiatric Association.

Andreasen, N.C. (1987). Creativity and mental illness. *American Journal of Psychiatry, 144*, 1288-1292.

Anthony, E.J. (1987). Risk, vulnerability and resilience: An overview. In E.J. Anthony and B.J. Cohler (Eds.), *The invulnerable child* (pp. 3-48). New York: The Guilford Press.

Antonietti, A. (1997). Unlocking creativity. *Educational Leadership, 54*, 73-75.

Aponte, H. (1994). How personal can training get? *Journal of Marital and Family Therapy, 20*, 13-15.

Aponte, H.J. and Van Deusen, J.M. (1981). Structural family therapy. In A.S. Gurman and D.P. Kniskern (Eds.), *Handbook of family therapy*, Volume 1 (pp. 310-360). New York: Brunner/Mazel.

Ariel, S. (1992). *Strategic family play therapy*. Chichester, NY: Wiley.

Arieti, S. (1976). *Creativity: The magic synthesis*. New York: Basic Books.

Baer, J. (1993). *Creativity and divergent thinking: A task-specific approach*. Hillsdale, NJ: Erlbaum.

Barron, F. (1963). *Creativity and psychological health*. New York: Van Nostrand.

Barron, F. (1988). Putting creativity to work. In R.J. Sternberg (Ed.), *The nature of creativity: Contemporary psychological perspectives* (pp. 76-98). New York: Cambridge University Press.

Barron, F. (1995). *No fruitless flower: An ecology of creativity.* Cresskill, NJ: Hampton Press.

Barron, F.X. and Harrington, D.M. (1981). Creativity, intelligence, and personality. *Annual Review of Psychology, 32,* 439-476.

Beavers, W.R. and Hampson, R.B. (1990). *Successful families: Assessment and intervention.* New York: W.W. Norton.

Beck, A.T. and Emery, G. (1985). *Anxiety disorders and phobias: A cognitive perspective.* New York: Basic Books.

Benjamin, L. (1984). Creativity and counseling. *Highlights: An ERIC/CAPS Fact Sheet* (ED 260 369). Ann Arbor: School of Education, University of Michigan.

Berg-Cross, L. (2000). *Basic concepts in family therapy: An introductory text,* Second edition. Binghamton, NY: The Haworth Press.

Bernard, J.M. (1979). Supervisor training: A discrimination model. *Counselor Education and Supervision, 19,* 740-748.

Bernard, J.M. and Goodyear, R.K. (1992). *Fundamentals of clinical supervision.* Needham Heights, MA: Allyn & Bacon.

Bertolino, B. and O'Hanlon, B. (1999). *Invitation to possibility land.* Philadelphia: Brunner/Mazel.

Black, D. (1984). Laughter. *JAMA, 252*(21), 2995-2998.

Bleedorn, B.B. (1982). Humor as an indicator of giftedness. *Roeper Review, 4,* 33-34.

Blissett, S.E. and McGrath, R.E. (1996). The relationship between creativity and interpersonal problem-solving skills in adults. *The Journal of Creative Behavior, 30*(3), 173-182.

Blocher, D.H. (1983). Toward a cognitive developmental approach to counselor supervision. *The Counseling Psychologist, 11*(1), 27-34.

Boorma, D. (1999). *The family play genogram: A guidebook.* Summit, NJ: The Family Play Therapy Press.

Borders, L.D. (1986). Facilitating supervisee growth: Implications of developmental models of counseling supervision. *Michigan Journal of Counseling and Development, 17*(2), 7-12.

Bordin, E.S. (1983). A working alliance model of supervision. *The Counseling Psychologist, 11*(1), 35-42.

Boscolo, L., Cecchin, G., Hoffman, L., and Penn, P. (1987). *Milan systemic family therapy: Conversations in theory and practice.* New York: Basic Books.

Botkin, D. (2000). Family play therapy: A creative approach to including young children in family therapy. *Journal of Systemic Therapies, 19*(3), 31-42.

Botkin, D. and Raimondi, N. (2000). Children in family therapy: A training model for family therapy programs. Preconference institute conducted at the 58th annual Conference of the American Association for Marriage and Family Therapy, Denver, CO, November.

Bowen, M. (1978). *Family therapy in clinical practice.* New York: Jason Aronson.

Bowlby, J. (1969). *Attachment and loss* (Volume 1: Attachment). New York: Basic Books.

Bowlby, J. (1988). *A secure base.* New York: Basic Books.

Bradley, L.J. (1989). *Counselor supervision: Principles, process, and practice* (Second edition). Muncie, IN: Accelerated Development, Inc.

Britsch, S. (1992). *The development of "story" within the culture of preschool.* Berkeley, CA: University of California.

Brown, L.H. and Unger, M.A. (1992). *Sentence completion series: Professional user's guide.* Odessa, FL: Psychological Assessment Resources, Inc.

Brown, R.T. (1989). Creativity: What are we to measure? In J.A. Glover, R.R. Ronning, and C.R. Reynolds (Eds.), *Handbook of creativity* (pp. 3-32). New York: Plenum Press.

Bugental, J.F.T. and Sterling, M.M. (1995). Existential-humanistic psychotherapy: New perspectives. In A.S. Gurman and S.B. Messer (Eds.), *Essential psychotherapies: Theory and practice* (pp. 226-260). New York: The Guilford Press.

Carson, D.K. (1999a). Counseling. In M.A. Runco and S.R. Pritzker (Eds.), *Encyclopedia of creativity* (pp. 395-402). San Diego: Academic Press.

Carson, D.K. (1999b). The importance of creativity in family therapy: A preliminary consideration. *The Family Journal: Counseling and Therapy for Couples and Families, 7*(4), 326-334.

Carson, D.K. (1999c). Intuition in marital and family therapy. *Annals of the American Psychotherapy Association, 2*(5), 4,10.

Carson, D.K. and Becker, K.W. (2000). Marriage and family therapy supervision: An integrative approach and case illustration. *Annals of the American Psychotherapy Association, 3*(6), 6-9.

Carson, D.K., Becker, K.W., Vance, K.E., and Forth, N.L. (2003). The role of creativity in marriage and family therapy practice: A national online study. *Contemporary Family Therapy, 25*(1), 89-109.

Carson, D.K., Bittner, M.T., Cameron, B.A., Brown, D.M., and Meyer, S.S. (1994). Creative thinking as a predictor of school-aged children's stress responses and coping abilities. *Creativity Research Journal, 7*(2), 145-158.

Carson, D.K. and Chowdhury, A. (2000). Family therapy in India: A new profession in an ancient land? *Contemporary Family Therapy, 22*(4), 387-406.

Carson, D.K. and Runco, M.A. (1999). Creative problem solving and problem finding in young adults: Interconnections with stress, hassles, and coping abilities. *The Journal of Creative Behavior, 33*(3), 167-190.

Carson, D.K. and Skarpness, L.R. (1988). Contributors to children's coping: A developmental overview. *Wellness Perspectives, 5*(2), 21-25.

Carson, D.K., Swanson, D.M., Cooney, M.H., Gillum, B.J., and Cunningham, D. (1992). Stress and coping as predictors of young children's development and psychosocial adjustment. *Child Study Journal, 22*(4), 273-302.

Cashdan, S. and Welsh, G.S. (1966). Personality correlates of creative potential in talented high school students. *Journal of Personality, 34,* 445-455.

Christensen, A. and Jacobson, N.S. (2000). *Reconcilable differences.* New York: The Guilford Press.

Cohen, L.M. (1989). A continuum of adaptive creative behaviors. *Creativity Research Journal, 2,* 169-183.

Cohler, B.J. (1987). Adversity, resilience, and the study of lives. In E.J. Anthony and B.J. Cohler (Eds.), *The invulnerable child* (pp. 363-424). New York: The Guilford Press.

Cole, H.P. and Sarnoff, D. (1980). Creativity and counseling. *Personnel and Guidance Journal 59,* 140-146.

Coll, R. (1986). Power, powerlessness and empowerment. *Religious Education, 81*(3), 412-423.

Corey, G. (1991). *Theory and practice of counseling and psychotherapy* (Fourth edition). Pacific Grove, CA: Brooks/Cole.

Cornelius, G. and Casler, J. (1991). Enhancing creativity in young children: Strategies for teachers. *Early Child Development and Care, 72,* 99-106.

Cousins, N. (1979). *Anatomy of an illness.* New York: W.W. Norton.

Cowan, P.A., Cowen, C.P., and Schulz, M.S. (1996). Thinking about risk and resilience in families. In E.M. Hetherington and E.A. Blechman (Eds.), *Stress, coping, and resiliency in children and families* (pp. 1-38). Mahwah, NJ: Erlbaum.

Crane, D.R. (1996). *Fundamentals of marital therapy.* New York: Brunner/Mazel.

Cropley, A.J. (1990). Creativity and mental health in everyday life. *Creativity Research Journal, 3,* 167-178.

Csikszentmihalyi, M. (1996). *Creativity: Flow and the psychology of discovery and invention.* New York: HarperCollins.

Csikszentmihalyi, M. (1997). *Finding flow.* New York: Basic Books.

Csikszentmihalyi, M., Rathunde, K., and Whalen, S. (1993). *Talented teenagers: The roots of success and failure.* Cambridge, UK: Cambridge University Press.

Curran, D. (1983). *Traits of a healthy family.* San Francisco, CA: Harper and Row.

Dacey, J.S. (1989a). *Fundamentals of creative thinking.* San Francisco: Jossey-Bass.

Dacey, J.S. (1989b). Peak periods of creative growth across the life span. *Journal of Creative Behavior, 23*(4), 221-247.

Dacey, J.S. and Lennon, K.H. (1998). *Understanding creativity.* San Francisco: Jossey-Bass.

Dacey, J. and Packer, A. (1992). *The nurturing parent: How to raise creative, loving, responsible children.* New York: Simon and Schuster.

de Shazer, S. (1985). *Keys to solutions in brief therapy.* New York: W.W. Norton.

de Shazer, S. (1988). *Clues: Investigating solutions in brief therapy.* New York: W.W. Norton.

de Shazer, S. (1991). *Putting differences to work.* New York: W.W. Norton.

de Shazer, S. (1994). *Words were originally magic.* New York: W.W. Norton.

Deacon, S.A. (1998). The talk about game. In L.L. Hecker and S.A. Deacon (Eds.), *The therapist's notebook: Homework, handouts, and activities for psychotherapy* (pp. 269-270). Binghamton, NY: The Haworth Press.

Deacon, S.A. and Piercy, F.P. (2001). Qualitative methods in family evaluation: Creative assessment techniques. *The American Journal of Family Therapy, 29,* 355-373.

Deacon, S.A. and Thomas, V. (2000). Discovering creativity in family therapy: A theoretical analysis. *Journal of Systemic Therapies, 19*(3), 4-17.

DeGenova, M.K. and Rice, F.P. (2002). *Intimate relationships, marriages, and families,* Fifth edition. Mountain View, CA: Mayfield Publishing Company.

Dellas, M. and Gaier, E.L. (1970). Identification of creativity: The individual. *Psychological Bulletin, 73,* 55-73.

DeMaria, R., Weeks, G., and Hof, L. (1999). *Intergenerational assessment of individuals, couples, and families: Focused genograms.* Philadelphia: Brunner/Mazel.

Derks, P. (1985). Abstract: Creativity in Shakespeare's humor. *Journal of Creative Behavior, 19*(3), 218.

Dickey, J.P. and Henderson, P. (1989). What young children say about stress and coping in school. *Health Education, 20,* 14-18.

Dimmer, S.A., Carroll, J.L., and Wyatt, G.K. (1990). Uses of humor in psychotherapy. *Psychological Reports, 66,* 795-801.

Ditlow, F. (1993). The missing element in health care: Humor as a form of creativity. *Journal of Holistic Nursing, 11*(1), 66-79.

Dowd, E.T. (1989). The self and creativity: Several constructs in search of theory. In J. Glover, R. Ronning, and C. Reynolds (Eds.), *Handbook of creativity* (pp. 233-242). New York: Plenum Press.

Dugan, D.O. (1989). Laughter and tears: The best medicine for stress. *Nursing Forum, 24*(1), 18-26.

Duhl, B.S. (1983). *From the inside out and other metaphors: Creative and integrative approaches to training in systems thinking.* New York: Brunner/Mazel.

Duhl, B.S. (1999). A personal view of action metaphor: Bringing what's inside outside. In D.J. Wiener (Ed.), *Beyond talk therapy: Using movement and expressive techniques in clinical practice* (pp. 79-96). Washington, DC: American Psychological Association.

Eberle, R.F. (1971). *SCAMPER: Games for imagination development.* Buffalo, NY: D.O.K. Publishers.

Edwards, M.R. and Sproull, J.R. (1984). Creativity: Productivity gold mine? *The Journal of Creative Behavior, 185,* 175-184.

Eisenman, R. (1997). Creativity, preference for complexity, and physical and mental illness. In M.A. Runco and R. Richards (Eds.), *Eminent creativity, everyday creativity, and health* (pp. 99-105). Greenwich, CT: Ablex.

Elkind, D. (1988). *The hurried child: Growing up too fast too soon.* Reading, MA: Addison-Wesley.

Ellis, A. (1977). Fun as psychotherapy. In A. Ellis and R. Grieger (Eds.), *Handbook of rational-emotive therapy* (pp. 262-270). New York: Springer.

Ellis, A. (1989). Rational emotive behavior therapy. In R.J. Corsini and D. Wedding (Eds.), *Current psychotherapies* (Fourth edition) (pp. 197-238). Itasca, IL: F.E. Peacock.

Eysenck, H.J. (1982). *Personality, genetics, and behavior selected papers.* New York: Praeger.

Eysenck, H.J. (1993). Creativity and personality: Suggestions for a theory. *Psychological Inquiry, 4,* 147-178.

Eysenck, H.J. (1995). *Genius: The natural history of creativity.* Cambridge: Cambridge University Press.

Farber, E.A. and Egeland, B. (1987). Invulnerability among abused and neglected children. In E.J. Anthony and B.J. Cohler (Eds.), *The invulnerable child* (pp. 253-288). New York: The Guilford Press.

Fenell, D.L. and Weinhold, B.K. (1997). *Counseling families: An introduction to marriage and family therapy* (Second edition). Denver, CO: Love Publishing Company.

Fisch, R., Weakland, J.H., and Segal, L. (1982). *The tactics of change: Doing therapy briefly.* San Francisco: Jossey-Bass.

Fisher, B.J. and Specht, D.K. (1999). Successful aging and creativity in later life. *Journal of Aging Studies, 13,* 457-471.

Fisher, M. (1981). *Intuition.* New York: E.P. Dutton.

Flach, F. (1988). The creative process in psychiatry. In F. Flach (Ed.), *The creative mind* (pp. 1-22). Buffalo, NY: Bearly Limited.

Flach, F. (1990). Disorders of the pathways involved in the creative process. *Creativity Research Journal, 3,* 158-165.

Fleming, J. and Benedek, T. (1966). *Psychoanalytic supervision.* New York: Grune and Stratton.

Framo, J.L. (1982). *Explorations in marital and family therapy.* New York: Springer.

Frankel, A.D. (1993). Using a funeral ritual in therapy: Changing rigid interaction patterns. In T.S. Nelson and T.S. Trepper (Eds.), *101 interventions in family therapy* (pp. 46-49). Binghamton, NY: Haworth Press.

Freeman, A. and Reinecke, M.A. (1995). Cognitive therapy. In A.S. Gurman and S.B. Messer (Eds.), *Essential psychotherapies: Theory and practice* (pp. 182-225). New York: The Guilford Press.

Freire, P. (1971). *Pedagogy of the oppressed.* New York: Herder and Herder.

Freud, S. (1940). *An outline of psycho-analysis* (Standard edition). London: Hogarth Press.

Frey, D.H. (1975). The anatomy of an idea: Creativity in counseling. *Personnel and Guidance Journal, 54,* 23-27.

Fry, W.F. and Salameh, W.A. (Eds.) (1987). *Handbook of humor and psychotherapy: Advances in the clinical use of humor.* Sarasota, FL: Professional Resource Exchange.

Galloway, G. and Cropley, A. (1999). Benefits of humor for mental health: Empirical findings and directions for further research. *Humor, 12*(3), 301-312.

Gardner, K.G. and Moran, J.D. III (1997). Family adaptability, cohesion, and creativity. In M.A. Runco and R. Richards (Eds.), *Eminent creativity, everyday creativity, and health* (pp. 325-332). Greenwich, CT: Ablex.

Garmezy, N. (1985). Stress-resistant children: The search for protective factors. In J.E. Stevenson (Ed.), *Recent research in developmental psychopathology.* (Book Supplement No. 4) (pp. 213-233). Oxford: Pergamon Press.

Garmezy, N. and Masten, A. (1990). The adaptation of children to a stressful world: Mastery of fear. In L. Eugene Arnold (Ed.), *Childhood stress* (pp. 460-473). New York: Wiley.

Gerstein, J.S. (1999). *Sticking together: Experiential activities for family counseling.* Philadelphia: Accelerated Development.

Gil, E. (1994). *Play in family therapy.* New York: The Guilford Press.

Gladding, S.T. (1995a). Creativity in counseling. *Counseling and Human Development, 28,* 1-12.

Gladding, S.T. (1995b). Humor in counseling: Using a natural resource. *Journal of Humanistic Education and Development, 34,* 3-12.

Gladding, S.T. (1998). *Counseling as an art: The creative arts in counseling.* Alexandria, VA: American Counseling Association.

Gladding, S.T. and Henderson, D.A. (2000). Creativity and family counseling: The SCAMPER model as a template for promoting creative processes. *The Family Journal: Counseling and Therapy for Couples and Families, 8*(3), 245-249.

Goldberg, P. (1983). *The intuitive edge.* Los Angeles: Jeremy P. Tarcher, Inc.

Goleman, D., Kaufman, P., and Ray, M. (1992). *The creative spirit.* New York: Penguin Books.

Goodyear, R.K. and Bradley, F.L. (1983). Theories of counselor supervision: Points of convergence and divergence. *The Counseling Psychologist, 11*(1), 59-67.

Gottman, J.M. (1999). *The marriage clinic: A scientifically based marital therapy.* New York: W.W. Norton.

Gottman, J.M. and Silver, N. (2000). *The seven principles for making marriage work.* Cincinnati: Three Rivers Press.

Greenberg, L.S. and Johnson, S.M. (1988). *Emotionally focused therapy for couples.* New York: The Guilford Press.

Grieger, R. (1986). *A client's guide to rational-emotive therapy.* Charlottesville, VA: University of Virginia Press.

Gruber, H.E. (1988). The evolving systems approach to creative work. *Creativity Research Journal, 1,* 27-51.

Gruber, H.E. (1995). Insight and affect in the history of science. In R.J. Sternberg and J.E. Davidson (Eds.), *The nature of insight* (pp. 397-431). Cambridge, MA: MIT Press.

Haig, R.A. (1988). *The anatomy of humor: Biopsychosocial and therapeutic perspectives.* Springfield, IL: Charles C Thomas.

Haley, J. (1984). *Ordeal therapy.* San Francisco: Jossey-Bass.

Haley, J. (1987). *Problem-solving therapy* (Second edition). San Francisco: Jossey-Bass.

Handly, R. and Neff, P. (1985). *Anxiety and panic attacks: Their cause and cure.* New York: Ballantine Books.

Harrington, D. (1990). The ecology of human creativity: A psychological perspective. In M.A. Runco and R. Albert (Eds.), *Theories of creativity* (pp. 143-169). Thousand Oaks, CA: Sage.

Haug, I.E. (1998). Spirituality as a dimension of family therapists' clinical training. *Contemporary Family Therapy, 20,* 4.

Hecker, L.L. and Deacon, S.A. (1998). *The therapist's notebook: Homework, handouts, and activities for use in psychotherapy.* Binghamton, NY: The Haworth Press.

Hendrix, H. (1988). *Getting the love you want: A guide for couples.* New York: Henry Holt.

Hennessey, B.A. and Amabile, T.M. (1998). The conditions of creativity. In R.J. Sternberg (Ed.), *The nature of creativity: Contemporary psychological perspectives* (pp. 11-38). Cambridge, UK: Cambridge University Press.

Heppner, M.J., O'Brien, K.M., Hinkelman, J.M., and Humphrey, C.F. (1994). Shifting the paradigm: The use of creativity in career counseling. *Journal of Career Development, 21,* 77-86.

Heppner, P.P., Fitzgerald, K., and Jones, C.A. (1989). Examining counselors' creative processes in counseling. In J.A. Glover, R.R. Ronning, and C.R. Reynolds (Eds.), *Handbook of creativity* (pp. 271-280). New York: Plenum Press.

Hess, A.K. (Ed.) (1980). *Psychotherapy supervision: Theory, research, and practice.* New York: Wiley.

Hobday, A. and Ollier, K. (1999). *Creative therapy with children and adolescents.* Atascadero, CA: Impact Publishers, Inc.

Hogan, P. (1988). Creativity in the family. In F. Flach (Ed.), *The creative mind* (pp. 23-50). Buffalo, NY: Bearly Limited.

Holloway, E.L. (1984). Outcome evaluation in supervision research. *The Counseling Psychologist, 12*(4), 167-174.

Holloway, E.L. (1987). Developmental models of supervision: Is it supervision? *Professional Psychology: Research and Practice, 18,* 209-216.

Holloway, E.L. (1995). *Clinical supervision: A systems approach.* Thousand Oaks, CA: Sage.

Holloway, E.L. (1997). Structures for the analysis and teaching of psychotherapy. In C.E. Watkins Jr. (Ed.), *Handbook of psychotherapy supervision* (pp. 249-267). New York: Wiley.

Holloway, E.L., Freund, R.D., Gardner, S.L., Nelson, M.L., and Walker, B.R. (1989). Relation of power and involvement to theoretical orientation in supervision: An analysis of discourse. *Journal of Counseling Psychology, 36,* 88-102.

Hoppe, K.D. and Kyle, N.L. (1997). Dual brain, creativity, and health. In M.A. Runco and R. Richards (Eds.), *Eminent creativity, everyday creativity, and health* (pp. 275-285). Greenwich, CT: Ablex.

Hovestadt, A.J. and Fine, M. (Eds.) (1987). *Family of origin therapy.* Rickville, MD: Aspen.

Huber, C.H. and Baruth, L.G. (1989). *Rational-emotive family therapy: A systems perspective.* New York: Springer.

Humke, C. and Schaefer, C.E. (1996). Sense of humor and creativity. *Perceptual and Motor Skills, 82,* 544-546.

Imber-Black, E., Roberts, J., and Whiting, R. (1989). *Rituals in families and family therapy.* New York: W.W. Norton.

Isaksen, C.G., Dorval, B.K., and Treffinger, D.J. (1994). *Creative approach to problem solving.* Dubuque, IA: Kendall/Hunt.

Jacobs, E. (1992). *Creative counseling techniques: An illustrated guide.* Odessa, FL: Psychological Assessment Resources, Inc.

Jacobson, N.S. and Margolin, G. (1979). *Marital therapy.* New York: Brunner/Mazel.

Jaquish, G.A. and Ripple, R.E. (1980). Divergent thinking and self-esteem in pre-adolescents and adolescents. *Journal of Youth and Adolescence, 9*(2), 143-151.

Johnson, S.M. (1996). *The practice of emotionally focused marital therapy: Creating connection.* New York: Brunner/Mazel.

Johnson, S.M. (1998). Emotionally focused couple therapy. In F.M. Dattilio (Ed.), *Case studies in couple and family therapy: Systemic and cognitive perspectives* (pp. 450-472). New York: The Guilford Press.

Johnson, S.M. and Greenberg, L.S. (Eds.) (1994). *The heart of the matter: Perspectives on emotion in marital therapy.* New York: Brunner/Mazel.

Kagen, N. and Krathwohl, D.R. (1967). *Studies in human interaction: Interpersonal process recall stimulated by videotape.* East Lansing, MI: Michigan State University Press.

Kane, T., Suls, J., and Tedeschi, J.T. (1977). Humor as a tool of social interaction. In A.J. Chapman and H.C. Foot (Eds.), *It's a funny thing, humor* (pp. 13-16). Oxford: Pergamon Press.

Keith, D.V. and Whitaker, C.A. (1981). Play therapy: A paradigm for work with families. *Journal of Marital and Family Therapy, 7,* 243-254.

Kerr, B. and Chopp, C. (1999). Families and creativity. In M.A. Runco and S.R. Pritzker (Eds.), *Encyclopedia of creativity* (Volume 1) (pp. 709-715). San Diego: Academic Press.

Kimchi, J. and Schaffner, B. (1990). Childhood protective factors and stress risk. In L. Eugene Arnold (Ed.), *Childhood stress* (pp. 475-500). New York: Wiley.

Kruse-Nordin, R. (2000). *After the baby: Making sense of marriage after childbirth.* Dallas: Taylor Trade Publishing.

Kubie, L.S. (1961). *Neurotic distortion of the creative process.* New York: Noonday Press.

LaGaipa, J. (1977). The effects of humor on the flow of social conversation. In A.J. Chapman and H.C. Foot (Eds.), *It's a funny thing, humor* (pp. 421-427). Oxford: Pergamon Press.

Laughlin, M.J. (2000). Teaching creativity in family therapy supervision: Looking through an improvisational lens. *Journal of Systemic Therapies, 19*(3), 55-75.

Lawson, D.M. and Prevatt, F.F. (1999). *Casebook in family therapy.* Belmont, CA: Wadsworth Publishing Company.

Lazarus, R.S. and Folkman, S. (1984). *Stress, appraisal, and coping.* New York: Springer.

Lazarus, R.S. and Folkman, S. (1989). *Manual for the Hassles and Uplifts Scale.* Palo Alto, CA: Consulting Psychologists Press.

Lester, D. (1999). Suicide. In M.A. Runco and S.R. Pritzker (Eds.), *Encyclopedia of creativity* (Volume 2) (pp. 585-589). San Diego: Academic Press.

Leuzzi, L. (1999). *A creative life: The young person's guide.* New York: Franklin Watts.

Lewis, H.C. (1983). Teaching therapists to use their right brains. *Journal of Strategic and Systemic Therapies, 2*(1), 44-56.

Liddle, H.A., Breunlin, D.C., and Schwartz, R.C. (1988). *Handbook of family therapy training and supervision.* New York: The Guilford Press.

Linesch, D. (1999). Art making in family therapy. In D.J. Wiener (Ed.), *Beyond talk therapy: Using movement and expressive techniques in clinical practice* (pp. 225-243). Washington, DC: American Psychological Association.

Loganbill, C., Hardy, E., and Delworth, U. (1982). Supervision: A conceptual model. *The Counseling Psychologist, 10*(1), 3-42.

Love, P. (1999). *Hot monogamy.* New York: Penguin Putnam.

Luquet, W.J. (1996). *Short-term couples therapy: The imago model in action.* New York: Brunner/Mazel.

MacKinnon, D.W. (1965). Personality and the realization of creative potential. *American Psychologist, 20,* 273-281.

MacKinnon, D.W. (1978). *In search of human effectiveness: Identifying and developing creativity.* Buffalo, NY: Creative Education Foundation.

Madanes, C. (1981). *Strategic family therapy.* San Francisco: Jossey-Bass.

Marshall, R.J. (1999). Facilitating cooperation and creativity in group supervision. *Modern Psychoanalysis, 24*(2), 181-186.

Martindale, C. (1989). Personality, situation, and creativity. In J.A. Glover, R.R. Ronning, and C.R. Reynolds (Eds.), *Handbook of creativity* (pp. 211-232). New York: Plenum Press.

Maslow, A.H. (1968). *Toward a psychology of being* (Second editon). New York: Van Nostrand Reinhold.

Maslow, A.H. (1971). *The farther reaches of human nature.* New York: Viking.

Masten, A.S., Best, K.M., and Garmezy, N. (1991). Resilience and development: Contributions from the study of children who overcome adversity. *Development and Psychopathology, 2,* 425-444.

May, R. (1975). *The courage to create.* New York: Bantam.

McBrien, R.J. (1993). Laughing together: Humor as encouragement in couples counseling. *Individual Psychology, 49,* 419-427.

McCollum, E.E. (1993). Termination rituals. In T.S. Nelson and T.S. Trepper (Eds.), *101 interventions in family therapy* (pp. 154-157). Binghamton, NY: The Haworth Press.

McCubbin, H.I. (Ed.) (1999). *Stress, coping, and health in families: Sense of coherence and resiliency.* Thousand Oaks, CA: Sage.

McGhee, P.E. and Goldstein, J. (Eds.) (1983). *Handbook of humor research* (Volumes 1 and 2). New York: Springer-Verlag.

McWhirter, E.H. (1994). *Counseling for empowerment.* Alexandria, VA: American Counseling Association.

Mellou, E. (1995). Creativity: The interaction condition. *Early Child Development and Care, 109,* 143-157.

Mendecka, G. (1996). Attitudes of parents and development of creativity. In A. Cropley and D. Dehn (Eds.), *Fostering the growth of high ability* (pp. 81-96). Norwood, NJ: Ablex.

Michel, M. and Dudek, S. (1991). Mother-child relationships and creativity. *Creative Research Journal, 4*(3), 281-286.

Miller, B.C. and Gerard, D. (1979). Family influences on the development of creativity in children: An integrative review. *The Family Coordinator, 28,* 295-312.

Miller, K.L., Serifica, F.C., and Clark, P.M. (1989). Interpersonal problem solving and creativity: A developmental analysis. Paper presented at the Annual Meeting of the American Psychological Association, New Orleans, LA, August.

Minuchin, S. (1974). *Families and family therapy.* Cambridge, MA: Harvard University Press.

Minuchin, S. and Fishman, H.C. (1981). *Family therapy techniques.* Cambridge, MA: Harvard University Press.

Mosak, H.H. (1987). *Ha ha and aha: The role of humor in psychotherapy.* Muncie, IN: Accelerated Development, Inc.

Mraz, W. and Runco, M.A. (1994). Suicide ideation and creative problem solving. *Suicide and Life Threatening Behavior, 24,* 38-47.

Murdock, M.C. and Ganim, R.M. (1993). Creativity and humor: Integration and incongruity. *Journal of Creative Behavior, 27*(1), 57-70.

Neill, J.R. and Kniskern, D.P. (Eds.) (1982). *From psyche to system: The evolving therapy of Carl Whitaker.* New York: The Guilford Press.

Nelson, M.L. (1997). An interactional model for empowering women in supervision. *Counselor Education and Supervision, 37,* 125-139.

Nelson, T.S. and Trepper, T.S. (Eds.) (1993). *101 interventions in family therapy.* Binghamton, NY: The Haworth Press.

Nelson, T.S. and Trepper, T.S. (Eds.) (1998). *101 more interventions in family therapy.* Binghamton, NY: The Haworth Press.

Nichols, M.P. and Schwartz, R.C. (1998). *Family therapy: Concepts and methods* (Fourth edition). Boston: Allyn & Bacon.

Nichols, M.P. and Schwartz, R.C. (2001). *Family therapy: Concepts and methods* (Fifth edition). Boston: Allyn & Bacon.

Nickerson, R.S. (1999). Enhancing creativity. In R.J. Sternberg (Ed.), *Handbook of creativity* (pp. 392-430). New York: Cambridge University Press.

Nilsen, D.L.F. (1991). Humor and creativity: Humor and health. *The Creative Child and Adult Quarterly, 16*(4), 245-249.

Noller, R. (1979). *Scratching the surface of creative problem solving: A bird's eye view of CPS.* Buffalo, NY: D.O.K. Publishers.

Nystul, M.S. (1993). *The art and science of counseling and psychotherapy.* New York: Macmillan.

O'Hanlon, B. and Beadle, S. (1997). *A guide to possibility land: Fifty-one methods for doing brief, respectful therapy.* New York: W.W. Norton.

Ollier, K. and Hobday, A. (2001). *Creative therapy 2: Working with parents.* Atascadero, CA: Impact Publishers, Inc.

Olson, D.H., McCubbin, H.I., Barnes, H., Larsen, A., Muxen, M., and Wilson, M. (1983). *Families: What makes them work.* Los Angeles: Sage.

Olszewski, P., Kulieke, M., and Buescher, T. (1987). The influence of the family environment on the development of talent: A literature review. *Journal for the Education of the Gifted, 11*(1), 6-28.

Openlander, P. (1991). Creativity and systems therapy. *Journal of Strategic and Systemic Therapies, 10*(2), 69-83.

Page, S. (1997). *How one of you can bring the two of you together.* New York: Broadway Books.

Papp, P. (1976). Family choreography. In P.J. Guerin (Ed.), *Family therapy: Theory and practice* (pp. 465-479). New York: Gardner Press.

Papp, P. (1984). The creative leap: The links between clinical and artistic creativity. *Family Therapy Networker, 8*(5), 20-29.

Phillips, L. (2000). Storytelling: The seeds of children's creativity. *Australian Journal of Early Childhood, 25*, 1-7.

Piercy, F. and Nelson, T. (1999). Flow in the consulting room. *Family Therapy Networker, 23*(1), 46-47.

Piercy, F.P., Sprenkle, D.H., Wetchler, J.L., and Associates (1996). *Family therapy sourcebook* (Second edition). New York: The Guilford Press.

Piercy, F.P. and Wetchler, J.L. (1996). Structural, strategic, and systemic family therapies. In F.P. Piercy, D.H. Sprenkle, and J.L. Wetchler (Eds.), *Family therapy sourcebook* (Second edition) (pp. 50-78). New York: The Guilford Press.

Pine, F. and Holt, R.R. (1960). Creativity and primary process: A study of adaptive regression. *Journal of Abnormal and Social Psychology, 61*, 370-379.

Plucker, J.A. and Runco, M.A. (1999). Deviance. In M.A. Runco and S. R. Pritzker (Eds.), *Encyclopedia of creativity* (Volume 1) (pp. 541-544). San Diego: Academic Press.

Raines, S. and Isbell, R. (1994). *Stories: Children's literature in early education.* New York: Delmar Publishers.

Reiner, P.A. (1997). Psychoanalytic approaches to supervising couple and family therapy. In T.C. Todd and C.L. Storm (Eds.), *The complete systemic supervisor:*

Context, philosophy, and pragmatics (pp. 135-155). Needham Heights, MA: Allyn & Bacon.

Reiss, D. (1981). *The family's construction of reality.* Cambridge, MA: Harvard University Press.

Rhodes, C. (1990). Growth from deficiency creativity to being creativity. *Creativity Research Journal, 3,* 287-299.

Ricchiuto, J. (1997). *Collaborative creativity: Unleashing the power of shared thinking.* New York: Oakhill Press.

Richards, R. (1990). Everyday creativity, eminent creativity, and health: Afterview for CRJ issues on creativity and health. *Creativity Research Journal, 3,* 300-326.

Richards, R. (1993). Seeing beyond: Issues of creative awareness and social responsibility. *Creative Research Journal, 6,* 165-185.

Richards, R. (1996). Beyond Piaget: Accepting divergent, chaotic, and creative thought. *New Directions for Child Development, 72,* 67-86.

Richards, R. (1997). Conclusions: When illness yields creativity. In M.A. Runco and R. Richards (Eds.), *Eminent creativity, everyday creativity, and health* (pp. 485-540). Greenwich, CT: Ablex.

Richards, R. (1999). Affective disorders. In M.A. Runco and S.R. Pritzker (Eds.), *Encyclopedia of creativity* (Volume 1) (pp. 31-43). San Diego: Academic Press.

Richman, J. (1996a). Jokes as a projective technique: The humor of psychiatric patients. *American Journal of Psychotherapy, 50*(3), 336-346.

Richman, J. (1996b). Points of correspondence between humor and psychotherapy. *Psychotherapy, 33*(4), 560-566.

Roberts, J. (1993). Termination rituals. In T.S. Nelson and T.S. Trepper (Eds.), *101 interventions in family therapy* (pp. 38-42). Binghamton, NY: The Haworth Press.

Rogers, C.R. (1961). *On becoming a person.* New York: Houghton Mifflin.

Rogers, C.R. (1986). Client-centered therapy. In I. Kutash and A. Wolf (Eds.), *Psychotherapist's casebook: Theory and techniques in the practice of modern therapies* (pp. 197-208). San Francisco: Jossey-Bass.

Rothenberg, A. (1990). *Creativity and madness: New findings and old stereotypes.* Baltimore: Johns Hopkins University Press.

Rothenberg, A. (1999a). Homospatial process. In M.A. Runco and S.R. Pritzker (Eds.), *Encyclopedia of creativity* (Volume 1) (pp. 831-835). San Diego: Academic Press.

Rothenberg, A. (1999b). Janusian process. In M.A. Runco and S.R. Pritzker (Eds.), *Encyclopedia of creativity* (Volume 2) (pp. 103-108). San Diego: Academic Press.

Runco, M.A. (1990). Editorial: Creativity and health. *Creativity Research Journal, 3,* 81-84.

Runco, M.A. (1991). *Divergent thinking.* Norwood, NJ: Ablex.

Runco, M.A. (1994a). Creativity and its discontents. In M.P. Shaw and M.A. Runco (Eds.), *Creativity and affect* (pp. 102-123). Norwood, NJ: Ablex.

Runco, M.A. (1994b). *Problem finding, problem solving, and creativity*. Norwood, NJ: Ablex.

Runco, M.A. (1999). Self-actualization. In M.A. Runco and S.R. Pritzker (Eds.), *Encyclopedia of creativity* (Volume 2) (pp. 533-536). San Diego: Academic Press.

Runco, M.A. and Bahleda, M. (1986). Implicit theories of artistic, scientific, and everyday creativity. *Journal of Creative Behavior, 20*, 93-98.

Runco, M.A, Ebersole, P., and Mraz, W. (1991). Self-actualization and creativity. *Journal of Social Behavior and Personality, 6*, 161-167.

Runco, M.A. and Richards, R. (Eds.) (1998). *Eminent creativity, everyday creativity, and health*. Norwood, NJ: Ablex.

Russ, S. (1999). Emotion/affect. In M.A. Runco and S.R. Pritzker (Eds.), *Encyclopedia of creativity* (Volume 1) (pp. 659-668). San Diego: Academic Press.

Rutan, J.S. (1992). *Psychotherapy for the 1990s*. New York: The Guilford Press.

Rutherford, K. (1994). Humor in psychotherapy. *Individual Psychology, 50*(2), 207-222.

Rutter, M. (1983). Stress, coping, and development: Some issues and some questions. In N. Garmezy and M. Rutter (Eds.), *Stress, coping, and development in children* (pp. 1-41). New York: McGraw-Hill.

Rutter, M. (1987). Psychological resilience and protective mechanisms. *American Journal of Orthopsychiatry, 57*, 316-331.

Satir, V.M. (1983). *Conjoint family therapy* (Third edition). Palo Alto, CA: Science and Behavior Books.

Satir, V.M. (1988). *The new peoplemaking*. Palo Alto, CA: Science and Behavior Books.

Sawatztky, D. D., Jevne, R. F., and Clark, G. T (1994). Becoming empowered: A study of counsellor development. *Canadian Journal of Counselling, 28*(3), 177-191.

Schaefer, C.E. (Ed.) (1993). *The therapeutic powers of play*. Northvale, NJ: Jason Aronson.

Schaefer, C.E. and Carey, L. (Eds.) (1994). *Family play therapy*. Northvale, NJ: Jason Aronson.

Scharff, D. (1992). *Refining the object and reclaiming the self*. New York: Jason Aronson.

Scharff, D. and Scharff, J. (1987). *Object relations family therapy*. New York: Jason Aronson.

Schnarch, D. (1997). *Passionate marriage*. New York: Henry Holt.

Schubert, D.S.P. (1988). Creativity and the ability to cope. In F. Flach (Ed.), *The creative mind* (pp. 97-114). Buffalo, NY: Bearly Limited.

Schuldberg, D. (1990). Schizotypal and hypomanic traits, creativity, and psychological health. *Creativity Research Journal, 3*, 219-231.

Schuldberg, D. and Sass, L.A. (1999). Schizophrenia. In M.A. Runco and S.R. Pritzker (Eds.), *Encyclopedia of creativity* (Volume 2) (pp. 501-514). San Diego: Academic Press.

Schwartz, R.C. (1995). *Internal family systems therapy.* New York: The Guilford Press.

Sears, S.J. and Milburn, J. (1990). School-age stress. In L.E. Arnold (Ed.), *Childhood stress* (pp. 224-246). New York: Wiley.

Selvini Palazzoli, M., Cirillo, S., Selvini, M., and Sorrention, A.M. (1989). *Family games: General models of psychotic processes in families.* New York: W.W. Norton.

Selye, H. (1988). Creativity in basic research. In F. Flach (Ed.), *The creative mind* (pp. 243-268). Buffalo, NY: Bearly Limited.

Sherman, R. and Fredman, N. (1986). *Handbook of structured techniques in marriage and family therapy.* New York: Brunner/Mazel.

Shondrick, D.D., Serifica, F.C., Clark, P., and Miller, K.G. (1992). Interpersonal problem solving and creativity in boys with and without learning disabilities. *Learning Disability Quarterly, 15,* 95-102.

Siegel, B.S. (1986). *Love, medicine, and miracles.* New York: Harper and Row.

Silverstone, B. and Kandel-Hyman, H.K. (1992). *Growing old together.* New York: Pantheon Books.

Simonton, D.K. (1988). *Scientific genius.* New York: Cambridge University Press.

Simonton, D.K. (1995). Many are called, but few are chosen. *Contemporary Psychology, 40*(8), 733-735.

Skynner, A.C.R. (1976). *Systems of family and marital psychotherapy.* New York: Brunner/Mazel.

Slipp, S. (1988). *The technique and practice of object relations family therapy.* Northvale, NJ: Jason Aronson.

Smith, G.J.W. and Van der Meer, G. (1990). Creativity in old age. *Creativity Research Journal, 3,* 249-264.

Stein, M.I. (1988). Creativity: The process and its stimulation. In F. Flach (Ed.), *The creative mind* (pp. 51-75). Buffalo, NY: Bearly Limited.

Sternberg, R.J. and Lubart, T. (1995). *Defying the crowd.* New York: The Free Press.

Stinnett, N. and DeFrain, J. (1985). *Secrets of strong families.* Boston: Little Brown.

Stoltenberg, C.D. and Delworth, U. (1988). *Supervising counselors and therapists: A developmental approach.* San Francisco, CA: Jossey-Bass.

Strong, S.R. (1968). Counseling: An interpersonal influence process. *Journal of Counseling Psychology, 15,* 215-224.

Stuart, R.B. (1980). *Helping couples change: A social learning approach to marital therapy.* New York: The Guilford Press.

Sween, E. (2000). Using the metaphor of teamwork in narrative couples therapy. *Journal of Systemic Therapies, 19*(3), 76-82.

Sweeney, D.S. and Rocha, S.L. (2000). Using play therapy to assess family dynamics. In J. Carlson (Ed.), *Techniques in marriage and family counseling* (Volume 1) (pp. 33-47). Alexandria, VA: American Counseling Association.

Taibbi, R. (1996). *Doing family therapy: Craft and creativity in clinical practice.* New York: The Guilford Press.

Takata, S.R. (1987). Learning by doing: The teaching of social research. *Teaching Sociology, 15*(2), 144-150.

Terr, L. (1999). *Beyond love and work: Why adults need to play.* New York: Scribner.

Thomas, V. (2000). Creativity in marriage and family therapy: A self exploration for therapists. Preconference institute conducted at the 58th annual Conference of the American Association for Marriage and Family Therapy, Denver, CO, November.

Thompson, R.A. (1996). *Counseling techniques: Improving relationships with others, ourselves, our families, and our environment.* Bristol, PA: Accelerated Development.

Todd, T.C. (1997). Purposive systemic supervision models. In T.C. Todd and C.L. Storm (Eds.), *The complete systemic supervisor: Context, philosophy, and pragmatics* (pp. 173-194). Needham Heights, MA: Allyn & Bacon.

Tomm, K. (1987a). Interventive interviewing: Part 1. Strategizing as a fourth guideline for the therapist. *Family Process, 26,* 3-14.

Tomm, K. (1987b). Interventive interviewing: Part 2. Reflexive questioning as a means to enable self-healing. *Family Process, 26,* 167-183.

Tomm, K. (1987c). Interventive interviewing: Part 3. Intending to ask lineal, circular, strategic, or reflexive questions? *Family Process, 27,* 1-15.

Torrance, E.P. (1961). Factors affecting creative thinking in children: An interim research report. *Merrill-Palmer Quarterly of Behavior and Development, 7,* 171-180.

Torrance, E.P. (1974). *Torrance Tests of Creative Thinking.* Bensenville, IL: Scholastic Testing Service.

Torrance, E.P. (1975). *Preliminary manual: Ideal child check-list.* Athens, GA: University of Georgia.

Torrance, E.P. (1982). Can we teach children to think creatively? *Journal of Creative Behavior, 6,* 114-143.

Torrance, E.P. (1988). The nature of creativity as manifest in its testing. In R.J. Sternberg (Ed.), *The nature of creativity* (pp. 43-75). New York: Cambridge University Press.

Torrance. E.P. (1995). *Why fly? A philosophy of creativity.* Norwood, NJ: Ablex.

Treffinger, D.J., Isaksen, S.G., and Dorval, K.B. (1994). Creative problem solving: An overview. In M.A. Runco (Ed.), *Problem finding, problem solving, and creativity* (pp. 223-236). Norwood, NJ: Ablex.

van der Linde, C.H. (1999). The relationship between play and music in early childhood: Educational insights. *Education, 119,* 610-617.

VanFleet, R. (1994). *Filial therapy: Strengthening parent-child relationships through play.* Sarasota, FL: Professional Resources Press.

Voss, J.F. and Means, M.L. (1989). Toward a model of creativity based upon problem solving in the social sciences. In J.A. Glover, R.R. Ronning, and C.R. Reynolds (Eds.), *Handbook of creativity* (pp. 399-410). New York: Plenum Press.

Walsh, F. (1998). *Strengthening family resilience.* New York: The Guilford Press.

Walsh, W.M. and McGraw, J.A. (1996). *Essentials of family therapy: A therapist's guide to eight approaches.* Denver, CO: Love Publishing Company.

Watzlawick, P. (1978). *The language of change.* New York: Basic Books.

Werner, E.E. (1990). Protective factors and individual resilience. In S.J. Meisels and M. Shonkoff (Eds.), *Handbook of early intervention* (pp. 97-116). New York: Cambridge University Press.

Western Psychological Services (2001). *Creative Therapy Store Catalog,* Fall.

Whitaker, C.A. and Bumberry, W.M. (1988). *Dancing with the family: A symbolic-experiential approach.* New York: Brunner/Mazel.

Whitaker, C.A. and Keith, D.V. (1981). Symbolic-experiential family therapy. In A.S. Gurman and D.P. Kniskern (Eds.), *Handbook of family therapy* (pp. 187-225). New York: Brunner/Mazel.

White, M. (1993). Deconstruction and therapy. In S. Gilligan and R. Price (Eds.), *Therapeutic conversations* (pp. 22-61). New York: W.W. Norton.

White, M. (1995). *Re-authoring lives: Interviews and essays.* Adelaide, South Australia: Dulwich Centre Pub.

White, M. and Eptson, D. (1990). *Narrative means to therapeutic ends.* New York: W.W. Norton.

Wiener, D.J. (Ed.) (1999). *Beyond talk therapy: Using movement and expressive techniques in clinical practice.* Washington, DC: American Psychological Association.

Wiggins Frame, M. (2000). Conducting religious/spiritual genograms. In R.E. Watts (Ed.), *Techniques in Marriage and Family Counseling* (Volume 1) (pp. 68-74). Alexandria, VA: American Counseling Association.

Wild, C. (1965). Creativity and adaptive regression. *Journal of Personality and Social Psychology, 2,* 161-169.

Winick, C. (1976). The social contexts of humor. *Journal of Communication, 26,* 124-128.

Wink, P. (1999). Self process and creativity. In M.A. Runco and S.R. Pritzker, (Eds.), *Encyclopedia of creativity* (Volume 2) (pp. 537-541). San Diego: Academic Press.

Witmer, J.M. (1985). *Pathways to personal growth.* Muncie, IN: Accelerated Development.

Wolin, S.J. and Wolin, S. (1993). *The resilient self.* New York: Villiard Books.

Woodman, R.W. and Schoenfeldt, L.F. (1990). An interactionist model of creative behavior. *The Journal of Creative Behavior, 24*(1), 10-20.

Worden, M. (1994). Family therapy basics. Pacific Grove, CA: Brooks/Cole.

Wuerffel, J., DeFrain, J., and Stinnett, N. (1990). How strong families use humor. *Family Perspective, 24*(2), 129-141.

Yontef, G.M. (1995). Gestalt therapy. In A.S. Gurman and S.B. Messer (Eds.), *Essential psychotherapies: Theory and practice* (pp. 261-303). New York: The Guilford Press.

Zimmerman, J. and Dickerson, V. (1996). *If problems talked: Adventures in narrative therapy.* New York: The Guilford Press.

Index